WOMEN'S NETWORKS

The Complete Guide to Getting a
Better Job, Advancing Your Career,
and Feeling Great as a Woman
Through Networking

CAROL KLEIMAN

LIPPINCOTT & CROWELL, PUBLISHERS
New York

FIRST EDITION

Designed by C. Linda Dingler

U.S. Library of Congress Cataloging in Publication Data

Kleiman, Carol.
  Women's networks.

  Includes index.
  1. Women's networks—United States—Directories.
I. Title.
HQ1883.K57 1980   305.4'025   80-11775
ISBN 0-690-01868-1
ISBN 0-690-01869-X (pbk.)

80 81 82 83 84 10 9 8 7 6 5 4 3 2 1

With deep respect and affection, this book is dedicated to Diann D. Smith, who has networked instinctively since the day she was born, and to Pauline B. Bart, who networks so well, compassionately, and consistently that one phone call to her and almost all problems are solved.

Contents

Acknowledgments ix

Introduction xi

1. | Networking:
What It's All About and Why It's Important to You 1

2. | Business Networks 13

3. | Professional Networks:
Doctors, Lawyers, Educators, Political Scientists, Architects, and More! 29

4. | Support Networks:
*Wives, Mothers, Divorced Women, Single Women,
Women over Forty, Teenagers, Displaced Homemakers,
Ethnic Women, Religious Women, Battered Women
—Women Helping Women* 42

5. | Health and Sports Networks 62

6. | Political and Labor Networks 84

7. | Artistic Networks:
*Painting, Sculpture, Music, Writing, Radio, Television,
Theater* 106

8. | Informal Networks 117

9. | How to Set Up Your Own Network 124

10. | Listings
*National, State, and Local Networks in the United
States* 130

Acknowledgments

This book came about by networking: Marilynn Preston, *Chicago Tribune* writer, creator of the nationally syndicated column "Dr. Jock," and author, said to me one day, "You should write a book about networking. You've been fascinated by it for years." Next, she called her book editor, Nancy Crawford, and said to her, "You should talk to Carol Kleiman. She has a good idea for a book."

Crawford called, I wrote, and within a very short time this book was in the works. So, many special thanks go to Preston and Crawford. I also want to thank Roger Kohn of Lippincott & Crowell for his invaluable help. For constant support and understanding, I want to thank my patient agent, Dominick Abel. Special thanks, too, to Rebecca Sive-Tomashefsky of the Midwest Women's Center; to Kaye Janus, for typing beyond the call of duty; and to my children, Cathy, Raymond, and Robert, for their encouragement and support.

And, special thanks to my researchers, Evelyn Engler and Susan Firkser.

Writing this book was networking in itself. Hundreds of phone calls were made to every state in the nation, and eager, helpful voices at the other end helped bring all these activities into sharp focus. Everyone was cooperative; everyone was willing to tell what they knew about the phenomenon known as networking. I want to thank most sincerely the following people in this newly created "*Women's Network* Book Network" who helped make this book possible:

Charlotte Adelman, Shauna Adix, Rosemary Aitken, Joanne Alter, Kay Anderson, Sharon Baldwin, Phillip Baretta, Cynthia Barrett, Kay Barrett, Sally Bender, Elizabeth Brenner, Lenore Borzak, Ann Brodie, Emily Brown, Ruth Campbell, Carol Carter, Elizabeth Chittick, Linda Coleridge, Huntley Collins, Doris Conant, Gena Corea, Belita Cowan, Doug Cox, Ellen Craig, Day Creamer, Sally Davis, Sharron Davis, Susan Davis, Nikki Deal, Elsie Dennisen, Dana Densmore, Janice Dinneen, Jean Donohue, Pheralyn Dove, Dorothy Downing, Aloha Eagles, Catherine East, Jean Edwards, Walter Y. Elisha, Dorothy Engles, Kathy Erwin, Joan Fortunata, Barbara Fox, Rona Frankfurt, Spring Friedlander, Hilda G. Frontany, Betty Garrett, Florence

Graham, Martin Glotzer, Sherry Goodman, Ruth Gundel, Mrs. Otis Hallaway-Owens, Mrs. Hamilton, Judy Harrington, Jane Harrison, Ann Haskell, Jane Haviger, Sue Hertz, Gloria Hochman, Stan Hochman, Jean Hoffman, Peggy Holman, Gloria Huguelet, Sonia Johnson, Louise Jones, Phoebe Jones, Jane Joost, Dorothy Jurney, Hope Kading, Joan Kaiser, Daire Kalmes, Deborah Kaplan, Vicki Kellinski, Jinnah Kelsen, Marilyn Kennedy, Coralee Kern, Pat Kizzier, Marilyn Kollath, Carolyn Mills Kroes, Lorraine Landelius, Phyllis Langer, Pam Lasser, Gloria Lewis, Diane Lichtenstein, Ann Marie Lipinski, Jeanne Lipscomb, Virginia Littlejohn, Jewel Russell Mann, Barbara McCullem, Tina McIntosh, Mary Lynn Meyer, Nancy Miller, Nancy Mills, Evelyn Moats Munger, Ada Munson, Judy Norsigian, Hester Newcomb, Thelma Norris, Carol Oglesby, Jean O'Hare, Becky Pack, Carol Parr, Mary Pineau, Allison Platt, June Pyskacek, Alice Quinlan, Hedy Ratner, Susan Rink, B.V.M., Henley Roughton, Marge Rossman, Muriel Rusten, Terry Saario, Bunny Sandler, Karen Saum, Ellouise Schoettler, LeAnne Schreiber, Sheryl Schreps, Diane Scully, Katherine Selden, Ruth Sherman, Laurie Shields, Penny Simkin, Joy Simonson, Marilyn Skinner, Tish Sommers, Betty Spencer, Kathy Stanwick, Ava Stern, David Stewart, Susan Strecker, Charlotte Taylor, Carol Thompson, Nancy Thompson, Jane Threat, Sheila Tobias, Joanne Vogel, Bari Watkins, Paul Weingarten, Jackie Wells, Judy Wesley, Carol Wheeler, Jane Whelan, Rosalee Whelan, Jackie Winnow, and Ilene Wolcott.

Introduction

At 5:45 P.M., Monday, June 18, 1979, I walked into the elegant Metropolitan Club, high in the Sears Tower, to attend the first meeting of The Chicago Network. The name tags of the women in the room—and their titles—would make a Who's Who of their own. Even more importantly, the names would also make a Who Will Be.

Gathered in this room were seventy-five of the most important and powerful women in Chicago, women who had never gotten together in one room before, and never for this reason: to help each other advance in their careers. And, just as important, to help advance their own careers.

It was all out in the open. It was a network—business, political, educational, medical, legal, and media women, women at the top, women who run things in corporations and professions, women with clout gathered together informally to meet one another and discuss mutual concerns.

The women in The Chicago Network span a variety of political beliefs. Most are conservative business and professional women, such as Hanna Gray, president of the University of Chicago. A few are feminists, such as Susan Davis, founder of *The Spokeswoman*, one of the early feminist newsletters, and today vice-president of the South Shore Bank. The Chicago Network spans race, religion, age groups, and economic classes too. What we all have in common is unabashed self-interest: We want to get ahead in our chosen fields. And we feel a commitment to help other women do the same.

At that meeting was Betty M. McFadden, one of the highest-paid women in retailing in the United States; she's president, Direct Marketing Division, Jewel Companies. Anne L. Barlow, medical director of Abbott Laboratories Hospital, was present. So were Evangeline Gouletus, executive vice-president, American Invesco; Addie Wyatt, international vice-president of the United Food and Commercial Workers, AFL-CIO; Eva Jane Milligan, senior vice-president, Marshall Field; Betsy Ann Plank, assistant vice-president, Illinois Bell Telephone; and Christie Hefner, corporate vice-president of Playboy Enterprises, Inc. The names, titles, and rankings were a staggering collection of women who had made it.

If they were so important, why were they here? One of the striking truths of the get-together was that these highly successful, important women had never before, in most cases, met face to face, and this is true of similar women throughout the United States. Certainly it was true for me, even though I had been writing about women and women's issues for the *Chicago Tribune* for more than a decade. Many of the women were the only women officers in their companies—not a surprising fact since the isolation of women who are successful is universal. That was an underlying reason for these busy women to take time out from their pressurized schedules to attend the first meeting of The Chicago Network: We knew we needed to know each other, just as business and professional men need to know each other and, indeed, do already know each other.

If we had been men, we would have naturally met many times before, all of us, at the Union League Club, the University Club, the Chicago Athletic Club, board meetings, or in the course of daily business life. But the clubs I've mentioned—and even the most prestigious golf club of all, Butler National Golf Club, where literally millions of dollars in business casually takes place on its greens—are male domains. Women have to create their own meetings and their own meeting places, and that is just what we are doing throughout the United States. Everywhere, women are organizing to help one another, from the Philadelphia Forum for Executive Women, to the Front Porch Committee in Birmingham, Michigan, to the Professional Women's Alliance of San Francisco, to an international network of nuns.

The network I belong to has no subcommittees or projects. We have several dinner meetings each year. The shoulder-rubbing during the cocktail hour before dinner is when the real networking takes place, just as men converse in private clubs, locker rooms, and on the golf course. And the same exchanges are made: information, tips, advice, moral support.

Even at the very first meeting of The Chicago Network, a lot of things happened for me. First of all, I had the opportunity to see and hear in person the first woman mayor of the city of Chicago, Jane Byrne, the network's kickoff speaker. Mayor Byrne is a busy woman and was especially busy then because it was so soon after her election. Many organizations were inviting the new mayor to speak, and almost all were turned down. But she couldn't say no to this group. She had to appear.

Mayor Byrne could not turn down this group and its collective clout, much as she could not and did not turn down powerful bankers and business leaders, all male, who were inviting her to their breakfasts, lunches, and dinners.

In her wonderfully direct manner, Mayor Byrne departed from her written speech to tell The Chicago Network that a few days after her election she was asked to meet with some prominent business leaders in the community who were concerned about her plans for industrial growth. "I went to the meeting and there were fifteen men there, men who could make important decisions," said Mayor Byrne. "The next few days were filled with many such meetings called by businessmen. Each group had a different name, but they were always the same fifteen men! Where are the women?"

Chicago's prominent businesswomen had decided to do something about always being left out when important decisions were being made. As women throughout the country were beginning to realize, the answer was networking, where the impact of the whole is greater than the sum of its parts. Three hours later, when the talking and dinner were over, after each woman had stood and announced her title and affiliations, something else had happened to me: I was very consciously going over the list that the network organizers had compiled and distributed, with name, title, and phone number of every member. I was checking the names of the people I wanted to call, women with incredible credentials, women I needed to know—in my case, as sources for stories and information. Most of the other women were doing the same, for their own reasons.

What we were doing, naturally and easily, was networking. In Chicago, women with similar interests had reached out to one another before, but we never came up with precisely the structure that answered our needs until the idea of networking was born. Most of us, working independently of one another, had worked in the dark. We formed circles of women friends and business acquaintances that were comfortable, but because they were circles, they didn't go anywhere. I, too, made my own attempts to bring women together ten years ago, without knowing exactly what I was doing. I was writing a column called "Working Woman" for the *Chicago Tribune,* and in the course of my assignments I met some of the most exciting women in the city, women doing things, women proud to be women, who were willing to share their successes and failures with other women. The fact that there were so many active, accomplished women in Chicago astounded me. I wanted them all to know one another. So every Tuesday we had "Great Women" luncheons. These meetings were exciting and important, and deep friendships still exist from those days. We gave each other mutual support, a lot of creative ideas, and much warmth for several years—but very little light. Unlike networks, we had no direction, no goal, no stated purpose of helping each other, ourselves, and other women. The luncheons ended, and it wasn't until I began reading about women forming networks in art, health, sports, business, and politics that I understood more of what I had been trying to do, what we were all striving for: We needed more than simply to know each other. We needed a support group, a personal network, even for our own self-interest. We needed to exchange helpful information.

Many of the "Great Women" are now members of The Chicago Network. One of them, Diann Smith, is its president. We had been searching for the right setting in which to grow and "do our thing," and in networking we have found it. This book—a form of networking in itself—tells you what networks are all about, how they work and how they can help you, and the many kinds of networks that already exist. It tells you how to form your own in your own city, town, or block; the benefits, the pitfalls to avoid; the ways in which women's networks differ from "Old Boy Networks."

And why every woman, no matter who she is or what she does or what she wants to do, needs a network of her own.

1 | Networking:
What It's All About and Why It's Important to You

Network   1. Any arrangement of fabric or parallel wires, threads, etc., crossed at
regular intervals by others fastened to them so as to leave open spaces.   2. A
system, etc., of interconnected or cooperating individuals.
—*Webster's New World Dictionary*

Roxanne Mankin, real estate syndicator and president of her own company, was in the women's washroom of a downtown San Francisco hotel. Frankly, she was in a stall, going to the bathroom. Mankin, co-founder of the Professional Women's Alliance of San Francisco, was taking a brief break from a luncheon her network had arranged, with Sarah Weddington, special assistant to the President for women's issues, as guest speaker. Some 400 women—active, energetic, eager businesswomen, women on their way up—had been admitted to the luncheon. Some 200 more, equally impressive women, were turned away simply for lack of space.

While Mankin mused on the excitement and "incredible energy" of the women assembled, she overheard a conversation between two women washing their hands at the sink. Both were clearly guests at the luncheon. One asked the other what she did, and the woman replied that she was an executive with a high-level search firm, specializing in finding good jobs for people in finance. Mankin hadn't meant to eavesdrop, but something clicked: At the time, she was looking for a comptroller for her company. Maybe this woman could help her. Still sitting in the stall, Mankin called out, "Wait a minute! Don't go away! I want to talk to you!"

She came out, introduced herself to the search firm executive, Joan Mills, and they exchanged business cards. They promised to call one another the next week, and not only did the woman try to help Mankin solve her business problem, *she* is now interested in investing in some of Mankin's projects.

What Women's Networks Are

What Mankin was doing was networking, a new "arrangement of parallel wires" that is exploding in popularity through the United States today, not just among businesswomen, and not just among top businesswomen, but among all women who want to get something done, who want to move upward, who know full well it isn't only what you know but *who* you know that matters. Obviously, washrooms are not the only places networking occurs; it happens whenever and wherever women get together. Once you learn the secrets—and rewards—of networking, as Roxanne Mankin has, you don't stop because you happen to have to go to the bathroom. Networking works so well that once you learn the ins and outs it becomes second nature, automatic. No opportunity to network is permitted to slip by, whether it's to locate new personnel, as Mankin did, or to help women learn to breast-feed their babies, as the network of women in La Leche League does. The results are too far-reaching to miss out on. And that is why women who want to achieve their goals are joining forces, from the five women in Tish Sommers's Cancer Support Group in Oakland, California, to the thousands of women in the national Displaced Homemakers Network, based in Washington, D.C.

Why Women's Networks?

Women's networks are the new wave of the eighties. This new form of the "buddy" system is an outgrowth of the women's movement and the increasing awareness among women that we do, indeed, need one another; that men help each other almost automatically, and that if we want to go somewhere in business or get something done in the community, we must do the same. Networking is so important it can't be ignored, especially in the world of business where the exclusion of women can be measured statistically: *The U.S. Bureau of Labor Statistics shows that almost half—48 percent—of all jobs come through personal contacts.* Most people believe this a very conservative figure, for the higher you are in the executive tower, the more jobs that are filled by word-of-mouth. Nationwide, in 1978, more than 400 women climbed from lower-management jobs into top-level executive jobs never before filled by women, up 28 percent from the year before. How did women get those jobs? A fair guess is through networks—women's networks.

In the past decade, the media have bombarded women with an idea that for centuries has been one of the best-kept secrets in the world: Women are competent human beings. The nitty gritty of that belief is the business world, a junglelike environment at best. There, men seem to cling together, leaving women to fend for themselves. But the problems of not knowing what's going on, not being able to communicate new ideas, not being able to make people accountable for actions exist beyond the world of business, too, as women who simply want to learn to sail or ride in rodeos will tell you, and as women who are "DES daughters," victims of drugs used on their mothers to prevent miscarriages, will also report. These women are now talking loud and clear, through networks. For all these women, women's networks are a means of survival. And that is why they are so important to you. Especially if you are a working woman, networking resembles an oasis in the desert. If you're still not convinced, just look at the most recent statistics: *Women working full-time earned 59 cents for every dollar earned by a man, and the gap between female and male earnings has been widening*, not decreasing, as you might expect.

The "Old Boy" Network

Why do the best jobs go to men? Why do they know about them before anyone else does? Why do men seem to know what grants will be awarded for research, and why do they get them? Why are sports dominated by men? When President Carter appointed his old buddies to high government posts, what was that all about?

The questions about why women are left out and men counted in, almost automatically, are many. The answer is singular: the "Old Boy" Network. To women, even the title evokes the image of a secret fraternity, an exclusive, informal agreement among men, meeting in shadowy, clubby, smoke-filled backrooms, to help other men. It is in this stereotype setting that men give advertising accounts to other men, earmark their fellows for promotion, and leak information about proposed mergers and net sales; here that political candidates are given a shot at top elective posts, names of potential clients are proposed, topics of research are decided.

It *is* secret and it *is* informal, but it is such an inbred, automatic response that men don't think twice about it. "Good Old Boys" don't say, "Well, today is the day to pick one of our own as the new vice-president in charge of transportation." They just do it. What it comes down to is that men play the leadership game better than women. Because of their socialization, men grow up knowing all about how to network. They play team sports. They are taught how to collaborate and work with each other. They learn not to hold grudges. They learn to share. Along with reading, writing, and arithmetic, they absorb the fact that *they need each other*.

Most important, these boys grow into men who can get along with each other in order to achieve individual and group goals—whether they like each other or not, in the name of team spirit. They learn not to take things personally. And from early on, boys and men have their own support group: the Old Boy Network.

The informal sticking together of young boys becomes institutionalized through camps, high schools, colleges, fraternities, country clubs, and other private clubs. Good Old Boys grow up to be men who have group skills, who know how to work in and through organizations, who can solve problems by picking up the phone and calling another Good Old Boy with whom they are on a first-name basis. Meanwhile, the most highly honed Good Old Boy, with his school tie, fraternity pin, college beer mug, membership at the best private clubs, and golf bag firmly in hand, knows how to use the network to move ahead. That's all part of being an Old Boy, with self-interest and group interest as the basic motivations.

The "Old Girl" Network

Women, first as girls, and then as adults, have traditionally been left out of this socialization process, and not until recently have we made serious efforts to form a women-only counterpart to the Old Boy Network. "It isn't because men are better competitors," says Sally Bulkley Pancrazio, manager of the research and statistics bureau of the Illinois Office of Education and an active force in a network of women school administrators. "Females learned early in grade school how to win in the classroom—after all, girls generally earn higher grades in elementary school. The big difference is that males learned to be competitive in such a way that the process taught them to compromise, cooperate, and collaborate. The same process teaches young girls how to win as individuals only, and to distrust other females."

Today, because of the consciousness-raising of the past decade, much of that socialization is changing. And women who missed out on the early years of working together are joining forces now to help one another, to get things done—like the networks of women who want to be named to regulatory and government boards, the women who want to have babies at home, the women who simply want to see artist Judy Chicago's monumental work about women, "The Dinner Party," which major museums refuse to exhibit.

Women want to melt the resistance to our presence in the mainstream of life, and the most effective way to accomplish this is through networking. Today, even women who have been taught to distrust one another are *purposely* forming networks, swapping skills, creating new ideas, giving each other support at such a rapidly growing rate it's hard to keep up with them. In this book, we have listed 1,400 national and local networks, in every state and major city throughout the country, but it's only the tip of the iceberg. There are hundreds more, changing in shape and purpose, forming each day to counter the Old Boy Network, to make things happen for women.

Overnight, networks for women have cropped up with names like Front Range Women in the Visual Arts (artistic network); Wages for Housework (political); Women Can Win (business); American Mothers' Committee (family-oriented); Sociologists for Women in Society (specialized professional); Pillsbury Bake-Off Girls (women who hate cooking), and the Gourmet Exchange (women who love cooking). There are networks of women lawyers who want to play basketball and soccer. There's even the Creative Mundanes, a network of women who informally barter time and skills with each other.

Tens of thousands of women of all ages are actively involved in helping other women find out about job openings; getting needed legislation passed; forming support groups to help other women through emotional crises; networking together to face problems of poverty, old age, widowhood, single parenting, for the fun of cooking gourmet meals, running, enjoying the outdoors, improving women's studies. Women are learning quickly and well how networks can dramatically change their lives—for the better. The Old Girl Network has evolved because women need it, and need it badly, and now.

How Women's Networks Evolved

"The past ten years have aroused the hunger among women to work with each other," says Dr. Rosabeth Moss Kanter, professor of sociology at Yale University. "We hunger for contacts with one another. Women have left the isolation of their kitchens and are seeking the sisterhood they once had."

For women got together for sociability and comfort long before the network explosion of today. Nancy Cott, American historian, says she discovered examples of such bonding from Colonial days to the Jacksonian era. Informal connections among women have always existed: having coffee together, helping out in emergencies, handing down clothes for kids, even forming car pools. Our own personal telephone book, the names of people we call when we need help, is a portable network we carry with us wherever we go.

Handing out a business card is networking too. Institutions such as YWCAs, sororities, alumnae groups of women's colleges, and women's centers are powerful points of networking. So are the National Organization for Women, the Junior Leagues of America, the National Federation of Business and Professional Clubs, the Daughters of the American Revolution, the National Society of Colonial Dames of the Seventeenth Century, and the League of Women Voters. Other forms of networking are newsletters, like *KNOW* and *The Spokeswoman*. Women are publishing directory listings of important women, such as the *Directory of Significant 20th Century American Minority Women*, and of organizations and referral services, such as the *Women's Action Almanac*. Caring women have formed hotlines for rape victims and battered women, for crisis counseling.

But what is *new* today is the formation of networks with the expressed purpose of women helping women. The idea of creating for ourselves what the Good Old Boys do so naturally seems to have hit everyone at the same time. Bridge clubs, bowling leagues, and canasta games are fun, but networking is a statement of support. And more and more women are eager to make that statement, from a network of baseball players' wives who need each other for an extended family, to a network of radical intellectual lesbians with author Kate Millett among its members. What has been missing from women's lives is power, and women have decided to do something about that lack together.

The Rungs Up the Ladder: How to Be a Successful Woman

There is no doubt that the operative word among women today is *networking*. A few years back, it was *role model*. Then, women starting in business, women starting lives as wives of doctors and dentists and clergymen, were told to find a role model and emulate her. Two generations ago, women grew up admiring women like Eleanor Roosevelt, Pearl Buck, and Marian Anderson; today's women have chosen Margaret Mead, Gloria Steinem, Barbara Walters, Patricia Harris, Billie Jean King. Next, women were told to "go out and hire a *mentor*," the advice of Dr. Mary P. Rowe of the Massachusetts Institute of Technology, among others. Mentors are women who are already successful in their chosen field of endeavor, women on the inside who have made it and who generally are probably earmarked for further success. They are the ones best equipped to show the ropes to other women who are on the way up.

But a beginner—she doesn't necessarily have to be young and is often a mature woman—who can find someone to be her mentor is the lucky exception. Mentors are hard to come by, and a successful woman, the most desirable mentor, is often too busy to have much time to spend with the neophyte, no matter how willing she might be to help. In addition, women at the top are still a scarce commodity, and in many organizations where women have not yet penetrated the upper echelons, they simply cannot be found.

Why Women's Networks Are Formed

Certainly, role models and mentors are helpful, but even if you are lucky enough to find a mentor to help guide you in your career, becoming a success is still a slow, evolutionary process. Networking accelerates that process. Networks are a step beyond role models and mentors, a necessary next step for women to take if they want to achieve their goals.

"A group of us decided that what we wanted was to form a network," says Betsy Gemmill, attorney and vice-president of the Girard Bank in Philadelphia. "I knew other women in banking, and another woman in insurance knew more women in insurance. But I didn't know women in insurance and she didn't know women in banking." The result, in 1977, was the Philadelphia Forum for Executive Women. "The point," says Gemmill, "is to provide a network for women to come together, not to make great achievements for society, not to be do-gooders, but to get to know one another."

The need to know other women with similar concerns is one of the strongest factors in networking. In 1974, Lore Caulfield, founder of Women in Business in Los Angeles, gave a workshop at the University of California on Women, Work, and Power. "Something chemical happened among the women attending the seminar," says Caulfield, who designs and manufactures a line of silk lingerie. "We all clicked. We didn't want to lose track of one another."

In the workshop, Caulfield outlined the most effective ways women get power. One of the avenues was to form a support group to bolster self-esteem, confidence, and awareness. The women in the workshop decided to be their own support group and had informal meetings for one year. Then, in 1975, the group incorporated as a formal network. "I didn't necessarily want it to be so structured," says Caulfield, "but the members did, and we run it democratically."

At almost the same time, in Denver, eighteen high-ranking women formed the Women's Forum of Colorado—for many of the same reasons. "Several women became aware that they were not in touch with their colleagues," says Elizabeth Wright Ingraham, an architect and president of the Wright-Ingraham Institute who is a granddaughter of architect Frank Lloyd Wright. "We set out to find who the high-level women in Denver were, and if they were interested in forming a network. We found many high-caliber women *were* interested. We were surprised."

The isolation of the "token" women made Ingraham's peers eager to meet one another. And the architect makes an important observation about networking, one women are beginning to deal with together: "Women are interested in power," she says. "We should be. We're out there in the everyday world and we have to deal with it. By forming a network, we do not mean what we are interested in is just grasping power. We want to understand it and to humanize it."

Who Belongs to Networks?

Some of the most intensely individual women belong to networks. Jean Allard, prominent attorney and member of the board of directors of four major corporations, is clearly a woman who has made it. Yet she wholeheartedly espouses the idea of networking.

"I'm in a network because I've been 'networked' myself," she says. "I'm a product of networks, of male networks. I wouldn't be where I am without one. I was passed around because I produced. Networks work and they ought to be extended. They need to be created, so I'm helping do that."

Even such super achievers and well-connected women as Patricia Wyskocil, vice-president and director of marketing for the First Los Angeles Bank, have a personal need for networking. "Men bond naturally and network instinctively," Wyskocil observes. "We need to make the buddy system work for women." And Elinor Guggenheimer, former New York City Commissioner of Consumer Affairs, told Enid Nemy of the *New York Times* that networking becomes almost a matter of which locker rooms you are allowed to use.

"The men in those locker rooms get a lot of information," says Guggenheimer, describing how astounded she used to be when her husband mentioned the amount of business conducted in locker rooms. "I can't tell you how often they help each other. It's amazing the number of contacts they make just by changing shoes." That is the reason Guggenheimer belongs to the star-studded Women's Forum, Inc., of New York, which also includes Barbara Walters, Bella Abzug, and Erica Jong among its 155 members.

Not only the "stars" are networking, though the impact of their encouragement and interest helps all women. The majority of women in networks are not high-status, highly visible women. They are women of all ages from all walks of life, women in business and the professions as well as homemakers, women with diverse backgrounds and interests, who share a common bond: the desire to be successful in their chosen endeavors and to be taken seriously in a male-dominated society. Many are women on the "outside," women stymied at one level in the business world, such as highly qualified secretaries, who often watch men get promoted while they get to train them. Some networks, like the New Girl Network of Winston-Salem, North Carolina, include all levels of business and professional women; others, like the National Women's Health Network, based in Washington, D.C., are even broader, including not only professional women but all women concerned about their bodies. Neighborhood women, too, are banding together to help change their lives, forming networks such as Chicago's Mujeres Latinas en Accion. Even midwives are forming networks.

Women of all ages belong to networks. Except for networks specifically devoted to older women, there are no age limits. Men help one another on a peer-group basis, which generally means the same age group. Women, however, are more egalitarian in their networks. This lack of concern about age creates a wonderful mix and results in benefits and contacts that otherwise would not be possible, as women in the Pillsbury Bake-Off Girls and the

Women Can Win networks testify. The fact is, networks that include women in their early twenties as well as those in their late seventies and even eighties are simply more fun.

Thousands of women in every stratum of American society have learned the lesson: Women need other women and, more than that, we need to help and support each other. The women who belong to networks know this and are reaping the rewards.

What Women's Networks Do for You

This book describes how women's networks work for women, helping us to earn more money, to move ahead, to realize our goals more effectively, whatever they may be. Perhaps the most dramatic illustration of the need for women to network occurs in Washington, D.C., where the power of the Old Boy Network is most apparent. In 1977, in the capital city, women in government and business formed the Washington Women's Network. A thriving group with 1,000 members, its stated goals parallel those of most networks. For example:

• to facilitate communications among women leaders and executives
• to share support, information, and technical assistance
• to utilize and enhance the activities of women's organization
• to increase the visibility of women leaders

But networks have other goals and rewards besides increasing women's power base and helping women get the salaries and jobs they deserve. They also provide a number of emotional rewards and satisfactions that, while perhaps less tangible than a title or a paycheck, are just as meaningful. In recent years, for example, women have talked at great length about the need for increased assertiveness, but confident women do not have to learn to be assertive; they are, naturally. Through networks, individual confidence builds and grows.

"Every woman needs a network, a circle of women friends, for her survival," says Dr. Pauline B. Bart, sociologist in psychiatry. "Without networks, women don't know there are other competent women around. You think you're the only one. It's important to know you are not unique, that more than just one woman at a time can rise to the top." In a network, women learn that their problems aren't personal or unique. "You find, listening to stories of other women, that the same things that have happened to you have happened to them too," continues Dr. Bart. "It's reassuring to know that discrimination you meet is based on sex, not on ability. Realistically, something can't be wrong with *all* women!"

One of the greatest satisfactions from networking is the emotional reinforcement. "You feel better about the world and about yourself as part of a network," Dr. Bart observes. "Belonging to a network gives you validation and ego gratification. You know you're worth something." This increased sense of self-confidence holds true whether the network is for overweight women, single mothers, women with emotional problems, or women who are presidents of colleges and universities.

Dr. Rosabeth Kanter, who also heads her own high-powered management consultant firm, finds that when women join networks and profit from them, this act has a ripple effect. "We all do better when women do better," she says. "We need each other. The beauty of networking is based on the truism that each time you help another woman, you are helping all women—and helping yourself."

How Do You Join?

The Old Boy Network doesn't have formal meetings, officers, or a set of by-laws. It doesn't have to. But women's networks are a brand-new phenomenon, and women don't have the same well-established tradition of working together to draw on that men do. Women don't have established meeting places. We don't form links and bonds from drinking together at bars, as almost every beer commercial suggests men do. Women have to call formal meetings, at least to start. Networks meet at dinners, luncheons, kaffee klatsches, and teas. Some existing networks are open to anyone, such as the Washington Women's Network; others, like Denver's Women's Forum, are restricted as to title, responsibility, and salary. Some, especially the informal networks, are free—no dues, no fees; others, such as the high-level business and professional networks in New York, Chicago, and Los Angeles, cost hundreds of dollars to join. Some have paid directors; others are run by consensus. Some have projects and goals; others provide only the opportunity to meet other women with similar interests and goals—and what happens next is up to you.

Many of the prestigious networks in the business and professional areas have long membership waiting lists; networks in sports, politics (such as the Wisconsin Women's Network), health, and consumerism, and those for single or older women, are generally open to anyone who wants to join. Check the lists at the end of this book to see what networks exist already in your area. Chances are you'll find more than one network that suits your needs. Call up or write to find out how to join and what the stated objectives of the network are. Ask for names of other women who already belong and talk to them. If you find that the kind of network you need hasn't been formed yet, you can start your own simply by gathering together a few friends and colleagues (see chapter 9).

The Question of Elitism

With some networks based on special interests and others very carefully screening and limiting their membership, the question of elitism is raised. "We can't ask women to form alliances with other women doing very different kinds of jobs or at very different levels in the organization," says Dr. Kanter, "any more than we can expect men [the bosses] to relate across all sorts of boundaries. If I'm the only woman vice-president in the bank and all the other women are secretaries or tellers, it would be asking too much of me to expect me to form a network with those women because we don't have much in common."

Many organizers of networks, especially in business and the professions, believe there's no point in having a network if anyone, regardless of credentials, can belong. And it is a fact that top executives, for example, understand the problems of other top executives better than anyone else and are in a better position to help each other than people at other levels. The same principle holds true for secretaries, as well as for specialized women professionals, like doctors and lawyers. All are women whose need to be with their peers has never—until the emergence of networks—been satisfied.

"To work, a network must be exclusive," says Dr. Pauline Bart. "There's no point in having a network if anybody can get in it. Still, there are some things I'd like to see, such as secretaries being included in a businesswoman's network so secretaries, too, could hear about better jobs." Are women's networks, then, which in large measure are successful *because* they are exclusive and specialized, in danger of becoming just like the Old Boy Network?

Women, who for so long have been left out, are sincerely concerned about leaving out other women, a healthy commentary on where women are today. Many women who belong to networks cannot help but ask themselves, What are we getting into and where are we going?

"There is increased recognition that women can enhance themselves through networks, but there are several dangers," says Dr. Sally Bulkley Pancrazio. "Since networking is based on favors, loyalties, and personal influence, it provides the environment for cover-up and, at the worst, mediocrity. Kingpins are formed and kingmakers are revered. Networks exist to maintain power hierarchies, pyramid style. The system is still closed. Networks can close off healthy dissent, deviance, and creativity."

How, then, can women shape networks to be different?

The kind of networks women need, believes Dr. Pancrazio, are nontraditional, those which, first, increase individual success and, second, raise the overall impact level of women as a class.

In every network studied for this book, it was gratifying to hear the concern that the Old Girl Network not turn out solely to be the power game the Old Boy Network is. Most women feel accountable to other women. Most women who belong to networks have arrived where we are very gradually. We know from our own experience what it takes for a woman to succeed in a world dominated by men, and we support other women who are not successes in the traditional sense of the word, too. We do not intend to withdraw our support. On the contrary, women who belong to networks are making even stronger commitments to help other women get ahead. We are women who clearly welcome the opportunity to band together to enjoy the fruits of our labor and to increase our own and our women colleagues' positions.

Whatever our individual needs, women are eagerly seizing on networks as a potent mechanism to help break down the barriers that keep us underpaid, underemployed, and uninformed. To conceive such alliances shows that women want to move ahead and that we realize we can help each other achieve a common goal. Through networking, we can make inroads and changes. At present, the Good Old Boys have a fairly firm grip on running the show and reaping the profits, but they are vulnerable. Jane Byrne managed to slip by them. You can too. But it is almost impossible to do it alone. Through the collective clout of networking, you will be able to advance your career, improve your life-style, make more money, gratify your own self-interest, and at the same time help other women to move ahead right along with you. And that is precisely what women's networks are all about.

2 | Business Networks

... women often have wrong expectations of strong women. That is, such women are expected to be Self-sacrificing for their sisters, rather than Self-affirming.
—Mary Daley in Gyn-Ecology

Nearly everyone knows that Philadelphia is a financial town. And that's why the Philadelphia Forum for Executive Women is business-oriented, with a membership made up of a high percentage of women in banking and insurance and a generous sprinkling of management consultants. Of the seventy members of this well-functioning network, not one is the least bit embarrassed about being "Self-affirming." These strong women take—and give—as a matter of course. Their daily dealings with the hard realities of the business world, where women are more often than not left out of important decisions and important opportunities, have motivated the forum members to join forces. Networking, of necessity, has become a way of life in Philadelphia and other cities among women who want to make money, who want more power, who want to make it.

Even though business networks are a relatively new phenomenon, women are learning quickly how to use them, for their own advancement and for that of other women colleagues. Betsy Gemmill, for example, one of the original members of the Philadelphia Forum, believes women in business must help other women in business, so when she was made vice-president of the Girard Bank, she didn't hesitate a moment. There was a terrific job opening: her former job of general counsel and secretary-treasurer in the bank's operation division. Gemmill moved quickly to fill the spot with another woman who was a competent lawyer. "At the Forum, I had met Libby Fishman, an attorney for the Franklin Mint Corporation," Gemmill says. "We became friends. I told her about the opening."

Today, Libby Fishman is general counsel, secretary-treasurer, and vice-president of the Girard Bank. Her colleague and fellow Philadelphia Forum network member, Betsy Gemmill, is also a vice-president.

Why Business Networks?

All over the United States, businesswomen like Fishman and Gemmill are forming networks. Their chief motive: profit. Most of the women in the hundreds of business networks in the United States today have never joined anything before; rather, they are women who are so committed to their careers they have no time for anything so "frivolous" as women's organizations. But their good business sense tells them right away that networking is *not* frivolous. They know it is vital for them as professional and career women to exchange relevant career information, to provide support for problem solving, and to help develop skills and a sense of professionalism. They know, too, that business networks are the best means for them to do this, and that is why they are members.

Business networks are booming everywhere. Among them are the Women Entrepreneurs of Portland, Oregon; the Westchester County (New York) Association of Women Business Owners; the Women's Business Council of Dade County, Florida; The Network, Atlanta, Georgia; the Woman's City Club in Cincinnati; All the Good Old Girls (AGOG) of Minneapolis, and CAN, a network of business and professional women in Columbus, Ohio, whose openly exhortative name, an acronym for Career Advancement Network, reflects the spirit typical of women networkers. These business networks are highly professional, organized groups of women who meet on a regular basis and work to help one another find out about business opportunities, job openings, and what's going on in the marketplace.

Often, the network itself provides an opportunity for women to exhibit— and to practice—leadership. So whether the network is made up of five women in various professions or hundreds in the same business, the process of networking is beneficial as far as job skills are concerned. Many networks are formed around shared professional commitments. Others are in-plant, networks of women who work for the same company. Some of the most successful business networks are made up of women in the same industry, such as the National Association of Bank Women and the Women's Media Group of New York, networks that actively pursue better job opportunities for their members. Women business owners, too, are increasingly banding together in networks.

Who Joins Business Networks?

Ava Stern, author of *The Self-Made Woman*, has some interesting observations about women in business. "They are extremely independent and difficult to organize, because they are basically rebels," she says. Within existing networks, Stern finds that women who have participated in other business groups can get more out of and put more into their network than women who have never joined anything. Stern's analysis is based on her experience as founding president of the New York Association of Women Business Owners and publisher of the business monthly *Enterprising Women*.

That solitary, almost inaccessible person, the "token" woman, is, surprisingly, one of the most avid networkers. As a direct result of the past decade, during which women have lobbied for equal rights and representation, many corporations named one woman to a top post, local governments put one woman in a high position, and the media have one or two women in visible spots. Women, one by one, are getting more responsible jobs, and their tasks and the weight of what they do hang heavier on them just because they *are* women. Because they are "token," it isn't politic for them to show any doubts or confusion, as a man in the same position might do. These women, then, are spearheading the formation of business and professional networks throughout the United States. By joining forces with one another, they give and get mutual support and also provide the climate for more women to enter management. Here again, they themselves profit from helping others: The more women in management, the less "token" the original solitary woman is.

Networks are as plentiful among "beginners" as they are among the more established businesswomen. The smart career woman sees women's networks as the difference between making it and making it big. "Look at it this way," an eager middle-management woman points out. "If you're competing with a woman who is in a network and that network is staunchly behind her, you are at a distinct disadvantage if you don't belong to one. It would take a roomful of mentors, role models, and then some to make up for *that* handicap!"

Women have always shared job information, but by joining formal or informal networks we commit ourselves to helping other women. Sometimes, however, the exchange of information is overwhelming for those in demand as role models and mentors. This situation has led one network in Los Angeles, the Organization of Women Executives, to keep a very low profile. Jane Wilson in *Savvy* magazine says that in order to survive as a network for its members, the group strenuously avoids publicity and remains a strictly private sisterhood of heavyweights in the business world who wish to communicate at a more sophisticated level than is possible in the presence of beginners.

Whatever level you are at on the business ladder, the woman who wants to get ahead doesn't want to be left behind. As well as being frustrating and disappointing, being left behind is not conducive to earning money for things like feeding yourself and your family.

How Business Networks Are Born

Instead of dwelling on feelings of resentment at being left out of the mainstream of business activity, women are now forming networks to become active participants. The Women's Lunch Group in Boston, born in 1975 out of hunger for an equal shot at making it in the world of business, is one example of women in business who are making inroads through networking. Bobby Altman and Nancy Korman, founding members of the Women's Lunch Group, are partners in 760 Associates, a graphics and public relations firm in Newton, Massachusetts, a suburb of Boston. Altman and Korman have been in business together since 1969.

"Nancy's in charge of contacts, of making the phone calls to pick up new customers," Bobby Altman explains. "One day she decided to call an old political friend, one she had done a lot of favors for. She asked for a meeting, so we could make a presentation. But he said that would be impossible. He belongs to a breakfast club, and all his business goes to the breakfast club member who does public relations and graphics."

Later that same day, Altman recalls, Korman called another old friend with the same request. He had the same answer.

"Nancy was livid," says Altman. "We had lunch in Boston that day with some other women. One was an international economist, another ran a headhunting firm for managerial women, and a third is now director of the Mayor's Office for Cultural Affairs. Nancy was fuming. She said she couldn't stand it anymore. We decided to form our own network and to have lunch meetings because none of us were free for breakfast or dinner. The next time we met there were ten of us, and we became the Women's Lunch Group."

The group now numbers eighty—"It's impossible to be loyal to more than eighty people at a time," says Altman—and they're all in there pitching for one another and for themselves, in the best networking tradition.

And, in the best networking tradition, Korman isn't so livid anymore, because *her* contacts are now paying off in contracts. "It took us at least two years for our Women's Lunch Group to take off and get going, but the contacts we have made there resulted in actual business, not just directly but indirectly, too," says Altman.

The Women's Lunch Group meets once a month at the Harvard Club in Boston, and, says Altman, the choice of location was an important consideration. "At first we thought we'd hold our meetings at the Woman's City Club, but then we decided we had to be where the action is. You know, we discovered you can meet new people and even do a lot of business while taking an elevator to the thirty-eighth floor!"

The Women's Lunch Group is successful, and Altman attributes much of that success to the fact that it was set up properly and concentrates solely on being a network. "We never mention kids," she says. "We are not a consciousness-raising group. Our members discuss how they *feel* elsewhere. At our meetings, we discuss business only."

Networks of Women Business Owners

Though Korman and Altman are business owners, they chose to form a network that cuts across professions and specific management responsibilities. Other women who own businesses feel the need to network with women who share precisely their concerns. One of the largest of these networks is the National Association of Women Business Owners (NAWBO). Nine different networks belong to the umbrella group and they represent all kinds of businesses, from catering services to selling photographic equipment. The groups are active on a local basis in Minneapolis, Chicago, Pittsburgh, Houston, Boston, Miami, Durham, Washington, and Los Angeles. Their motive is a familiar one: profit. Though NAWBO members are allied, it is somewhat typical of women who are in business networks that each one of the chapters is intensely and fiercely local. And not all networks with the title "Women Business Owners" belong to the national group.

As in most business networks, NAWBO meetings begin with each member standing up and introducing herself and announcing her business connection and the kind of clients she is looking for. At a recent meeting of the Chicago chapter, one member said she owned a flower shop and wanted to rent plants. A woman who owns and manages apartments quickly signed her up to supply greenery for the lobby of her buildings. At the same meeting, a woman explained the workings of a wholesale fruit and vegetable supply business she ran. Present that evening was a woman who owns a restaurant. The restaurant owner is now being supplied with produce by her network colleague.

Women who own businesses are perhaps even busier than other women. "Our members spend an enormous number of hours on their businesses," says Virginia Littlejohn of Women Entrepreneurs of San Francisco. "Our group started out small and informal, and today it is one of the largest single unaffiliated groups. We have some four hundred women who are making a go of their business, spend fifty to eighty hours a week at it, but who find networks germane and important."

And in Philadelphia, women who will one day be owning and operating businesses are already networking to make sure thay reach their goal; women with masters' in business administration—that much talked-about and important MBA degree—from the Wharton School of Finance of the University of Pennsylvania have their own network. Taking their cue from their Old

Boy peers, the women are forming their own power base, establishing the contacts they know will help them in the years ahead.

Forum—The Popular Business Network

The buzz word in business networks is "forum," a sophisticated word that matches the desire of many women executives for their network to have a dignified and businesslike name. The forums, which include the Women's Forum of Colorado, the Albany (New York) Women's Forum, the Philadelphia Forum for Executive Women, the Women's Forum of North Carolina, the Bay Area Executive Women's Forum in San Francisco, and New York's powerful Women's Forum, are not affiliated with each other. Their birthings were spontaneous, with a little help from friends in other states, though there are efforts to unite the forums nationally.

According to Margaret Price in *Industry Week*, the forums are "real old boy stuff—without the cigars." They are blatantly elitist; only the top, most powerful women belong. Some, like New York's Women's Forum, which numbers 155 extremely successful and powerful women, are even formidable. Price gives two examples of what networking means at top levels of the power structure, above and beyond the advice and support businesswomen give each other through their networks: When Carol Bellamy, a Women's Forum member, was running for president of the New York City Council in 1977, her network urged other members to aid her campaign, which they did. Bellamy rolled up 83 percent of the vote, and became the first woman ever elected to citywide office in New York. And Lee Lowell, executive director of the Women's Forum, says that just after both President Carter and New York's Mayor Edward Koch were elected, their respective staffs called the Forum seeking applicants for top-level administrative jobs.

More testimony to the power of women's networks comes from Sherrye Henry, charter member of the Women's Forum and host of the Sherrye Henry program on WOR radio in New York. "I have a real advantage in that I can check things out, easily, with other women in the Forum," says Henry. "That's the advantage of a network. I've had one third of the membership on my show. The women say yes because they know me, and the radio exposure helps them, too. I never go to a Forum meeting that I don't find good program ideas. Members call me and suggest ideas that would be helpful for them and interesting for me to do." And, because of her membership in the network, Henry, who has given much to her colleagues, has gotten something extra in return. "Through the Forum, I've been hired as a consultant to the *Ladies' Home Journal*," she says with delight.

The excitement of making contact with other businesswomen with the expressed purpose of helping one another is almost universal in networks. Elizabeth Wright Ingraham talks about the Women's Forum of Colorado: "The thrilling part is in the colleagueship developed. We know what women are doing things and where. We're sharing work experiences. Everybody in the group feels that during the first two years, we have opened up and started to know one another. We're included in things that happen in business. We get referrals from other network members. We have entrees we'd never have otherwise because of our network connections. Right now, in fact, we're expanding our horizons and moving into the fabric of the business, social, and political world."

Because of such testimony and the many successes of Forum networks, new networks springing up are eager to adopt the name. Anyone can, of course, as all the Forum groups, so far, are not officially connected to one another.

Where Do Business Networks Meet?

Because even the most prestigious women do not usually belong to private clubs or established institutions in which we can hold network meetings—we certainly do not have any permanent domains such as the Union League or other private men's clubs—we have to come up with our own meeting places. Busy businesswomen have been extremely innovative in this area. There seems to be universal agreement that meeting in each other's homes is counterproductive: It diminishes the aura of professionalism most business networks need to create to get ahead, and, more practically, most women are too busy and hold transportation time at too high a premium to attend any meeting away from the downtown area they most likely work in. Because of these factors, women's business networks meet in company and school cafeterias, restaurants, exclusive private clubs to which their corporations belong, and, in one case, even at a yacht club!

The New Girl Network in Winston-Salem, North Carolina, for example, meets quite conveniently in the cafeteria of Salem College, a small liberal arts college for women. Its founder, Martha Fleer, is Salem's director of continuing education and counseling. "We meet one day a week and have lunch together," she says. "Everyone stands up and introduces herself. This leads to jobs." The New Girl Network consists of business and professional women but is also open to secretaries who want to advance in their careers, and the informal meeting place permits a more egalitarian atmosphere to prevail than if the meetings took place at an expensive downtown club. The cafeteria reflects the network's openness to all.

The meetings of the Orange Coast Network have quite a different setting, according to Susan Strecker in *The Executive Female*. The members meet at a local yacht club. As Strecker says, why not? It's in sunny Newport Beach, California, and consists of a well-rounded group of fifty area women in high positions from both the private and public sector. It's not known if any of the members own yachts yet—but they will.

Strecker also reports that Pittsburgh's Executive Women's Council meets informally each week at a downtown department store and formally at the Press Club; another network meets informally in the privacy of the "ladies' room" of a major New York bank, and CAN (Career Advancement Network) of Columbus, Ohio, has its monthly get-together at the "Spare Room" of Lazarus Department Store.

There is the possibility in the not too distant future that businesswomen will establish their own Union Leagues, athletic clubs, and university clubs with athletic facilities and private dining rooms, just as the men have done. A portent of things to come is the Women's Athletic Club of the Boston YWCA, which opened in 1979. With the membership come exercise rooms, reading rooms, telephones, photocopy machines, typewriters, catered luncheons—and networking.

The Business of Business Networks

Because of the explosion in popularity of women's networks throughout the United States, some networks are in the business of establishing networks for other women as a commercial enterprise. And women eager to network flock to them. Women Can Win, based in Los Angeles, is clearly one of these. Judi Hochman, president and founder of Women Can Win, is a therapist with a degree in social work who has counseled many women. A former psychiatric social worker and college counselor, Hochman has talked to hundreds of women on a one-to-one basis, women concerned about themselves and where they are going, women who want to get there. "Always, there was something missing," Hochman says. She believes what was missing is networking.

In response to this need, Hochman runs weekend seminars once a month in Los Angeles and Newport Beach and at various locations in the San Fernando Valley. The two-day seminars cost $250 per person. So far, each seminar has been attended by an average of some twenty women. The seminars include intense career boosting, time management training, brainstorming, and self-actualization. There are workbooks, exercises, and a reading list that runs the gamut from *Look Your Best*, by model Candy Jones, to *Executive Jobs Unlimited*, by Carl Bowl. Hochman's staff includes two women who have advanced degrees in business and psychology.

The Women Can Win seminar is attended by diverse kinds of women from all levels of business. Many are mature women re-entering the labor market. A good number are displaced homemakers. Some are women on their way up; others are established career women who feel isolated in what they do. Through Hochman, they are "linked up." At the end of the two-day seminar, she divides them into smaller groups of from five to ten women. That is their network. And, like other business networks formed out of self- and group interest, they work. Each network then continues to meet, once a month, at members' homes.

"A woman who had worked for a large newspaper as a graphic arts director always wanted to do something on her own," says Hochman. "Somehow, she never got around to taking that step. She had many excuses: She was married, had two children, couldn't take a chance. But in our seminar, she learned she didn't need a lot of money. She needed clients. From our group of twenty women at her weekend seminar, she got five clients."

Hochman is just one of many professionals now in the business of *teaching* the art of networking. Almost every career conference, seminar, or workshop given for women today includes at least one session on how to network—such as the full-day seminar on networking recently given at Macy's department store in New York. According to Biffie Estabrook of Macy's, fifty women who planned to re-enter the job market and wanted to learn how to climb the corporate ladder spent $15 each and learned to network. The workshop, says Estabrook, was a resounding success. And at the New York YMCA, a semiannual "contact" seminar organized by Christine Filner draws hundreds of women who want to learn to network. The women wear name tags, exchange business cards, and make luncheon dates and business appointments with the women they meet that day. The charge: $12.00 each.

How Seminars and Workshops Work

Does for-profit networking work? Yes, just the same as teaching law prepares people to become lawyers. Law school is not free. What is different about the business of networking as contrasted to other commercial enterprises is that networking's results are more subtle and often take longer to materialize. But the results are impressive. Network entrepreneurs point to many successes on the part of their clients, such as this story Hochman tells:

Janet McKinley, twenty, is a young, very talented designer who attended a Woman Can Win seminar. At the time, she was designing clothes from her home. Because of her limited quarters, she had been able to produce only ten original designs.

Through Women Can Win, McKinley met Jo Lathwood, seventy-eight, who was the first woman to design a bikini. The senior designer showed the young woman how to get into production, how to handle more than five or six items in one line. She introduced McKinley to a fine professional seamstress. The result: McKinley is in business, has had her own fashion show, has her garments in Bullock's and Robinson's department stores in Los Angeles, and is making it.

Now, Let's Talk About Money!

The politics of career advancement are new to most women who, until the past decade, believed like Elsie Dinsmore that virtue shall triumph. Perhaps it does, but businesswomen, especially in California, seem to pick up on the notion rapidly that you also need all the help you can get.

If you like to talk about lots of money and true success stories, talk to Joy Davis of Women in Business in Los Angeles.

Davis was an original member of the board of the network. When it was organized in 1974, she was an assistant manager at a small bank. One of the things she learned at network meetings was that contacts are money. Back at the bank, Davis realized she had lots of contacts in film, which is really where she wanted to be. So, in 1975, she took the plunge. She gave up her job, became an assistant producer, quickly rose to producer, and today is an executive producer of successful commercial films, some of which have been shown at the Cannes Film Festival. Further testimony to her financial success: Davis has had to buy a fleet of ships for a tax shelter!

"She's made a fortune," says Lore Caulfield, founder of Women in Business.

Davis is not the network's only major success story. There's Caulfield herself, who switched from film making to becoming a lingerie manufacturer, and Sandra Winston, who is president of a management consulting firm and author of *The Entrepreneurial Woman*. Winston, married and the mother of three, was once a full-time homemaker; today she is a confident, dynamic businesswoman who has gained national recognition as an expert in her field. Winston herself attributes many of her insights about business and much of her success to her network and is active in helping other women get ahead.

Other members of Women in Business include Elaine Wegener, founder of PACT, a consultant firm. Wegener told Kathleen Hendrix of the *Los Angeles Times* that PACT exceeded $350,000 worth of business in 1979; her other business, Quest, had revenues of $1 million. Sylvia Kirts, a British-born clinical psychologist in private practice with Gestalt Associates in Santa Monica, is also a Women in Business member. Before she joined, Kirts had not been involved in investments. Through the network, she got the courage and confidence she needed to start business investments and became an investor in Streel Fuels, Ltd., a Delaware-based company. Kirts so impressed the company that she is now one of their representatives—as well as being involved in other lucrative business ventures of her own.

Advancing Your Career Through Networking

How can women move ahead in business? How can women get appointed to important committees and government posts? Business and professional women have observed over the years that the prestigious appointments almost invariably go to men before they ever hear about them. Women who work in offices know if they can find out about a job opening early, they have a much better chance to apply for it and get it. But who will tell the career woman about these opportunities? The answer throughout the country—and the only answer so far—is women's networks. It was specifically for this purpose that a San Francisco network of business and professional women was formed.

The Professional Women's Alliance (PWA) in San Francisco is a highly structured, high-level network that was founded with the express intent of satisfying the needs of upper-level management women, women who could fill government appointments when the specific request came for women. They got what they wanted. When the Federal Reserve Bank called the network to ask if they had any women who could serve, they were able to give the bank several résumés. In fact, the PWA has one member who acts as referral person. "The network works to help other women," says Roxanne Mankin, co-founder, "It's important that our referral person and all our members not be so competitive that they don't want to recommend someone better suited than they for these important posts."

PWA boasts another real advancement for women in the area of top government jobs. Sharlene Hirsch, who is manager of the Tennessee Valley Authority's office of community development but who is not in the network, told Diane Winokur, a PWA member and management consultant, that the Tennessee Valley Authority was looking for someone to head it. Winokur, who also belongs to the Bay Area Executive Women's Forum, told Hirsch, "Marilyn Taylor, who was the major labor negotiator on behalf of management for the Kaiser Sand and Gravel Company and is one of our PWA members, would be perfect for that." As it turns out, Taylor was: She got the job and moved to Tennessee, where she heads a staff of 30,000 persons. That might not have happened without PWA.

No one seems to be holding back. Cindy Cotter, first woman contractor in the state of California, also belongs to the network. Through PWA, Mankin and Cotter are jointly negotiating to become part of a $6 million condominium project in Arizona. If they make the deal, they'll sell the condos for $11 million. "That's an alliance that wouldn't have happened without the network," says Mankin. "And," she adds, "without PWA, I would never have met Cindy." The two women have also put together another real estate deal: a $15 million office building.

The Media Take Note of Business Networks

As networks begin to precipitate millions of dollars in business and powerful directorships, business publications are taking notice of them. After all, those millions of dollars and powerful directorships would have gone to members of the Old Boy Network if Old Girls hadn't interfered in the process. The *Wall Street Journal, Business Week, New York Magazine, MBA* magazine, *Newsweek, Industry Week, Savvy, Working Woman, Ladies' Home Journal, Female Executive Digest,* and even *Women's Wear Daily* have done serious studies of the impact of networking. *Newsweek* describes Old Girl Networks as gatherings "for the unabashed purpose of making contacts." The magazine has focused on the Washington Women's Network, Houston's exclusive River Oaks Business Women's Exchange Club, San Francisco's Women's Forum-West, Los Angeles' Women in Business, the Professional Women's Association of Chicago, Atlanta's The Network, and an informal group of corporate wives in Detroit who report openings to other women—openings in their husbands' corporations.

In-House Networks: The Wave of the Future

In-house networks are networks made up of women employees in the same company. These are rare. Alina Novak formed an in-house network called Networks at Equitable Life Assurance Society in New York City in 1977. At that time she worked in the benefits and compensation areas of the company. Novak, an economist, learned so much about the firm in the network that she earned a promotion to executive assistant to the president in 1978. More recently, she was promoted to senior financial analyst. The network has 450 members in the company. Equitable approves of the network and even helps finance it with $3,000 annually. Novak believes so strongly in the value of networking that she has started another network for women in business. It is called the Fortune 500 Business and Professional Women's Club, and its ninety members meet the fourth Thursday of every month at the Harvard Club. The club is committed to elevating the status of women and to the passage of the ERA. Dues are $35 a year.

In-house networks like the one at Equitable can work wonders. Another,

Alliance for Women, started at AT&T in New York in 1973, no longer exists, but in-house networks at Metropolitan Life Insurance Company, the Columbia Broadcasting Company (CBS), the Port Authority of New York, and at several affiliates of the Corporation for Public Broadcasting are active. In-house networks are naturals; they are the logical alternative to the Old Boy Network for women who want to get ahead in the company where they now work. They are also an ideal means of keeping abreast of job openings and other important in-house information. But not all companies are as liberal as Equitable or Metropolitan Life, and at this time in-house networks are still few and far between.

Many experts, such as Rosabeth Moss Kanter, management consultant and Yale professor, believe the future of women's networks lies in in-house networks. It will take gutsy women to set them up and get them going—and *then* ask their employers' permission to have one. But women who work in offices where they watch men with only mediocre talents get promotion after promotion might decide to risk forming a network. If you're a business-woman, it may be the only way to succeed.

Women who want to have an in-house network often begin just by going to lunch with three other women, which is a good nucleus. Discussions of lack of opportunity, waste of money, oppressive policies in the office are the general topics of office lunch groups anyway, regardless of gender. But if the working woman adds to these natural and informal lunches a *focus*, a way out of the tunnel, so to speak, they will be productive luncheons. They will also be networks.

Taking the energy expended in legitimate and necessary complaints and gripes and deciding to do something about them, to look out for one another, to have regular luncheon meetings to figure out what to do, can be the best thing a working woman has going for her at the office. To know that, on the job, there are a handful of people with your best interests in mind, who are there to lean on, to share information with, who *care* about what happens to you—especially when so often the Big Bosses are invisible and do *not* care— can make moving ahead on the job a real possibility. And the road to better jobs, better pay, better working conditions need not be so filled with frustration, barriers, and lack of information. Instead, it can have good feelings— and positive results—connected with it.

Networking at the office is worth a try.

National Efforts at Networking

Although it has already made impressive inroads in the traditionally male-dominated business sector, networking is still, by and large, such an untapped source for women that it hasn't even been "nationalized" yet. True, the National Association of Women Business Owners does have nine local networks, but, as we have seen, they are independent. Efforts are being made to affiliate existing Women's Forums under one umbrella and to set up more in other cities and states. So far, this "nationalization" hasn't jelled. The National Alliance of Professional Women's Networks also is working to form national links.

In addition, the National Women's Education Fund, which organized the Washington Women's Network (see chapter 6), received an anonymous grant to help join together all networks. In March, 1979, a meeting was held in Washington with twenty representatives of ten networks in a four-state area. Plans were not completed, but the representatives were asked, upon returning home, to seek out and document all networks in their area—a huge task because of the nascent state and somewhat amorphous structure of so many of the networks.

The women's media are also using their influence to spur the movement to national networks. *Working Woman*, one of the first magazines—regardless of gender—to recognize networking and its importance, has asked its readers to send in the name of every network they know of, with the hope of compiling a national networking directory. *The Executive Female*, magazine of the National Association for Female Executives (NAFE), asked its readers— 38,000 women executives—to send in names and addresses of networks too. And they went one step further: In its May/June issue, 1979, it announced it was setting up its *own* NAFE Networks. "NAFE," it promised in an editorial, "will help NAFE members in your area to exchange ideas, share job and career information, discuss common problems, and in general offer each other the advantages of shared individual resources." NAFE offered to list names of people who requested to be NAFE Network Directors for their area. Then it would be up to the director to get in touch with everyone in her city who got in touch with her through the magazine and to establish a network. NAFE promised to produce a special network newsletter to keep everyone informed.

By the time the next issue had come out, some 500 NAFE members had sent in their names and addresses to get NAFE networks off the ground. The enthusiasm was overwhelming. Wendy Rue, president and executive director of NAFE, says the network will have definite political overtones in meeting the needs of its members. "Some of the first issues we will be focusing on are: iniquities of the single income tax return; iniquities of the double paycheck family—which bite most often into the female executive's earnings—and our current Social Security laws, which fail to take into account the fact that women comprise 50% of the American workforce," Rue told her readers. She sees the NAFE networks as making a difference in the area that spells true liberation for women: "$$$$!" as she puts it.

National vs. Local Networks

As the power and the tangible results of women's networks become more obvious, many women in local and regional business networks are feeling the need to extend their connections to a national level. Sister Colette Mahoney of New York's Women's Forum talks about a national "shoulder touching" of networks. "There is a movement that wants to be tied together," says Mahoney, who is president of Marymount Manhattan College and on the board of directors of several large corporations. "A national charter would be a long-dreamed-of opportunity for women of some achievement to communicate with one another."

The high, the excitement women feel from simply meeting other women in local networks who have achieved in business—without anyone else's knowing of their existence—would naturally heighten at a national level. Some women in local networks state firmly that they feel it is their right, finally, to know and to be known nationally, even internationally. Perhaps these dimensions will be a part of networking in the future, but today the most dominant aspect of business networks seems to be the one-to-one contact among women and the feeling of solidarity that results from working together—at a local level—to achieve a common goal. Any reservations about the formulation of national business networks are limited only to the chances of achieving the goal, not to their value.

There is concern that, at a national level, business and professional women would lose the intimate, even precious functions that local networking provide. National networks are seen by some as a kind of businesswomen's Chamber of Commerce, which businesswomen, who are excluded from most all-male business organizations, badly need.

The weekly or monthly meetings, the phone calls, the accidental meetings in the street, the sharing of knowledge of job opportunites are by their nature localized. That particular aspect of networking might be lost in national umbrella groups. There are those, however, who envision national business networks functioning as strong lobby groups, as distributors of newsletters, and as a political fist for local network arms. Just as networking evolved from role models and mentors, perhaps the next step from networks will be strong national business associations, with the stated purpose of working for the advancement of women's careers. They would be wonderful and vital organizations. But they would not be networks.

The beauty of networking *is* that it is new and can change and grow to suit the needs of its members. Clearly, even in these early days of women's networks, it is a potent force for change. While it might not be the answer to every working woman's fondest dream, it is a strong, assertive step in the right direction.

If you are a career woman, out in the work world, putting in long hours of hard work, you owe it to yourself to explore the possibility of networking, what it can do for you and what you can do for it. Through networking, you will find the group support you now lack, a circle of friends who understand the reality of working 9 to 5. You will find through networking you'll be privy to what is going on in other businesses and in your own company too. You'll hear about job openings; you'll learn when people are leaving to go on to other jobs or have been promoted. Instead of having a worm's-eye view of the world of business, you'll be a confident and active participant. Networking is one of the few springboards today's businesswoman has to success. Don't leave home without one.

3 | Professional Networks:
Doctors, Lawyers, Educators, Political Scientists, Architects, and More!

Fewer women hold high-ranking jobs not only because of overt discrimination and exclusion but because their sex status places them disadvantageously in the structure of their profession.
—Cynthia Fuchs Epstein in *Woman's Place*

Like business networks, professional networks are booming in the United States. Like businesswomen, professional women see clearly the need to band together and network in order to get top appointments and more money and to learn what's going on in the world of research, grants, and honorary positions. Unlike business networks, however, professional networks are formed around specific interests and do not cut across a wide variety of jobs or careers.

Honing in on one field of interest, rather than many, is the basis of the success of such professional networks as The Queen's Bench in Portland, Oregon (for lawyers); the Alaska Council of Administrative Women in Education in Juneau; the Association for Women Attorneys in New Orleans; Archives of Women in Architecture, New York; Sisters for a Human Environment, Seattle (also architects); the National Women's Studies Association; the national Women's College Coalition, based in Washington, a network of presidents of women's colleges; and the Neylan Conference, an offshoot of the coalition, made up of nuns who are college presidents.

All over the United States, doctors, lawyers, architects, sociologists, psychologists, and educators have formed networks for women colleagues. Despite the fact that networking is so new, the networks command increasing influence, and results—profitable ones—are already being seen.

The professional woman who does not join a network is at a distinct disadvantage in these sophisticated fields where men have mentors and women by the hundreds are joining the scores of professional networks dedicated to the advancement of their members.

Who Joins Professional Networks?

Professional women are still so few in number within any given institution, corporation, or business firm that most women who are doctors, lawyers, architects, sociologists, or other professionals are considered "token," one of a kind. Their feelings of isolation are similar to those of women in top corporate jobs. And, as you might expect, their reasons for joining networks are the same: the opportunity for better jobs and more rapid advancement, higher annual incomes, and the chance to know and have access to their peers, other women who are in the same field and who they can count on to work *for* them, not against them.

In the past, many women have dropped out of the professions, and their reasons are understandable—especially in those professions which require long years of education and training and more long years to get established. These are lonely years for most women, and, in the majority of cases, professional women (or those who aspired to become professionals) had to make it on their own, without benefit of mentors or female colleagues who had made it and were willing to lend a hand to the neophyte. The past scarcity of women professionals—and their continued scarcity—in fields like engineering and physics stifles the progress of women who choose to enter these fields and, worse, often acts as a deterrent to young women who might otherwise have entered them.

But recently, despite the continuing bleak picture for women professionals insofar as tenure, promotions, appointments, or funding is concerned, the rate of attrition of women in professional fields is on the decrease. The difference: networks. Women preparing for professions are now joining networks, formal and informal ones, which provide a support group and a source of confidence and strength that women need to succeed. Oddly enough, the very isolation of women in professional fields is viewed by women who belong to networks as an advantage. Says sociologist Arlene Kaplan Daniels, "The sense of working together as an embattled few can provide a sense of solidarity and an impulse to develop greater esprit de corps."

What Professional Networks Do for You

Women doctors, women lawyers, women administrators of schools and colleges have long been invisible, not only to male colleagues and the outside world but also to themselves. One of the first goals of the new professional networks springing up all over the United States is to locate and identify the women in the field. If you are a physicist, how many other women physicists do you know? Probably not many, unless you belong to a network like the Association for Women in Science. So the first task of organizers of networks such as HERS (Higher Education Resources Services) is to make as accurate a count as possible of their colleagues in the same field. After locating, contacting, and forming networks with other professionals, the real work of professional networks begins.

The profit motive is a primary goal of professional networks, and most of them have newsletters or other methods of directly—and quickly—contacting members to inform them of job openings. Dr. Reatha Clark King, for example, president of Metropolitan State University in St. Paul, Minnesota, and one of only three black women to be president of an American college, is a product of networking. Back in 1975, she was a resource person at a HERS workshop in Philadelphia. Dr. King has her master's degree in business administration from Columbia University and was then assistant dean of York College of the City University of New York. Also at the workshop were officials of Metropolitan State University in St. Paul. The university was looking for a new president and was impressed with Dr. King. Next, the university checked with Donna Shavlik, associate director of the Women's Office for Higher Education in Washington. She recommended Dr. King for the position. And so did Cynthia Secor of HERS–Mid-Atlantic. "It's very helpful to be part of the education network," says Dr. King. Help is needed because in 1979 there were only 182 women college presidents and 2,318 men college presidents. The inroads of networking here, however, are making a difference.

Support is another purpose of professional networks. Boosts to the morale may not result immediately in higher annual incomes, but they do give you the courage to hang in and keep trying to move forward. Professional networks such as the American Association of Women Dentists, Association for Women in Science, American Women in Psychology, National Women in the Law Conference, and Women in History are gearing up to move their members into the mainstream and decision-making levels of their fields. Their route: networking.

Communication, Research, and "Doing Good"

Communication is also a goal of professional networks. Newsletters such as the one Sarah Slavin Schramm edits for the Women's Caucus for Political Science, in Pittsburgh, keep members abreast of what's going on in their field. Encouraging students to enter the professions is another networking aim; the New Orleans chapter of the American Medical Women's Association, for example, has a special program to link up with premedical and medical students. The feeling of being a part of something important is an ingredient of the professional networks.

Through networks, women are trying to break down traditional barriers in the professions that keep them in low positions and at low salaries for so long. Often, the route to moving ahead in the professions is research. And women, through networking, are making that happen too. Myra Dinnerstein, for instance, head of women's studies at the University of Arizona in Tucson, is creating a southwest network among women doing research on pioneer women, both contemporary and historical. Her group, located in an area which has a high representation of ethnic and rural women, is called Southwest Institute for Research on Women in the Western Frontier; its aim is to give support to those in the field, to encourage research, and to work to get funding for relevant projects.

Funding for research has always been a problem for women. A report sponsored by the Ford Foundation found that of the more than $2 billion in private foundation grants in 1976, only six tenths of one percent (0.6%) went to women's projects. Paltry as it is, this figure represents a considerable improvement over previous years; grants from private foundations to women's projects had increased from $1.7 million in 1971 to some $12 million by 1976. That increase, however small, is due in large part to the activities of women in networks—women insisting on being heard, insisting on a fair share. There are also networks that help women master the technique of acquiring grants. "I spend a lot of time helping groups learn how to play the funding game," Nancy Castleman, grants administrator at the Fund for the City of New York, told the *New York Times*. And Leeda Martin, manager of national contributions for the Levi Strauss Foundation, got down to brass tacks: "We're talking about redistribution of power," she told the *Times*.

While everyone likes to make money, most professional women also have a commitment to "doing good." Many women in the networks of doctors, nurses, lawyers, and teachers are idealistic—they want to help others, to see ideas for research that might ultimately help others bear fruit. The professional networks tell their members something they don't hear in too many other places: It's okay to want to change the world. It's okay to want to make a difference, to feel an obligation to help, to want to relieve pain and suffering. It's okay to give back.

How Professional Networks Work

While traditionally women have been viewed as suspicious of one another, at each other's throats, and knifing each other in the back at every opportunity, networks are a clear statement that this simply is not true. Instead, not only are women professionals finding out about those few jobs in their fields and sharing the information, many networking women who move up in their professions are filling their vacant jobs with other networking women—who then look out for the best interests of still more networking colleagues. In this way—at last—professional women are beginning to be in touch with each other and with what is happening in their fields.

Hedy Ratner, now assistant commissioner for public affairs of the U.S. Office of Education, formerly a division of that huge superstructure called Health, Education, and Welfare (HEW) and now the Department of Education, can testify just how a network of women in the American Association of School Administrators (AASA) worked for her.

In 1977, Ratner, then assistant superintendent of Cook County schools in the state of Illinois, was one of seventy-five women singled out as a top school administrator by AASA and the Ford Foundation. A special seminar was held for these women in Los Angeles, and a strong bond—called networking—formed among them. Two years later, Ratner realized her career had nowhere to go but sideways with the Illinois Board of Education, and she began looking for a new job.

A founder of the Illinois Women's Political Caucus (IWPC), a chapter of the National Women's Political Caucus, Ratner got in touch with a friend from the IWPC, Linda Frees, who was living in Washington and promised to help. Frees contacted one of *her* friends, Peggy Rhoades, who had the HEW job then that Ratner has now.

"I went to Washington looking for a job and stayed with my old friend Linda," recalls Ratner. "She introduced me to Peggy Rhoades. Rhoades was moving on to the Social Security Administration and was trying to find a replacement for herself. Rhoades introduced me to Eileen Shanahan, who was assistant secretary for HEW in charge of public affairs. Eileen had been interviewing people for various jobs in the department and was trying to place feminist women in public affairs."

Ratner was interviewed intensely and her credentials checked out, by many HEW officials and by Rhoades and Shanahan in particular. Ratner got her initial interview, however, because of network contacts, which gave her the credibility she needed to get a foot in the door. Her networking with Frees in the Illinois Women's Political Caucus, even after Frees left Chicago, and the fact that Rhoades and Shanahan already knew Ratner from the school administrators' network and Shanahan also knew her from the National Women's Political Caucus—all these networks made it possible for Ratner to have her qualifications examined just like Old Boys do, cutting through the bureaucracy and red tape of the mammoth HEW structure.

There was something else working for Ratner, in addition to the fact that she was the right person for the job. Both Rhoades, now associate commissioner for public affairs for the Social Security Administration, and Shanahan, a former *New York Times* reporter and now assistant managing editor of the *Washington Star*, have a commitment to hiring competent women, especially feminists. Ratner's networking over the years led to a prominent post for herself. Today, she has the job she sought in Washington, earns $39,000 a year, and has a staff of forty-four. And the government has a valuable employee.

Specialized vs. General Networks

The woman who is in a profession has an advantage over the woman in business: She can join the many networks for business and professional women, and she can also join a specialty network for her own profession. In addition to establishing contacts in her own field, the professional woman can cross over to be part of the very prestigious Forums and other business networks that include doctors, lawyers, architects, educators. The advantage is, of course, that she has increased her exposure to include a variety of women in different fields with different professional contacts and connections.

The specialized professional networks have their own distinct advantages. "It's important for networks to be specialized," points out Rosabeth Moss Kanter. "The more specialized the network is, the more helpful it is to women in specific professions." The American Association of School Administrators is an example of a specialized professional network intensely concerned that its members move onward and upward.

On the other hand, professional networks, too, are trying to stretch across traditional disciplinary boundaries and form coalitions, such as the Association for Women in Science, an umbrella group for natural and physical scientists. Today, the growing strength of the Federation of Organizations for Professional Women suggests the continual reaching out to one another by professional networks, using local networks to form strong national umbrella groups.

The professional women is lucky. She doesn't have to make a choice. She can belong both to business networks and to networks of other women in her specialty. She can belong to local networks and to national ones. And, as most professional women will testify, she will need all the help she can get.

Education Networks

Of all the specialized professional networks, the education networks are the strongest, most active, and most effective. There are thousands of women professionals in education, at every level, and they, like women everywhere, are tired of being left out of important, well-paying jobs. They are joining networks with enthusiasm and vigor; they know networking is a path to moving ahead.

In education networks, women aspiring to move on know whom to contact. The names of Bernice Sandler, Effie Jones, Betsey Wright, Donna Shav-lik, Emily Taylor (all in Washington, D.C.), and Dr. Cynthia Secor (in Phila-delphia) are mentioned over and over again by women describing how they got the administrative post or teaching position they presently hold. These women have single-handedly connected women in education with one an-other—and with jobs. They are "extremely supportive," as Hedy Ratner de-scribes them.

One of the "oldest" educational networks is HERS (Higher Education Resource Services), with chapters in Philadelphia, Wellesley, and Salt Lake City. The first was HERS–Mid-Atlantic, funded by the Ford Foundation in 1974 and headed by Dr. Secor at the University of Pennsylvania. Next came HERS–New England at Wellesley College, and most recently funded is HERS–West, at the University of Utah.

The groups' aim is the advancement of women in education. Since 1975, HERS–Mid-Atlantic has held 3½-week seminars each summer in con-junction with Bryn Mawr College. The seminars draw mostly middle-level women from colleges and universities in the United States, Canada, Nigeria, and Great Britain. The seminars are thorough and to the point: Workshops are given in computer training, management techniques, and professional development. Networking is strong, active, and encouraged among faculty and students.

"The way our network operates is first to have a network of women who participate in seminars as instructors and faculty," says Karen Byers, editor of the HERS newsletter, *The Network*. "Then we add a network of women who attend the seminars here each year. We tie them all together with our newsletter, which goes out to 533 women."

The staff is committed to the advancement of women and makes that clear at the seminars. Those attending are committed to moving ahead them-selves. Once again, two vital ingredients of networking are operative: self-in-terest and group interest.

"A lot of women who have attended the seminars report they are able to do their jobs much better and have gotten promotions within a year," reports Byers.

Another permutation of HERS is Carol Carter's network at the University of Massachusetts at Amherst, centered in its New Africa House. Carter's net-work is for minority women. Called the New England Minority Women Ad-ministrators, it locates minority women in administration in the New En-gland area as well as nationally. Minority women, like all women in education, have been invisible, but they are there. Carter's network helps these women cope with their special problems, including the fact that they are usually racially isolated, as at Dartmouth College, for instance, with its predominantly white student body and its distance from other cities.

HERS also has a forty-two-state project searching out women in higher education, researching the common problems and the regional differences. The center of information gathering, however, is the summer seminar at the University of Pennsylvania. And the support that builds at these meetings keeps members going for a long time.

"It's wonderful," says Karen Byers of HERS–Mid-Atlantic. "At the seminars, I see all the supportive things women do for one another, not just professionally but personally. A group of women went with one woman to get her hair styled, to make sure it was right for her. Some others went to help a woman buy a coat and a new wardrobe for a new job. Things like that make you keep fighting, even though it's so damn hard."

Out in the Southwest, Dr. Shauna M. Adix, director of the Women's Resource Center of the University of Utah, also talks about isolation. "Our first project at HERS–West will be to develop a network for women in this area," the social scientist says. "We are so isolated geographically. We do not have ready-made contacts. Our colleges don't even belong to athletic conferences. We are short of revenue, money for travel, for salaries. A lot of the women in this area went to the HERS seminars but they are never going to get back. So we have to be creative even to find out who we are so that some connections can happen."

Her target area is Colorado, Arizona, New Mexico, and Utah. Her budget: $25,000 over three years. Dr. Adix has set up a regional planning council of dynamic, energetic administrators as the basis of the new network. "We want to do additional career training here," she says, "and to establish a process for furthering our careers. We need to know each other."

"Educated" Education Networks

Despite their relative newness, some education networks are already so established they can actually point to specific jobs that are a direct result of networking. One such network is Oregon Women in Educational Administration in Portland, founded in 1977. Pat Schmuck, assistant professor at the University of Oregon and a member of the network, tells a "success" story about Margaret Trachsel, a teacher who attended a network conference. When she returned to her school, she decided what she really wanted to be was a high school principal.

"With the support of the members of the network, Trachsel had enough courage to go to her principal and superintendent—both men—and ask them to help her reach her goal," says Schmuck. "Eighteen months later, Margaret Trachsel became the fifth female high school principal in the state."

Another direct result of the Oregon network is the fact there are now six women superintendents of school districts in Oregon, as opposed to only two in 1972. And groundwork is being laid for further progress and change in the state's educational system. One school vice-principal, a member of the network, questioned her district's hiring two white male principals. That type of challenge takes courage, but she found it in support she got from the network. It gave her both authority and legitimacy to assume an advocacy position. The two principals were retained, but the district, at her suggestion, looked into the "chilling effect" hiring only white males was having on the educational system and the professionals in it.

Education networks are fascinating in their many aspects. Marcia Sharp, director of the Women's College Coalition in Washington, D.C., says her network is a voluntary organization of about sixty undergraduate women's colleges. It acts as an information resource and is an advocate for single-sex colleges. The coalition is an important network because presidents of women's colleges account for half the women who are college presidents.

Today, women in education are so alerted to the fact that they need each other to find out what's going on—something they have the *right* to know—that any and every get-together is a networking event. "Trading job information and finding jobs through networks happens all the time," says Bernice Sandler, director of the Project on the Status and Education of Women at the Association of American Colleges in Washington. Sandler is a member of the National Coalition for Women and Girls in Education, as well as the Washington Women's Network. Some sixty groups make up the Women and Girls Coalition, but in practice, says Sandler, regular attendance at the meetings numbers about twenty-five women—enough, however, to "keep posted on what's going on in the federal government so far as education is concerned."

Networks of Women Lawyers

In recent years, the number of women law students nationwide has increased dramatically from 2,500 in 1965 to more than 30,000 in 1977—and the potential that networking has for these thousands of women lawyers is just beginning to be realized.

For years, women have been members—silent and unseen—of male-dominated bar associations. Now they are forming their own law networks.

One very successful network is the Massachusetts Women Lawyers Association founded in 1978 by a group of eight women who decided that what they and the 2,000 other women attorneys in the state needed was an Old Girl network, the sort of informal system of contacts, case referrals, and job leads that has worked so well for Old Boy lawyers and judges since our nation was founded.

The primary aim of the group is to serve the needs of its constituents by providing an alternative to the Massachusetts and Boston bar associations. Kathy Clements of Boston, treasurer of the Massachusetts Women Lawyers Association and an attorney in practice for herself, explains why the network grew from twenty members in 1978 to more than three hundred in 1979.

"Being in the network lends credibility to what I do within the profession," she says. "The vice-president of the Massachusetts Bar Association calls me to have lunch so we can discuss similar problems. That helps me personally in my career and helps all women in the profession. Our members know they can contact us and we will try to put them in touch with jobs."

The network has a lunch club where women meet informally and talk over common problems. Through their formal meetings they have tried to set up a job bank so that when federal, state, or local officials ask for names of qualified women for appointive positions, they have a list ready. The women in the network are trying, with some success, to sit on the boards of delegates of their professional associations and have some imput there too.

The group doesn't always wait to be asked, either. It also suggests women who it believes deserve to be named to the bench. And Judge Margaret Burnham of the Massachusetts network has proposed that the association study the situation in the court system's own back yard—in the clerk's office, where nearly all the low-paying, low-level jobs are held by women.

Because of what Judge Burnham calls the "debilitating isolation of women lawyers," some networks of female attorneys are purely social, still filling that important function of support. Compared to the highly structured, well-organized Massachusetts Women Lawyers Association, other groups seem random, but they still work.

In Portland, Oregon, a network with the delightful name of The Queen's Bench operates on an informal basis for women attorneys. The group was organized more than two decades ago, at a time when there were very few women lawyers in Portland—which makes it a grand foremother of networking. "We have lunch once a month and a picnic once a year," says Holly Hart, Portland attorney. "It's very informal, people make friends through it, and sometimes you call the people you meet, but our goal is not to make powerful connections. It is very low-key." Despite their low-key attitude, members do receive the benefits of belonging to a network—getting to know each other, hearing about jobs, and giving each other support and a feeling of solidarity.

Another network of women lawyers, the National Association of Black Women Attorneys, headquartered in Washington, D.C., has been effective in helping its members get clients and cases and appointments to important posts. Like other networks of minority women, the NABWA also tries to reduce the feelings of professional isolation its members feel.

Medical Networks

The world of medicine has been dominated by men in the United States for more than 200 years. But now, because of federal insistence, women are being accepted into medical school in greater numbers. At least one third of the first-year medical classes of the country's largest medical schools are female. But the old problem of being a woman, in the minority, in a setting that is geared to male students and run by a predominantly male faculty and administration, remains the same—except for networking. Networking is helping the woman who wants to become a doctor exactly at the source of her problem.

"Women starting out in the field of medicine are isolated and alienated," says Dr. Marilyn Skinner, a psychiatrist who heads the American Medical Women's Association chapter in New Orleans and has been in private practice since 1977. Skinner, like most women doctors, went through medical school with very little support from those who had been through already and had made it. "I would have appreciated it," she says. "Medical students lack personal contact." The New Orleans network was established to combat this problem. Consisting of 50 women students, residents, and doctors, the network has 250 women on its mailing list, with contacts at Tulane Medical School and Louisiana State University Medical School. More informal and social than scientific, the network gives a party each fall, to welcome incoming women medical students, and a big brunch honoring the graduating class in the spring. "In between, we keep in touch," says Dr. Skinner. "The network makes an enormous difference. The women feel less isolated. And they don't suffer as much from depression—a common problem in high-pressure fields such as medicine—as they would without the support of the network."

The members serve as role models, mentors, and friends to each other in a highly competitive field. The network also functions as a clearinghouse for jobs. "We give support and referrals," says Dr. Skinner. "I constantly get referrals from other women in the group."

Dental Networks

Giving students the chance to meet with professionals in their field is also one of the aims of the American Association of Women Dentists, a national organization consisting of several local district networks bound together by a newsletter that lists job opportunities.

President of the association is Barbara C. Kay, a dentist in private practice in Danvers, Massachusetts. "Through our membership directories, we help women who are moving to another area to relocate and to take their boards in another state," says Dr. Kay. "We also help them make contact with another member who lives there."

In this way, Pat Moss, a dentist from Virginia, contacted Dr. Kay when she moved to Boston. The result: Dr. Moss is now working in Dr. Kay's office. When women dentists have practices for sale, they call Dr. Kay and she tries to put them in touch with another member who may be interested. "We get calls about opportunities all the time," she says.

Another dentist was thinking about going into the U.S. Navy, so the network referred her to a member in California who is presently in the Navy. "But nothing we do is in a formal fashion," says Dr. Kay. "We handle each question or problem as it arises."

The network has organized student chapters in one fourth of the dental schools in the country, and a great number of students belong to the national association. Through the network, the students make important contacts and form valuable mentor and role-model relationships.

Other Professional Networks

Women historians, sociologists, architects—women in every kind of profession—are beginning to know each other through their conscious efforts at networking. Study groups of Archives of Women in Architecture, for example, are networking arms of the Architectural League of New York. And Sisters for a Human Environment, in Seattle, Washington, has about forty members, architects concerned about the world around them. Already, community spirit is paying off for network members. One such "success" story is told by Bari Watkins of Northwestern University, who, with her colleagues in history, belongs to an academic network. It is an informal group, with no meetings per se, but the women keep in touch "to help each other and to compare strategies for surviving," Watkins says.

The network connection paid off for Watkins at a recent meeting of the National Women's Studies Association. Watkins was on a panel called "New Directions in Women's History," and, because the woman who put the panel together is in Watkins's network, all except one panelist were friends from that network and had worked together. The women who knew each other delivered papers that meshed; they had talked to each other about the panel, had helped each other, and it showed. Result: The panel was far more cohesive than most, and the impact on the audience was greater.

Once again, the two important things that networks need to be viable entities—self-interest and group interest—were operating for Watkins and her colleagues. Granted, the results of Watkins's networking are tiny little steps, but they are moves forward, and, as Carolyn Dexter, sociologist at Penn State University and a member of the national Sociologists for Women in Society, points out, "careers are a series of small steps forward." Networks, she says, help keep her and her colleagues informed. The sociologists' network is a very strong support group; the women in it are close to one another and in constant touch. And a major thrust of the group is in keeping up with the field, finding out about research before it's published, and finding out about grants before they're awarded. That information is gathered from the network, and Dexter says it too is "survival."

Common experiences in sex-stratified professions finally have led women to join with one another to change the system by ourselves. If you are a professional woman, you know exactly what the barriers and handicaps are. Networking is one way to overcome them. And when you remember that just a few years ago the hundreds of professional networks active today did not exist, the range of these networks is even more impressive.

The reason they are thriving is that they *are* making a difference in helping their members: both to get and give referrals and to find out about the better jobs, about new research, about what grants have been given and when more will be given. Professional networks have already made an impact on women in the professions, from college students to established professionals. Not only are they a wonderful source of friendship, aid, and support—they also work. Professionally speaking, you can make them work for you, too.

Support Networks:

Wives, Mothers, Divorced Women, Single Women, Women over Forty, Teenagers, Displaced Homemakers, Ethnic Women, Religious Women, Battered Women—Women Helping Women

In an older American tradition, the women for whom a man took responsibility in his household often formed a very solid feminine front. This broke down under the newer expectations that widows and single women should accept responsibility for themselves.
—Margaret Mead in *Some Personal Views*, 1968

Anthropologist Mead would be pleased to know that a new form of cooperation has recently emerged among women who share common interests and responsibilities. The new cooperative is networking, and out of a mutual need for support, information, and community, older women, single women, new mothers, wives, displaced homemakers, ethnic women, rural women, minority women, religious women, battered and abused women, and prostitutes have joined together in networks to make life more equitable, easier, and in many cases more fun for themselves.

What Are Support Networks?

Business and professional networks are changing the reality of women's work lives, but the supportive networks, like California's Doctor's Wives, Michigan's Front Porch Committee (made up of gifted women and teenage girls), South Dakota's Women in Transition—these networks are where most of us *live*, for they touch the things that matter most to us and help change them for the better. Throughout the United States, there are hundreds of supportive networks which aim not to increase annual incomes for women—though that certainly can and does happen—but to improve the quality of our lives.

Women have always networked as a support group. Ask any woman who works what she would do without her friends who do not work. Ask any homemaker what she would do without her neighbors—and they without her. Women have always networked to help their communities, schools, and social clubs. Now, in addition to these more traditional support groups, we are also networking for our own self-interest. Networks of support groups are growing by the hundreds in the United States today. Many do not have official names, but their members know who they are and come through for each other. Most support networks function on a limited local basis, one to one, such as the Pillsbury Bake-Off Girls. A few reach out and touch thousands of women in need, such as Displaced Homemakers and a network of shelters for battered women, both national groups. The deep concern and caring feelings women have for one another, and the universal need for a little help and understanding from a friend, make the support networks a moving and enlightening experience for members.

Perhaps more than anything else, a feeling of camaraderie is the basis of the support networks, especially those of new mothers, single mothers, widows, divorced women, and older women. Author Marilyn French describes these easy and natural feelings women have for one another. Against the background of the maternity ward where Mira, heroine of French's penetrating novel *The Women's Room,* has her first baby, French hits the point of networking right on the head: "They talked and talked and talked, but with great delicacy. . . . She [Mira] was drawn to these women because of their warmth and their easy acceptance of her." Later, when she returns to her suburb, Mira forms strong networks with her neighbors, warm yet delicate. Without them, she would not have survived those years. Later, at Harvard, Mira becomes part of another close network: different women but the same immediate support, understanding, and acceptance.

The Goals of Support Networks

Support networks rise from a need: emotional, physical, or mental. Their goals are to give help where needed, to give insight, and to help relieve the pain of facing problems alone, such as the many networks of rape victims and single parents do each day. Communication among women is another goal carefully attended to by networks. Women are isolated from one another, even those who live in the same crowded apartment buildings and housing projects. Rural women, farm women, and older women often feel alone and *are* alone. Today, hundreds of women are joining networks to discuss common problems, to find solutions, and often just to be together.

The real beauty of support networks is their goal of helping you feel better about yourself. The excitement of being with a group of other women who feel the same way you do about things has the end result of making you feel *great* as a woman—not a bad feeling at all! This is accomplished through the very serious efforts of groups like Colorado's Clergymen's Wives, who try to understand each other and themselves in probing, frank discussion, but the same euphoric feeling comes from networks like the Gourmet Exchange and the Creative Mundanes.

One woman who feels absolutely wonderful about who she is and what she is doing is Spring Friedlander of Oakland, California. She's in the Gourmet Exchange network: six members who meet once a week and cook one great meal for each other and their families. The "easy camaraderie" Marilyn French describes makes this network even more fun. And Friedlander continues this feeling of cheerful give-and-take in another network she belongs to, the Creative Mundanes. The latter network is made of women who barter time and skills with one another, such as food shopping for house painting. The various talents and expertise are exchanged on the basis of time and task by direct negotiations between the women themselves. And they feel great about their trade-offs!

Friedlander's supportive networks are helpful and fun, but they also have a more serious purpose and goal: their commitment to the emerging strength of their members. Supportive networks make a contribution that extends far beyond their immediate function because they know that *when you feel better about yourself, you do better for yourself.*

How Support Networks Form

Many networks begin as consciousness-raising groups, a popular activity of the 1960s and early 1970s. From there, however, they take off and fly when their members decide they can *do* something about the conditions that seemingly control their lives. Just getting together was the basis of the early meetings of the Pillsbury Bake-Off Girls of Sioux Falls, South Dakota, in 1975. A dozen friends of one particular woman—women who previously did not know each other—were invited to join, and the meetings were held at a member's home. The name of the group was a humorous way of attracting interest.

The group was made up of all kinds of women: single, married, divorced, widowed. Their ages were from twenty-five to sixty-two, a wonderful range for a network. "Most of us couldn't have cared less about cooking," says Libby Shreves, one of the original members. "We just wanted to get together and visit." At the early meetings, each women told her life story and everyone listened. Fun weekends and parties were planned. The women enjoyed these early days—having a psychic at their meetings, reading their own poetry, baring their souls to one another—but consciousness-raising is a phase, albeit an important one, and the women soon outgrew it.

The monthly meetings have now evolved to less frequent get-togethers. The group has changed, too, as women move away and new members join. Today, the group calls itself Women in Transition and is made up of ten women who are concerned about their own personal growth and that of each other. They are now down to the serious business of networking, dedicated to moving ahead in the world, making life happier for themselves and for all other women. Among the network's important accomplishments is that the women in the group have moved upward in the world of business. Almost all had been in lower-level, no-place-to-go jobs. Today, the "Girls" have as members a media consultant, a lawyer, a government assistant, and a public relations adviser. Libby Shreves herself is an example of what supportive networks can do for you. She was in real estate in 1975 when the group was formed and went on to become a candidate for the legislature, which whetted her interest in the political arena and in improving the quality of life for all women. Married, Catholic, the mother of eleven children, Shreves is now state organizer for South Dakota's Abortion Rights Action League. The network continues to contribute to her growth.

"It's hard to explain what the Pillsbury Bake-Off Girls means to me today," she says, "but every time I bump into someone from the group, I feel very close, very close."

Networks of Wives

During the Civil Rights marches of the 1960s, a popular song among the marchers was "We Are Not Alone." The phrase was sung over and over again, almost like a hymn. The conviction you are *not* alone is one of the things that makes you feel good about yourself and your daily responsibilities. And it leads from a sense of despair, which is a direct result of feelings of isolation, to the courage to face your problems and the strength to handle them.

Being a wife is a full-time job, and often women need to get together just to talk about the realities of marriage. It's hard, in many cases, to be viewed as somebody's wife instead of your own person, an alter ego, defined only by the man you are married to, much as the First Lady becomes an extension of the President and seemingly has no life or personality of her own. Wives of famous or important men often struggle hard to find their own identity. Through networks, they are succeeding.

Doctors' Wives

Doctors' wives often find marriage to a doctor isn't so easy as it seems. Many young women are brought up to believe that marrying a doctor connotes prestige, power, and lots of money and that the best marriages are made in hospitals. Often this is true, but doctors' wives also find they are very lonely because their husbands are so busy and tend to be so involved with their patients and their work. Despite the fact that doctors' wives tend to be proud women themselves and may find it hard to admit they are lonely, they, like other women today, *are* reaching out to one another, given the chance to do so. One such chance was a course entitled "Doctors' Wives—No Bed of Roses," given in 1978 at the extension division of the University of California at San Diego. Some twenty women enrolled.

The first thing that struck the women was the shock of recognition in describing common problems. "We don't really have our husbands very much," says Margaret Harris, one of the women who enrolled in the class and who is now a member of the network of doctors' wives which evolved. "They're dedicated to medicine. Other women, whose husbands are dedicated to their careers, are allowed to feel resentful and jealous, but a woman married to a doctor has a hard time working out the guilt feelings. After all, he's out helping the sick and needy. How can I complain? Still," she adds, stating a problem homemakers have long lamented, "it's hard to raise kids without their father around the house."

Through the course, sharing the common problems that belonged to all the women, Harris gained the perspective she needed to cope. "I learned I can't feel guilty because I want to see him when he's out saving lives. You think you're the only one, and it's not so. It's neat to share experiences and find that other women are married to the same problems."

In the course, the doctors' wives learned to be assertive and to deal with their husbands' egos. "They're God to a lot of people," says Harris, "but they can't make us feel guilty when they don't take responsibility for things like child rearing and companionship." And, just as important, the women learned to express their needs, to feel that they are human beings too. Out of this tremendous enlightenment came a very special relationship with the other women in the class who were going through the same process.

"I feel I can call any of the girls up any time and talk to them," says Harris. "I knew that what I was saying in class was not going to be blabbed around town, that my privacy was respected and that it still is. I feel about the support group the way I feel about Transcendental Meditation: I don't practice it every day, but it's good to know it's there."

Clergymen's Wives

If doctors' wives realize that people think their husband is God, imagine the feelings of clergymen's wives, whose husbands are not considered gods but are certainly expected to have a direct pipeline to heaven. What is it like to be the wife of a man of the cloth? Often wonderful; once again, often very, very hard and lonely.

Clergymen's wives are often as reluctant to admit any marital problems as doctors' wives, politicians' wives, or wives of other service-oriented professional men. Yet these women also are getting together and forming supportive networks. Clergymen's wives, dedicated to the idea of helping others, are realizing that they too need to air their feelings. An active network of supportive clergymen's wives is headed by Virginia E. Pike of Grand Junction, Colorado. And Clara Bing Binford of Houston, Texas, married for twenty-two years to a clergyman, mother of four children, and author of a column for clergy wives called "Talk 'n' Thought," has formed a network of some ten women, married to ministers, who share her concerns.

"Clergymen's wives are isolated," says Binford, a sympathetic, giving woman. "Our network is an attempt to develop a sense of community with each other. There is a mystique about clergymen's wives that we all feel. People think that we are holy and not really people."

In their dialogues, the clergy wives have identified their problems: People think they are "holier than thou." They live in a fishbowl. There are a lot of expectations about the woman and her children. The wife tends to "pick up" criticism that might not go to the clergyman himself—and she is expected to deliver the message. And there are always financial problems. The very description "clergyman's wife" is an indication of the scope of the problem: Clergy wives are viewed as extensions of the clergymen. They lose their identities. The women are not in power positions where they can gracefully handle the problems of their roles or the criticisms they are vulnerable to. And that's where networking comes in.

"Our group has definitely made me feel less reticent," says Clara Bing Binford. "Clergy wives are reluctant to mention any problems, but we can voice them to each other because none of us will be surprised. People tend to think that since we are so happy to be Christians, we are happy all the time. But no one is happy all the time. It just isn't true."

Farm Wives

Loneliness—and powerlessness, too—has long been the condition of farmers' wives. Now they too are seeking each other out for mutual aid, comfort, and networking. Wisconsin Women for Agriculture (WWA), based in Cato, is typical of the many networks for farm women in the United States. An articulate spokeswoman for the group is Joanne Vogel, who is concerned not only with the isolation of being a farmer's wife but also with the legal rights of these women, who often work side by side with their husbands in the field but who have no real property rights to either the farm or the crop.

Another spokesperson and active worker for WWA is Sister Thomas More of the Franciscan Sisters of Christian Charity at Silver Lake College.

She's an American history professor who also teaches economics and political science. Sister More told Richard Orr of the *Chicago Tribune* bluntly that WWA is "a bunch of broads who are sick and tired of sitting there waiting for the fairy godmother to come and get the show on the road." "And," she adds, "members look at farming as an industry that is an essential part of the entire system of providing food and fiber to the consumer. Farm wives have a double stake in the effort because they are consumers as well as producers."

Helping each other to be heard, wives of cattlemen, dairy farmers, potato growers, and the like have formed a national coalition of twenty-two networks like WWA, called American Agri-Women, representing about 15,000 women in fifteen states.

Rural Wives

Farm women have their farms, but rural women rarely own property. Isolation, poverty, and a struggle for survival typify their problems. Rural women have long had informal networks to give each other support and direction; now, rural wives, like wives of other men, are discovering the importance of a more formalized system of linking, weaving, and working together for personal growth.

Rural American Women is a network organized to help rural women recognize their own needs and lobby for legislation that will benefit them. Headquarters are in Washington, D.C., but the individual groups within the network are diverse in their setups and independent of central control. In Williamsburg, Kentucky, a network of low income rural women is called The Fellowship Center. Rural women in Bozeman, Montana, have organized a network called Focus on Women; its coordinator is Suzanne Wellcome. And in Orangeburg, South Carolina, rural women in transition who are in need of employment counseling and a best friend get both through their network, Transition Resources. This unique group has come up with a creative idea to help rural women help one another: Advice and guidance on how to get a job provided by Transition Resources is backed up by assigning each woman a "buddy." According to Jean Lipscomb of Transition Resources, the rural woman who needs a friendly ear calls her buddy—and her buddy listens. This form of networking is helping to forge strong bonds among women who have not been in touch with one another before and who have been socialized to "hide" any family problems they may have.

Networks of Women with Children: Mothers Who Care

Having children is both a time of joy and a time of stress. It's easy to talk about the joys in a country that ostensibly worships Motherhood, but talking about the problems is a little more difficult. Yet talking about them is a form of survival for mothers, and that is precisely what they are doing in hundreds of networks all across the country. Networking around parenting is just as important to many mothers as making a million-dollar deal is to the woman in the business network. Mothers are a group that too often is not taken seriously by the public—you never see a "mere" mother on any television panel show of "experts" on children—but in networking, mothers are important people whose goals for their children are treated as serious concerns.

There are thousands of women involved as mothers in networks. Boston is the home of COPE (Coping with the Overall Pregnancy Experience). Sioux City, Iowa, has a group called MOM (Moving On to Motherhood), a network of new mothers. In the same city, there's another support network for single women who are pregnant, organized by Catholic Charities of Sioux City. This network consists of single mothers who give care and emotional support to other single mothers who have opted to keep their babies. In Pontiac, Michigan, there's a network of women called Parent to Parent, organized under an Oakland County Cooperative Extension Service program. In it, one parent is matched to another parent, with the "volunteer" parent acting as a friend and confidante to the troubled parent. One such duo is Diane Duffie, divorced and supporting three children on welfare, and Sandy Murphy, her new friend, who lives with her husband and two children in an attractive new development. "Talking together makes all the difference," says Duffie.

Another example of a network that provides direct benefits to the women in it is the Sisterhood of Black Single Mothers, located in the Bedford-Stuyvesant section of Brooklyn. Organized in 1974 by half a dozen women who wanted and needed to share their experiences as single mothers, the group pairs single mothers in their twenties and thirties with adolescent mothers. Women in the network help one another find housing, jobs, and baby-sitters. They intervene with city agencies, sponsor family outings, and have guest speakers who discuss everything from birth control to safety. In six years, the network has grown to 256 members and has branches in the Bronx and Westchester. It works, Nadine Brozan says in the *New York Times*, because its members know firsthand what it is like to be young, single, and a mother.

Through networking, women are also organizing to do something about their children's education. Lois Steinberg, sociologist and visiting senior study director at the National Opinion Research Center, has a contract from the National Institute of Education to study mothers involved in educational issues. And one of the major involvements is networking. Dr. Steinberg is interviewing members of six groups in suburban Westchester County, New York, looking for the factors in community and school programs that promote networking. She will then compare her findings in the East with research on five communities in the Midwest.

"What I'm doing is looking at how women use social contacts to cope with the bureaucrats and the federal decision makers," says Dr. Steinberg. "This is particularly relevant to women because most women don't know how to cope with bureaucracy and must network with other women to stand up to it."

Networking, the sociologist observes, will give women the power base to fight back against the socialization process that for centuries has taught women to be altruistic and deferential to authority. As she also notes, women recognize that they have to take political action, and the variety of issues concerning their children that mothers are networking around dramatizes this new awareness in women.

Some of the networks Dr. Steinberg has found that are organized by mothers include those concerned with special education, such as learning disabilities; lunch programs; open classrooms; and administration of a local high school. Two networks are on black issues—one to retain Title I federally funded programs and another of middle-class black parents who feel teachers are not sensitive to the needs of their children.

Another thing parents worry about is teenagers. And teenagers worry about themselves, too: the rapid changes in their lives, physically and emotionally; their conflicts, fears, rebellions. Networks have not neglected teenagers. In Columbus, Ohio, is a helpful network called Friends in Action, which works with troubled teens. And, to be a teenager, female, and extremely gifted is so difficult in our society that a network of women, all of whom had been intellectually gifted girls themselves, decided in 1976 to band together to help other young and gifted girls. The name of this group of concerned business and professional women reflects its approach: The Front Porch Committee of Birmingham, Michigan. Through their network, many of the women who had been lonely as girls and later as adults are forming supportive friendships too, for the first time in their lives. If only there were more networks of this kind!

Networks of Ethnic and Minority Women

Ethnic women have always been close to one another. Anyone who has been to an ethnic picnic or party notices right away how the women literally dash to each other, eagerly and naturally showing affection, love, and concern, while everyone else seems to be more interested in eating, drinking, and having a good time. The same strong bond is carried over to the self-help networks being formed constantly by Latina women, black women, and native

American women. Among the networks are Women of All Red Nations, for which Lorelei Means of Porcupine, South Dakota, is a spokesperson, and the National Council of Negro Women, which is based in Washington but has local networks that form around its outreach programs.

In January, 1979, the council's program to find employment for black women received an allocation of $200,000, and, according to Alma Brown, director of the council's division of employment opportunity, the funding of training programs is going to make a great deal of difference for rural black women, who have different problems from white rural women. Currently, in Okolona, Mississippi, for example, the program is training rural black women for nontraditional jobs, such as those in the automotive and furniture industries. Through the office in Okolona, the staff locates underemployed women—and the women locate each other. In Issaquena County, Mississippi, another council program is working with fifty black women, and once again the women are networking with each other.

Religious Networks

Networks of women in various religions are time-honored, potent forces in our society. Nuns, for example, have networked with one another successfully for centuries. Today, networks of nuns are international; a nun always knows that wherever she may go, she has friends and a free place to stay. An important network of nuns is the National Assembly of Women Religious. There are networks of ex-nuns, who help each other adjust to civilian lives, and networks of former nuns who are now married. There are also networks of nuns who want to be ordained priests, and they spoke up loud and clear when Pope John Paul II visited the United States in 1979. Women of other religions have formed networks too, such as the Jewish Women's Caucus, organized in Washington, D.C., by Betty Shapiro. In Chicago, a small informal group of Greek Orthodox women got together with a woman who is a church official and formed a study group—and a network—to try to learn more about women's role in the Greek Orthodox Church. Concerned Catholic Women is an active national network of lay women. And Campus Ministry Women is a national network of Catholic, Protestant, and Jewish women who provide campus ministry and work to advance women's issues.

Networks of Women Who Are Prostitutes

Prostitutes, long the outcasts of every society, are banding together to end their oppression. Regardless of how you feel about prostitution—in addition to those who believe it is immoral, it is also *illegal*, tainted with the problems of corruption, vice, and criminal influences—women who are prostitutes realize they need each other, that they are their only allies. At the same time that the need to help one another is growing, the number of prostitutes is also on the increase. Prostitution is becoming visible and increasing in large cities everywhere. There are no official counts of how many women are prostitutes—the U.S. Census Bureau does not list prostitution among the occupations for which it keeps statistics—but more and more housewives, students, and young girls are turning to prostitution as a means of making money. Some are forced, some are "recruited," some become prostitutes willingly. It is a sad commentary on women's wages to realize that prostitution pays much better than secretarial work.

Prostitutes are networking in every major city. The names vary: Missouri's Ocelot, Atlantic City's Hush, the West Coast's COYOTE (Call Off Your Old Tired Ethics), and, in New Orleans, PASSION (Professional Association Seeking Sexual Identification Observant of Nature). In Boston, at a public rally, "Ms. Anonymous Prostitute," speaking for PUMA (Prostitutes' Union of Massachusetts), told the large crowd in the Boston Common, "My crime is not actually having sex—work which all women are supposed to do for free—but rather demanding money for it."

Margo St. James is coordinator of COYOTE, a network founded in 1973, that has as its goal the local regulation of prostitution. "We feel that is the least abusive way to regulate prostitution," St. James says, "if prostitution must be regulated and licensed."

St. James says her network collects information, documents abuse of prostitutes, stops arbitrary quarantining of prostitutes for venereal disease, raises funds, lobbies state legislatures for decriminalization, and has even achieved United Nations Nongovernmental Organization status. "We're a support group for prostitutes, who are so often attacked, robbed, and raped," says St. James. "We get women into rap groups, urge them to press charges, force district attorneys to prosecute, and provide moral support for prostitutes during the trial." To keep the women in the network in touch with one another, COYOTE publishes a newsletter called *Coyote Howls*.

Networks of Battered Women

Some of the most important networks formed in recent years are those organized by women to help other women—women who are abused and battered or who are rape victims. The issue of violence against women has touched every sensitive woman, and many are moved to act, through crisis centers, telephone hotlines, and support groups.

Throughout the country, hundreds of women volunteer to help the battered woman, to stand by her, to go to court with her, to help her seek medical aid, and to listen to and try to alleviate her despair. Women identify more than any man can with the plight of other women who are victims of rape, battery, and violence, crimes which touch the core of our being. It is to our self-interest, too, to work to stop the victimization of women, and this common thread touches all women, including those who have been victims themselves.

Patricia Hearst of Los Angeles, who was kidnapped by the Symbionese Liberation Army, is a woman who can relate to the problems of other battered women from personal experience. Loath to discuss her ordeal, Hearst seems only to want to regain a semblance of a normal life and the privacy she had before her world was disrupted so violently. Understandably, Hearst avoids public appearances and speaking with the press. But one thing does make her speak out, and that is the subject of battered women. In 1979, in an act of real courage, Hearst held a national press conference to urge battered women to seek help.

"Having been a victim of violence, this is the reason I'm so concerned," Hearst said. She hoped to persuade battered women that police are willing to help them, a situation she apparently sees as analogous to her own distrust of law enforcement during the time she was held captive. "I understand how helpless and desperate these women feel," she says. "They are afraid to call the police because they don't think they will help them. I identify with the desperateness of the situation."

Hearst's story is dramatic and draws media attention, but hundreds of women whose names are not known do the same and more, every day in every city in the country. The Phoenix House in Columbus, Ohio, has a network of battered women. Women Against Rape in New Orleans is a network organized to fight battery and rape. In San Francisco, there is a network of Women Against Abuse, organized by the Women's Liberation Union. In Philadelphia, Women Organized Against Rape painted signs on those streets, street corners, and alleys where women had been raped. Though Philadelphia police had not acted to protect the women from rape, the city moved quickly this time—to have the painted signs erased. An international network, Women Against Rape (WAR), is known in Britain for invading courts, government offices, exclusive private clubs, and the most exclusive private male club of all—newspapers—to denounce the lack of protection for women and the failure to punish rapists.

The terrible problems inflicted on battered women are so manifold that women are only just beginning to realize all the factors involved and the variety of solutions necessary. A chain of networks in western states addressed itself to a basic problem of abused women: a place to stay. Many cities have come up with much-needed shelters where battered women can find refuge, but the western network, knowing women are frequently followed to shelters in their own city, works at arranging for women to move from shelter to shelter, city to city, as necessary.

The Committee to Aid Abused Women in Sparks, Nevada, is a shelter that covers all of northern Nevada and is affiliated with the Western States Shelter Network and the National Coalition Against Domestic Violence. According to Joni Kaiser, coordinator, the network provides direct aid to battered women and educates the public about domestic violence in order to generate peer pressure against it. The Sparks network is also part of an underground network for battered women who are forced to leave one state and go to another to escape their pursuing husbands or boyfriends.

At the shelter, which was opened in 1977, the networking and bonding that are so necessary for battered women have a warm and friendly setting. Kaiser tells how the network helped a woman in her early twenties, a diminutive woman, just five feet tall and weighing about 100 pounds, who had been beaten repeatedly since her marriage four years earlier. The woman had two small children and came to the shelter through a referral. She had been forced to leave her children at her husband's family's home, a family known for violence.

While she was at the center, she got her children back and remained there with them for five weeks. The network helped her obtain a divorce, and *another battered woman she met at the center testified for her.* After her divorce, she moved to a shelter in another state. "She couldn't have made it alone in Nevada," says Kaiser. "Her children were under age two, and there's no day care for children of that age. She couldn't get welfare, either, because we wouldn't release her address at the shelter."

At the center, battered women often sit up all hours of the night talking, becoming close friends. Once again, the requisites for networking are present: self-interest and group interest. The Committee to Aid Abused Women counseled 450 women between December, 1977, and August, 1979. "The exciting thing," says Kaiser, "is that because women are getting together and helping each other, there is a change, a real change. Women are learning with other women who are going through the same things. In the end, it is the battered women who help each other." And that is what networking is all about.

Networks of Middle-aged Women: Single Women, Women over Forty, Divorced Women, and Displaced Homemakers

Women who have not been in touch with other women, who have always felt they did not need other women, suddenly learn the value of cooperation—and networking—with one another when they reach middle age. Necessity is often the mother of networking, and in our society, with its high divorce rate, empty nests, and, above all, increased life spans for women, that necessity arises more vividly as we age.

"This is not a good society in which to grow old or in which to be a woman," says Dr. Pauline Bart, sociologist, who has researched depression among middle-aged women. But while the problems of middle age more often hit women harder than men, all is not bleak. Many older women, freed from family responsibilities, are coming into their own for the first time in their lives, daring to try new careers and businesses, becoming active and positive forces in their communities; and, everywhere, networks are giving them the support they need to get where they want to go. The supportive networks attempt to meet the needs of middle-aged women, needs that are the result of all the significant changes in their lives: familial, occupational, social, educational, financial, and medical.

Single Women

The enormous phenomenon of middle-aged women dealing with their problems through networks is only beginning. Today, there are 28.4 million American women between the ages of 40 and 64. More than 5 million are widowed or divorced. Between 1990 and 2010, the U.S. Census Bureau predicts that the number of women between the ages of 45 and 64 will skyrocket to 36 million! And many will be widows because women have a longer life expectancy than men.

It is not surprising, therefore, that networks of widows and older women are springing up everywhere. There is a network of widows in Sioux City, Iowa, called Solitaires. The Older Women's Network of Wolf Creek, Oregon, a network that finds places for older women to stay as they travel throughout the country, has a newsletter called *Our Own*. Options for Women over Forty in San Francisco has a newsletter cheerfully named *Broomsticks*. Jobs for Older Women Action Project is a network in Berkeley, and PHASE (Project for Homemakers in Arizona Searching Employment) is located in Tucson. The Older Women's League Educational Fund, a network organized by Tish Sommers and Laurie Shields as "a new voice for middle-aged and older women who are taking responsibility for the rest of their lives," is in Oakland. There are networks of older women who are re-entering college or the job market after a hiatus of many years, and who need strong supportive services, as well as networks of single older women and of married older women, of displaced homemakers, and of unmarried older women with low incomes (72 percent of the elderly poor in this country are unmarried older women).

Women over Forty

Elisa Van Til of San Francisco, a woman who has never been married and is the mother of one child, is a member of Options for Women over Forty. This supportive network has enriched Van Til's life in many aspects.

"I've had to work all my life and I've been single all my life," Van Til says. "Though I have a college degree, I had to go on welfare for a while when my son was younger. I had been a secretary and a teacher, and my focus was to make it in a man's world. I realized I was trying to get where men are, and that I had placed women, including myself, somewhere below men. Fortunately, in 1974, I came to Options."

Van Til became involved in a network with women who understand, and she found the courage to face another problem: overweight. "I joined a network called Fat, Female, and Forty," she says. "The women met in groups two hours a week and rapped. We had barbecues and picnics and did exercises together."

Van Til had still another problem. She needed a job. And then she had an inspiration: Options needed a publicist. She asked for the job and got it. "I am qualified, you know," she says. "I have my master's degree."

Van Til's life has changed very much for the better. "I feel really excited about where I am now," she says. "I wouldn't change it for the world. Things still aren't perfect, but I'm feeling totally different. I can see the change in myself even in the last two years. Being here at Options is a mind-blower."

Divorced Women

While Van Til was going through the process of taking a good hard look at her life on the West Coast, on the East Coast, in Philadelphia, another woman was taking an equally serious look at hers.

In 1978, Fritzie Dichter, a recently divorced woman who works at the American Law Institute in Philadelphia, decided to stop in at the offices of Women in Transition, located in the same building where she works. Women in Transition (WIT), which started out in the basement of a church in 1970, now has a staff of seventeen and a reputation for helping women through professional counseling, peer counseling, self-help, and networking. (The Philadelphia group, incidentally, is not connected with the "Pillsbury" Women in Transition network.)

Dichter has two grown children, had been married for twenty-five years, and had worked the last ten years of her marriage as a secretary. "I needed help in dealing with my problems," she said. "I felt overwhelmed.

My marriage was over, my daughters grown, I felt I had no life to look forward to. I needed to be with other women with the same experience."

Ditcher had one advantage: a skill that was in demand. She also had a job. But still, she needed support and she knew it. "Eight women met once a week for twelve weeks with the WIT staff," she recalls. "We covered different topics of interest to women, ranging from money—the biggest problem, especially when you don't have it—to sex, the law, motherhood, depression. We were all ages, from twenties to the forties. All different types, but so many things in common. We didn't condemn. We tried to be of help. And we were."

Today, Dichter still maintains her contact with her WIT network. "It means so much to see you're not alone," she says. "Especially when you believe you are. You see other people in the same position who *are* managing, and gradually you become strong enough to know that you, too, will be able to do the same. I looked forward to those meetings so much."

Displaced Homemakers

When a marriage breaks up or the husband dies and an older woman is forced back into the labor market during this time of personal insecurity and trauma—especially if she has not worked outside the home for years—she is at a distinct disadvantage.

There are so many women like this today—the U.S. Census Bureau in 1976 counted 4 million women thirty-five and over without income or jobs because of years of homemaking—that the category has a name: displaced homemaker. The term was created by Tish Sommers, president of the Older Women's League Educational Fund, in 1973 when she was trying to get the older mature women included in CETA training funds. In 1978, she and a grass-roots coalition of concerned women *did* get budgetary funds for displaced homemakers, and the name has been in general use ever since.

People concerned about displaced homemakers, and displaced homemakers themselves, are beginning to realize that society has let them down: In our society, homemaking has little status and no monetary worth. The valuable skills we acquire as homemakers and services we render have never been understood, assessed, or appreciated by society, the government, or our own families—and often not even by ourselves.

"The women in this younger generation still suffer discrimination, and I don't mean to minimize it," actress Marlo Thomas testified before the Senate Committee on Human Resources on the special needs of women re-entering the job market, "but they've been the beneficiaries of the legal and attitudinal changes of the past ten years. Their future looks promising."

But for the woman of thirty-five or fifty or sixty-five," Thomas pointed out in *Ms.* magazine, "the future is *right now*. And it's not a comforting one."

Writing in the *Chicago Tribune* on the Supreme Court's decision that state laws requiring husbands but not wives to pay alimony are unconstitutional, Joan Beck, columnist and child-care expert concerned about homemakers, describes the homemaker's dilemma.

"It is another stiff reminder to women that traditional assumptions about the financial aspects of marriage are rapidly changing and that opting out of the work force for years to be a traditional, full-time wife and mother is an enormous financial gamble," Beck comments. And then she asks: "Do women dare risk letting themselves become financially dependent on a male—dare to drop out of the job market and gamble that the relationship will last, knowing one out of every two marriage fails and every year of not working lessens their value on the job market compared to that of their spouse?"

Even the so-called "modern, liberated" law which created no-fault divorce works against displaced women, increasing their numbers more easily than should be possible. "For older women, no-fault has been a disaster," says Tish Sommers. "It has been especially hard for older women who have been homemakers and who assumed that marriage was till-death-do-us-part. The career world has passed them by, and they cannot hope to find well-paying jobs that will enable them to support themselves or to provide for old age."

According to the U.S. Department of Labor, 15 million women over forty work full-time. Most are employed as retail clerks, industrial workers, or in service industries. In 1976, their mean income was $8,914 a year, compared to $16,551 for males in the same age group. For many of these women, women who are not covered by a private pension plan and whose Social Security benefits will be based on low average covered wages, the present is a time of struggle and the future also looks bleak.

That is what it's like to be a displaced homemaker; and that is precisely why networks of support such as the national Displaced Homemakers Network and WOMAN (Woman, Owner, Manager, Administrator, Networking) of Chicago, which specifically invites the displaced homemaker to join with professional women and young women just entering the labor market, are forming around these women.

The Displaced Homemakers Network is a national network that was created in 1978 as the result of the first national training conference held on displaced homemakers in Baltimore. Director of the network is Cindy Marano. "We now have a grass-roots organization of nearly 2,000 service agencies, displaced homemakers, and supportive organizations and individuals," she says. The networks' national office in Washington, D.C., serves as headquarters for the development of programs and services for displaced homemakers through resource assistance, staff training, information, and the *Network News*.

The network, funded by donations, membership fees, and corporate grants, also distributes a training manual for the centers and agencies that provide training and counseling to displaced homemakers—an estimated 200 organizations and growing daily.

Shirley Sapin is Region 5 representative for the Displaced Homemakers Network. She is director for special projects for the Union of Experimenting Colleges and Universities in Cincinnati.

A displaced homemaker herself, Sapin was counseling displaced homemakers in a Cleveland YWCA program while she was married. (Sapin was married for thirty years before her divorce.) Originally, she notes, networks concerned with displaced homemakers attempted to reach middle-aged women only. "We know that younger women feel trauma and have problems when displaced," Sapin says, "but in a competitive society, there's more room for the twenty- or thirty-year-old than there is for the fifty- or sixty-year-old." Sapin, who has helped so many other displaced homemakers get a new start in life and feel good about themselves, says she has benefited from the network too. "Just being able to counsel other women has been helpful," Sapin says.

One of the ideas the network promotes is that displaced homemakers are naturals to start their own businesses, businesses that capitalize on the real skills they have acquired over years of homemaking. One such enterprise is contracting to clean other people's houses, a venture that Leilani Lovern, owner of Magic Mop, a home-cleaning business in Baltimore, has found makes very good economic sense. Lovern and her husband separated in 1974, at which time she went to work as a school-bus driver to support her three children. Then she trained at the Maryland Center for Displaced Homemakers, a network whose staff, also displaced homemakers, have a commitment to helping other women during the difficult transition period. "They taught you to take what you've done all your life and make money at it," she says. Of the four women who finished training when she did, each now has an independent home-cleaning company—a 100-percent success rate!

"When I joined the network, I didn't know what I was doing or where I was going," says Lovern. "I was unemployed. They helped me get my head on straight and helped with immediate financial aid. The center has a job re-entry program. It helps you develop skills, even skills you don't know you have. I owe what I have to the training and to the network. They even helped with initial advertising—flyers and placing ads!"

Lovern doesn't need to go to regular meetings anymore, "but I know I can always go back whenever I need help." And she still gets business refer-rals from the center. "People call me who want to start their own business," she says. "I try to help them by telling them what to do and how to do it."

The Joy of Networks

Some of the excitement women feel in networking is due to the fact that the end results of networking are often such happy ones. Lovern *enjoys* running her new business, Magic Mop. Another friend of hers, a displaced homemak-er with sewing skills, is having the time of her life running *her* new business, Busy Thimble. Supportive networks make it possible for women who need help themselves to help others at the same time. The feeling of helping oth-ers is a good one, a valuable gift from someone who is in the same boat. And a glance at the listings of networks in the back of this book indicates how many supportive networks there are. Women who have survived ordeals in life they never expected to face and were never trained to handle are now bursting with life and excitement, having a good time with what they are doing, refusing to give in to seemingly overwhelming forces that threaten their well-being. No one can do this alone. Networks make the difference, and being in a supportive network is actually its own reward.

Peer Counseling and What It Means

Some of the real miracles networking has produced in the lives of battered women, displaced women, and women over forty might have taken years to achieve if attempted on the psychiatrist's couch. Often, the insights and sup-port of friends are just as effective as professional therapy. This type of infor-mal "lending a sympathetic ear" is called peer counseling.

"Peer counseling is not too different from the way women have always talked problems out in sewing circles, over coffee, at lunch, and on the tele-phone," says Dr. Gloria Lewis, professor of education at Loyola University and one of the first women in America to teach courses in peer counseling to college students as well as to mature women who attend non-credit courses and workshops.

The "official" peer counseling course is based on the first course in counseling in graduate school—same books, same techniques. "Peer counsel-ing is the answer for people with ordinary problems that don't need long-term therapy to solve. Peer counseling is self-help," says Dr. Lewis. "It's lay people helping lay people, one-on-one counseling, like Alcoholics Anonymous. What we are talking about are really just good communications skills, like distinguishing between actual content and emotional content of what someone says and learning to read nonverbal responses."

Academic courses in peer counseling are available and have been offered in this country since 1955, but they are not essential to acquire the necessary skills. Peer counseling is an important part of networking because it is an additional tool with which to help other women, such as rape victims, single mothers, divorced women, and those who need support. A logical outgrowth of peer counseling is a program many of the displaced homemakers centers have called Paid Peers, made up of displaced homemakers trained to counsel and advise other displaced homemakers. The word "peer" means equal. Equals who care.

"Some people are natural counselors," says Dr. Lewis. "A lot of people are good listeners, they tolerate ambiguity, are not defensive, and are comfortable with themselves. People gravitate toward them. After all, you can tell who cares."

There are few "entrance requirements" to join the supportive networks listed in this book. The best way to find one is to decide what it is you really need or are interested in and locate those in your area. Women's centers, which most large cities have, are incubators of networking and good places to start to find the support group you want to be a part of. But one of the most rewarding ways to get involved in issues that concern women, that touch us where we live in our souls and minds, is to form your own (see chapter 9). It may take courage to do this; it certainly takes time and effort. But it is one of the ways women today can express their own feelings, needs, and values. You will find that belonging to supportive networks will enrich your life. Through them, you will feel *great* as a woman.

5 | Health and Sports Networks

Women, like children, have told the stories in which the details are more
important than the plot, in which their own action is not possible, not imagined.
. . . Woman must learn to contrive plots in which she slays her own dragons.
—Carolyn G. Heilbrun in *Reinventing Womanhood*

A lot of factors go into making us feel great about ourselves as women: a
good job, a chance to advance, and a group of supportive friends go a long
way. But feeling great also means a healthy body, a sense of well-being that
is physical, emotional, and mental. Life isn't much fun if we're not healthy,
or if we can't experience the added fun and exhilaration that come from participating in sports. To make sure we know what our health problems are
and how to deal with them, to make sure women, like men, get a chance to
play and compete in whatever physical sports we want to, women throughout the United States are forming health and sports networks. For, as in other
phases of our lives, we *need* the help of networks—and each other—to
achieve these goals and to make sure our bodies *are* beautiful, in every way.

HEALTH NETWORKS AND HOW THEY WORK

- Do you want to learn how to breast-feed your baby?
- Do you want to know what drugs are dangerous?
- Are you in need of emotional support and guidance but afraid to go to a psychia-
  trist?
- Are you concerned that the birth control method you are using may be dangerous
  to your health?
- Are you concerned about reproductive freedom for all women?

If your answer to any of these questions is yes, there are networks of
women to answer them or to help you find your own answers. With women's
increasing realization that we are our own best friends, there is a renewed
search today to find out everything we need to know but were afraid to ask
about our bodies. There is nothing new about this quest. Women have always wanted to know, and, as Gena Corea points out in her book *The Hid-
den Malpractice*, it is only in recent history that men are the medical experts
and women almost completely ignorant of how our bodies function.

Today, women are forming health networks because we find our doctors will not share the information we need to know. Many health networks are formal, such as the famous Boston Women's Health Book Collective, San Francisco's Coalition for the Medical Rights of Women, Women and Chemical Dependency in Vermillion, South Dakota, and the Cesarean Support Group in Sioux City, Iowa. But informal networks also exist wherever women get together. Any woman who has ever gone to a gynecologist for a checkup notices how eagerly the women who are pregnant talk to one another and share advice, information, and support. In any pediatrician's office, mothers once again exchange symptoms and information about various childhood diseases that are making the rounds of the neighborhood. The need to know about our health and the health of our families is the reason health networks are forming—both on national levels, such as the National Women's Health Network, based in Washington, D.C., with its thousands of members, and on local levels, such as BABE (Better Alaskan Birth Experiences) in Eagle River, Alaska, with a small number of members.

Goals of Health Networks

Getting answers to questions we must know is the reason there are thousands of women in scores of health networks throughout the United States. Networks are an attempt to fill the man-made gaps between women and our knowledge of our own bodies. Through networking, women have a power base; we are no longer afraid to insist on having natural childbirth, for instance, if that's what we want. Through networking, women have successfully challenged drug companies that experiment with our bodies, such as the DES cancer cases. Through networks, women share common experiences— the good and the bad—as well as information about childbirth, menstruation, and menopause and about such diseases as endometriosis and cancer—all things we must know about in order to take charge of and preserve our lives. Women network to find the information we need for preventive health care, too.

Another important goal of health networks is to change things for women for the better, to have some muscle as a group, to improve medical services for all women. For by serving our own self-interests in our quest for better health, we help women everywhere.

The Most Successful Health Network of Them All

Certainly the best-known health network in this country is the Boston Women's Health Book Collective in West Somerville, Massachusetts, which grew out of a women's conference held in Boston in 1969. First known as the Doctor's Group, network members wanted to know more about their bodies, and so the idea for a book explaining women's health in simple, understandable terms, devoid of the medical mystique usually surrounding such discussions, was born. The excellent book which resulted, *Our Bodies, Ourselves*, a book by and for women, was an instant success and still, more than ten years after publication, is on best-seller lists—tangible proof of the responsive chord the network struck in millions of women all across the country.

For many women, opening the pages of *Our Bodies, Ourselves* was a revelation, an insight into a world we have no hope of penetrating through traditional medical institutions. Reading the clear, concise, nonsexist information about our bodies—anatomy, sexuality, relationships, nutrition, exercise, rape, venereal disease, masturbation, birth control, abortion, childbearing, menopause—was the first time many of us ever understood, or were permitted to understand, this vital information about ourselves. For many, it was also the first time we had ever read anything about lesbians that did *not* describe them as sick, lost women. The books was electrifying in its message and impact and was passed from friend to friend, mother to daughter, and from daughter to mother. And the network of eleven women who created that book and the one that followed, *Our Children, Ourselves*, still meets every Tuesday night and is still going strong.

Judy Norsigian, administrative coordinator of the collective, describes how the network has evolved after a decade of communicating health information to women.

"We're the repository for information about what other groups are doing," says Norsigian. "We act like the center of a wheel. We funnel out information to other groups and get people in touch with one another. We suggest that people from the same area join forces. We meet with people in small group settings. We do what we always have done: disseminate information on health. We produce a lot of literature, put out health packets. We ask women to report back their reactions. We want their input."

Since its inception, the Boston Women's Health Book Collective has done an outstanding job of educating us about our bodies. And, in keeping with its commitment to the good health of all women, the collective's tenth anniversary party in 1979 was a benefit for the National Women's Health Network. "Networking is one of the important tasks of the women's movement," declares Norsigian. "We need to share information, perspectives. We need to develop analyses and to build grass-roots constituencies. The way to do these things is networking."

The National Women's Health Network

The National Women's Health Network, Inc. (NWHN), based in Washington, D.C., is one of the most important women's health groups in the United States. It links networks to other networks, which gives it range and power.

Individuals can join, too, no matter where you live, and receive the latest information on health matters current and important to women, such as a drug to ease the pain of menstrual cramps, the pros and cons of hysterectomies, and suspected cancer-causative foods and drugs. Membership is $25 annually.

The National Women's Health Network was founded in 1975 by a group of concerned women, among them Barbara Seaman, Phyllis Chesler, Mary Howe, Alice Wolfson, and Belita Cowan. Their concern: There was no adequate women's health lobby. The group wanted to monitor the Federal Drug Administration, check out legislation that would affect the health of women, and bring together women's health networks.

In 1976, NWHN began picking up contacts with grass-roots organizations, according to Jenny Knauss, one of fourteen NWHN board members. "Some of the new members and board members questioned whether the network should be a lobby or an organization to tie together women's health groups," she says. "Some of the members wanted a broader-based group."

Today, NWHN is that broader-based group and among its affiliates are the Boston Women's Health Book Collective, American Foundation for Maternal and Child Health, East Harlem Council for Human Services, the Coalition for the Medical Rights of Women, and the Feminist Women's Health Centers. NWHN has a newsletter and a news alert system. When three board members agree an issue is important, NWHN sends out notices to all members. Knauss, training coordinator of the Health Systems Agency, explains how the news alert works:

"At 11 A.M. on August 11, 1977, NWHN had a national '11th Hour' demonstration against the Hyde Amendment in all cities with HEW regional offices. The demonstration was in response to the proposed amendment to stop the flow of HEW funds for abortions. It was also in response to an order from the then HEW chief, Joseph Califano, to HEW regional offices to cut off such funds. As soon as the Califano memo went out to stop funds, the news alert was under way. In five days, a nationwide demonstration was held. If you are able to organize a national demonstration in five days," adds Knauss, *"that's* networking!"

Among the NWHN member groups is the Reproductive Rights National Network, begun in 1979. Most NWHN groups involved in abortion issues are pro-choice. NWHN is basically feminist and also works with groups such as the Gray Panthers.

The NWHN "Lobby"

In 1978 alone, the American Medical Association spent $1 million and drug companies spent $4 million influencing Congress and federal officials. That same year, without lobbyists and with only $17,000 to use for women's health, the National Women's Health Network won some major victories:

- More than 200 network members successfully petitioned the FDA to alert women to new hazards of the birth control pill.
- A lawsuit against the Pharmaceutical Manufacturers Association, representing the drug industry, and the American College of Obstetricians and Gynecologists, forced the drug companies to provide women with printed warnings on menopausal estrogen drugs.
- Network pressure resulted in U.S. Senate hearings on obstetrical practices—the first in the nation's history.

And in 1979, the NWHN scored another major victory by establishing a national registry for women who were receiving the drug Depo-Provera, and injectable contraceptive that has not been approved safe for birth control by the FDA. According to *Media Report to Women,* the NWHN called attention to harmful effects of the drug at a press conference, adding, "Despite new evidence linking Depo-Provera to uterine cancer in monkeys, it continues to be used . . . especially among poor, minority, and institutionalized women."

NWHN was concerned that the FDA had taken no action to alert physicians and the public to this new evidence. So the network stepped in and established a national registry in order to identify and to assist women who may have been injured by the drug. "In the event that women bring lawsuits against their doctors or the manufacturers of the drug, the network will provide assistance," stated Belita Cowan, executive director of NWHN.

If you want to be part of an active network working daily to improve the quality of health of all women, or if you simply want to find out just what might be dangerous and even deadly for you, joining the National Women's Health Network is one of the most effective ways you have of being informed and making your voice heard.

The Variety of National Health Networks

The organization and scope of women's health networks make them a vital factor in the day-to-day lives of women. Some of the other far-reaching national health networks include the Women and Health Roundtable, a coalition of women in health-related groups that is part of the Federation of Organizations for Professional Women, and La Leche League, probably the largest health network in the world, with an international membership that believes in good mothering through breast-feeding.

The explosion of interest in such issues as home births, midwives, nurse midwives, and lay midwives is also reflected in the birth of networks like the

International Childbirth Education Network, with regional groups through the United States such as the network headed by Jane Wirth in Midland, Michigan. Women who want to control their reproduction have formed scores of national networks that range from the National Abortion Rights Action League to Catholics for a Free Choice (headed by Carol A. Bonosaro). Both groups are headquartered in Washington, D.C.

Feminist Women's Health Centers, founded by Carol Downer, are spread throughout the United States. And DES Action/National is a group that connects networks in Massachusetts, New York, Pennsylvania, Illinois, Washington, D.C., Michigan, Oregon, and California. As alcoholism increases among women, networks of women alcoholics, connected nationally through Alcoholics Anonymous, are forming, insisting that women with this problem get the same help as men do. Many other health "dragons" are being slain on a national level by networks of caring women.

The Variety of Local Health Networks

Local health networks also disseminate the information we need to know on important health issues, and they offer an additional advantage for members: direct and personal contact, and support in times of need. In Rockville, Maryland, women network through the Rural Health Research committee; in New York City, a network calls itself The Feminist Health Works. Another active local network is Rhode Island's Women's Health Collective, in Providence. And in New Haven, Connecticut, the Therapy Rights Committee, a network of women concerned about women's rights in therapy and mental health, has important impact for women with emotional problems. The Early Bird Support Group in Sioux City, Iowa, is a network that gives advice and support in the first three months of pregnancy, emphasizing the importance of a good nutritional start for the fetus—and the mother.

What One Health Network Has Accomplished:
DES Action/National

Getting out the word about dangerous drugs and their effects is an important commitment among health networks, which have often found the government and the medical profession will *not* do so, or, if they do, move very, very slowly. Because of this situation, an important network has formed around DES (diethylstilbestrol), a drug which was given to many pregnant women in the early 1940s to prevent miscarriage and which has been linked to cervical and vaginal abnormalities in daughters whose mothers took the drugs. It's also linked to an increased risk of breast and reproductive system cancers in DES mothers. In addition, Jan Loveland reports in *Ms.* magazine that, most recently, DES has been associated with genital tract abnormalities and possible testicular cancer in sons of DES mothers.

While the fact that DES was used on unsuspecting women in the first place is depressing, there *is* a feeling of uplift to see how the DES network has located and identified potential victims, given aid, support, and legal advice to those who file suit against the drug's manufacturers, and continues to press the government to expose fully the dangers of this drug—which is still being used by drug companies in hormone replacement therapy and in the "morning after" pill. The $500,000 that Joyce Bichler, a DES daughter, won in a suit against Eli Lilly & Co., a pharmaceutical concern that produced DES, and the $800,000 awarded Anne Needham in her suit against White Laboratories of New Jersey, which distributed the drug, show the real and practical power of health networks. DES Action/National, with its constant surveillance of this problem, is an awe-inspiring health network.

Mental Health Networks

Women going through a divorce, women who feel overwhelmed in their lives, women who are depressed and unhappy are increasingly seeking help for their emotional problems. In 1978 alone, it is estimated that from 21.6 to 32.4 million Americans received therapy—and more than 80 percent of those seeking professional help were women.

The area of mental health is so important to women that networks to make sure women get the kind of help they need, so that they do not feel alone and stigmatized, are forming throughout the country. Most women feel frightened when they realize they need professional assistance. They naturally gravitate to other women with their problems; men don't seem very sympathetic about emotional problems, one reason, perhaps, why so few men go for help themselves. And so mental health networks—women helping other women—are rapidly becoming the preferred choice for thousands of women who want and need therapy.

One of the most important kinds of mental health network is the feminist therapy network. Feminist therapy is an alternative to traditional therapy, which for the most part is male-dominated and consists of psychiatrists (who have a medical degree) and psychoanalysts schooled in Freudian therapy and techniques. Feminist therapists are women; most of them are psychologists, not psychiatrists. Many women today feel it is very important for women to have women therapists, women who understand, without the patient's feeling she needs to justify her condition. Women concerned about mental health believe that often the traditional male psychiatrist–female patient relationship devolves into a power situation in which the psychiatrist controls and wins—a relationship that can be extremely damaging for women in need of help. Feminist therapists differ in their relationship to their clients: There is more of a give-and-take, a *sharing* of problems. The feminist therapist does not play God. Often, clients work out contracts, goals, and expectations with feminist therapists. Traditional therapy does not allow for this kind of give-and-take which many women need to feel better about themselves and to understand themselves.

Networks of women in therapy are rarely formal. The truth of the matter is that women in therapy are often considered unstable, "sick," and their jobs could be in jeopardy if anyone knew they were seeking treatment. Concern about this situation has led to the formation of networks among professionals in the field who want to help and protect and inform women with emotional problems about their options. And the reality of the situation is that women professionals in mental health need support, too.

To answer these needs, the National Feminist Therapist Association, a network of women who are therapists in private practice, was formed in 1976. Carolyn Mills Kroes of Grand Haven, Michigan, is the group's founder. Its headquarters are in San Diego, and although the network lists 250 official members, "we figure we're reaching about 1,000 people," says Kroes. The network also has a bi-monthly newsletter.

Why a network of feminist therapists? "In 1976, I went into private practice and worked part-time at a women's center in Muskegon, Michigan," says the therapist. "One night I got a call from a woman who needed help. I had a client with me at the time, so I said I'd go to the woman's house when I was finished. When I finally got to her house—it took awhile because it was snowing—I knocked and there was no answer. Now, I don't usually go into people's homes, but this time I followed my instinct and went in. I found the woman lying on the floor by the phone.

"I called an ambulance and collected all the pill bottles in the house and took them to the hospital. I was sure she had overdosed on pills. But it seems what I had to say didn't matter. The physician at the hospital diagnosed her condition as an overdose of alcohol. He would not listen to me. *I realized then I was totally powerless in that hospital.* I was angry. I called a friend in Boston and said, 'Let's start our own organization.' I needed some communication with women who think the way I do, who have the same concerns.

"Later, the woman who had overdosed became my client. She told me she'd had only one glass of wine that night. She had overdosed on the pills."

Many therapists, says Kroes, work in traditional areas of mental health, such as institutions, and often they don't dare speak up against intolerable conditions or practices for fear they would lose their jobs. Now, because of the support of the networks, some of these therapists are speaking out. The accomplishments women's mental health networks have made are even more impressive when you realize that a few years ago, some of the present members of the National Feminist Therapists Association didn't even know there was a name for the kind of therapy they were doing—or that other women, also trying to remove sexism, racism, and elitism from therapy, were working toward the same goals as they. In this regard, therapy networks are similar to the business networks, forging new territory out of a situation where women had been so isolated that one businesswoman did not know that other businesswomen existed.

Kroes gets letters from members saying the network newsletter gives them strength to go out and do battle again. And she knows from personal experience the importance of communicating with peers: At age thirty-five, Kroes went back to school and there she learned an important quotation: "Therapy means *change*, not adjustment." "But you need support and communication to change," adds Kroes. She gets hers from her network.

The Largest Health Network in the World: La Leche

At least one million women worldwide annually turn to La Leche League International, Inc., a network devoted to helping mothers breast-feed, for information and support they can get nowhere else. La Leche was formed in 1956 in Franklin Park, Illinois, and today has grown into 4,300 groups of mothers who meet monthly in the United States, Canada, and forty-five other countries. The leaders of these groups number more than 11,000 mothers, women who themselves have breast-fed and are experienced in helping concerned mothers in their communities, either by telephone, monthly meetings, or correspondence. And after almost a quarter century, La Leche is still thriving; some 4,000 people attended La Leche's seventh international conference in 1979.

Even today, women who want to nurse their babies have unnecessary obstacles in their way, and that is where the powerful forces of networking come in. How do you prepare your breasts for nursing? How do you get the hospital to bring you your baby to nurse? Are supplemental bottles unhealthy and unnecessary for your baby? How can you possibly work at an outside job and nurse? How can you withstand the social pressure that still exists against nursing, one of the healthiest forms of nourishment, both physically and emotionally, you can provide for your infant?

Sally Murphy did volunteer work for La Leche for ten years until she was named a public relations assistant in 1979.

"I wanted to help, because La Leche had done so much for me," says

Murphy. She has two young children and had always planned to breast-feed. "I had a mother who breast-fed four children," she says, "so I thought you only had to put the baby to the breast and nurse." She found, with her first child, born in 1968, that it wasn't so simple. Murphy was unprepared for the social pressure she encountered *not* to breast-feed. And, since she was unprepared to nurse, she had cracked nipples from breast-feeding. "I was sore. I had a hard time. It hurt," she says. "I didn't know whether to use formula or not, as I was being urged to do. I didn't know what to do about breast-feeding at all."

But then she heard about La Leche, where her questions were answered kindly and intelligently and the support she needed was given. "I didn't go to meetings regularly with the first child, but by the time the second came along in 1970, I was going regularly," she says. "I liked the philosophy. It's nice being with mothers who like being mothers, where you *share* information rather than using children to compete with one another or to make comparisons. Through La Leche, I learned things can be relaxed and easy, that nothing is the end of the world."

The difference in breast-feeding her first and second child convinced Murphy that the league approach was for her, and over the years she became more and more involved. "I liked going to meetings where children were welcome, where mothers were breast-feeding babies. I feel the importance of the league only starts with breast-feeding and goes much further from there."

Murphy believes that babies need not only the milk "but the mother too." Though not everyone agrees that only mothers can take care of babies, it is the members' strong sense of nurturing that makes La Leche work as a network. Nursing is not as simple and uncomplicated as it should be in today's society. Often, mothers make frantic calls to La Leche in the middle of the night, when the baby is cranky and seems still to be hungry, even after nursing, and the mother is frightened and unsure. Someone is always on tap to answer those phone calls, giving encouragement, advice, and information when it is needed, counterbalancing a medical doctor's advice, which generally is the easy way out: Give up nursing or supplement with formula.

I myself made my share of those phone calls when my first child was born and I wanted to nurse her. Everyone was shocked that I wanted to do such a primitive thing—except La Leche. I vividly remember one night when I was frustrated because I felt I didn't have enough milk for my infant and the doctor had prescribed a formula to "keep the baby alive until the milk came in." My 3 A.M. call to La Leche was returned. I was comforted. I was told the formula often really isn't necessary. I learned, too, that some of the ingredients of the formula *undid* the helpful effect of antibodies in my milk—the very reason I was nursing!—and that if I nursed without formula, the milk would come in sufficiently. It would all work out. And it did.

I went on to nurse all three of my children, learning to cope with the problems of nursing as they arose, often only with the support of that voice on the other end of the telephone, a La Leche volunteer.

Networks for Third World Nursing Mothers

INFACT—Infant Formula Action Coalition—is a network of women activists trying to locate Third World new mothers who are being given formula for their babies, free, at time of birth. What happens is that the babies become dependent on the formula, the mother's milk dries up—and then there are no more free samples of formula available. The mother, impoverished to begin with, now has to *buy* formula. She cannot afford it, of course, but she is stuck. And the lack of money is only the tip of the iceberg; the truly frightening aspect of this situation is that many babies on formula become very sick because the water used to make the formula is often contaminated.

Alarmed that substituting infant formula for mother's milk can contribute to illness and death among babies, INFACT organized a boycott of the Nestlé Company, one of the largest food producers in the world. INFACT cannot stop Nestlé directly, nor does Nestlé seem to have halted its efforts to pursue this potential billion-dollar market. So INFACT is asking informed Third World mothers to warn other new mothers what starting to use the formula can mean. INFACT is distributing information, answering questions, taking its concerns to the women involved, and enlisting their help in spreading the word.

Networks Concerned About Giving Birth

Motherhood—including giving birth and the preparation for giving birth—is an important role in a woman's life, and women today are examining more carefully than ever before their options and alternatives to make childbirth a rewarding, meaningful experience—for themselves as well as for their husbands, their other children, and their babies. Women no longer want to be left out of the decision-making process when it comes to the birth of their children. They want to participate actively, to be able to choose for themselves what kind of delivery they will have, whether they will give birth in a traditional hospital setting or at one of the many new alternative birthing facilities, such as hospitals with nurse-midwives or maternity centers, or even have their baby at home.

Helping women to decide what is best for them are the scores of networks concerned with giving birth—networks like the Arizona School of Midwifery in Tucson; the Northwestern School of Practical Midwifery in West Linn, Oregon; the Maternity Center in El Paso, Texas, headed by Shari Daniels, a lay midwife; Better Births in Fayetteville, Arkansas; BABE (Better Alaskan Birth Experiences) in Eagle River, headed by Peg Newman; Birthplace, Inc., in Gainesville, Florida, headed by Judy Levy; and the Informed Homebirth Group in Boulder, Colorado.

"To me, home birth is one of the most special feelings a family can have," says Marianne Schroeder of Boulder's Informed Homebirth network. "It's not something you do and then forget about. It is a very intense experience. When it is over, the whole family is closer."

Yet women today who want to have home births face serious opposition from their doctors, and some state laws forbid midwives to supervise births. The many networks for home births have been formed in response to these problems. Nationally, Schroeder's group has some 600 members, 85 of whom are informed leaders, women who have been trained to teach classes preparing pregnant women for home births and assisting women to become midwives, attendants, and assistants in home births.

In 1977, Schroeder's baby was born at home. "It was beautiful, really neat," she says. "My husband and our first child were there. And because the household was not disturbed or upset, it made it much easier on all of us. There were other benefits, of course, emotional ones that never would have been the same in a hospital. A medical doctor and a homeopathic midwife were on hand. I felt my home delivery was much safer because in hospitals there are so many interventions from the medical staff to speed things up or to slow them down. It was a very private birth. I was the only patient, and I believe I got better care because of the one-on-one ratio."

Schroeder and her husband know they would like to have a third child sometime, so Marianne took a series of training classes to equip her to assist at births. Today, she teaches a series of training classes of from six to eight weeks that cover the prenatal period and educate prospective mothers about what home births are like and how to prepare for them—plus all the facts of childbirth and delivery, so they can recognize for themselves what is happening. The book she uses in her classes is *Special Delivery* by Rahima Baldwin, president of Informed Homebirth. Schroeder is now part of an ever-growing network of women who believe in home births.

Drugs and Alcohol Abuse

The commitment women feel toward one another is impressive in health networks, and because of this strong sense of responsibility and concern, networks are being formed among women who are aware of the dangers of drug and alcohol abuse among other women. Jennifer Rhodes of Vermillion, South Dakota, for example, gives a course at the University of South Dakota entitled "Women and Chemical Dependency." Her course trains former drug abusers to be counselors for other women; that is, to be peer counselors, an outgrowth of networking that is an extremely effective way of helping other women with the same problem. From her classes and seminars has evolved a network of women concerned about drug abuse.

"My motivation to do something in this area is strong," says Rhodes. "A close relative is a recovered alcoholic. My father died of alcoholism. I am especially concerned about women because they are more poly-drug users than men. They are more often prescribed Valium and Librium than men. When mixed with alcohol, the combination is deadly."

Rhodes sees many successes from her program and from the group support that follows. She cites the case of a former student who had been married and was physically abused by her husband. Her escape: drugs. But she did come to Rhodes's program, enrolled, took the course, and decided to go back to college and to become a social worker. She even became active in the local chapter of the National Organization for Women (NOW).

"Drug abuse is serious because women who are drug abusers tend to face reality by escaping through drugs, and then they become dependent on those drugs," says Rhodes. "They become out of touch with reality. They forget their responsibilities at work and at home. They lose their motivation. Instead, their life is spent trying to get high and maintaining that high. We work to change that process, through education, counseling, and support."

The university where Rhodes teaches has a women's Alcoholics Anonymous group which supplies extra support; a network of women in Yankton, South Dakota, also tries to help women drug abusers. The proliferation of treatment centers and networks of this kind that have sprung up all over the nation, such as Women for Sobriety, in Quakertown, Pennsylvania, prove that, given the proper help, women can successfully fight even the most painful addictions.

Networks of Women Health Professionals

One of the most exciting developments of health networks is the joining together of women who work in health and allied professions: nurses, doctors, laboratory assistants, nurse's aides, nutritionists, X-ray technicians, hospital social workers, pharmacists, health technicians, and assistants. In 1977, a seminar called Program for Women in the Health Sciences was held at the University of California at Santa Cruz, and the network of women health professionals was born. Founding mother was Dr. Maggie Matthews, and facilitators of the network are Patricia Bourne, Lucy Ann Geiselman, and Sheryl K. Ruzek.

The primary purpose of the group is to advance the careers of its members. But two of its goals show the sincere commitment of network members to the good health of all women: (1) To sponsor local, regional, and national conferences in order to identify and disseminate information on research, policies, and practices related to women's careers and women's health, and (2) the incorporation of the concerns and perspectives of Third World women into all activities.

The Future of Health Networks for Women

Health networks are only beginning to blossom. This is one area where there will be more and more growth, as women decide to do something about the health problems that concern us. If you live in a large city, you will most likely be able to find an already established health network that interests you. If you live in a smaller community, you may want to form your own and join the growing number of women in networks who are demanding to know the whys and hows of the world of medicine. Through health networks, the "dragons" are being met head on.

SPORTS NETWORKS

Running, sailing, horseback riding, tennis, rugby—all these sports are fun, and women want to be able to participate in them too. Businessmen who play squash or tennis at lunch, or who play touch football or golf with their friends on weekends, know how great it feels to be able to play a sport well and to release the tensions that often build up during the day through vigorous physical exercise. Likewise, women who have good body and muscle tone and who enjoy the outdoors find they concentrate better and feel more at ease, with themselves and with others around them. Whatever sport you enjoy, there is an active network of women enthusiasts making the sport happen.

Goals of Sports Networks

Women athletes and women who just enjoy team or individual sports find they need help to get started, to get playing time, to find other players, to enjoy the sport of their choice without being overshadowed by men. That is the fun part of sports networks—actively participating in any sport you want to play.

But there's a serious aspect too, and many networks of women athletes are working to bring about equality on the playing fields, in funding, and in facilities for all women athletes, from elementary school on. Working on behalf of equal opportunity in sports for the sexes are the National Association for Girls and Women in Sports and various sports networks that have grown out of the International Women's Year Conference in Houston. Women are forming networks because they want an equal chance to enjoy the camaraderie and sense of achievement that come from playing sports. Women's networks are combatting such things as the fact that in 1976, at one major midwestern university, more money was spent on men's hockey sticks than on any one women's sport.

The Variety of Sports Networks

Everyone is doing it—enjoying sports, that is. Women professional athletes in tennis and basketball have shown other women the joy of sports, and now more and more women are forming networks to make athletics part of their daily lives—networks like the Association for Intercollegiate Athletics for Women, a nationwide network for college athletes based in Washington, D.C., and, on the West Coast, the Women's Sports Foundation in San Francisco, which links athletes and sports organizations throughout the country. The scope of women's sports networks is breathtaking: Every major sport—tennis, rugby, running, softball, basketball, volleyball, badminton, hockey—has a nationwide network of athletes in touch with one another, organizing games, continuously boosting the sport of their choice. Internationally, Carol Oglesby of Temple University in Philadelphia represents U.S. athletes at meetings of the International Women's Year, networking among U.S. women and those all over the world to increase the opportunity of all women to participate in sports. A member of the IWY Committee on Women in Sports, Oglesby's expertise in sports networking has led to her nickname as the "guru" of women's sports.

Fun and Games—and Serious—Sports Networks

Some women network in sports merely for fun and games. An informal basketball league of women attorneys in New York, for example, plays regular games and is generally strict about permitting women attorneys only on the court. But now and then, when someone calls in sick and can't play, substitutes like LeAnne Schreiber, sports editor of the *New York Times*, are permitted to fill in. On the other hand, some women are deadly serious about their sports activities; they want to keep in shape for their own physical safety and to achieve the inner peace that comes from being able to take care of yourself in almost any circumstance. In Seattle, Washington, the Feminist Karate Union specializes in martial arts; so does the Artemis Institute of Medford, Massachusetts, which also instructs members in mountaineering. Informally, throughout the country, women teachers of the martial arts network with one another, sharing advice, expertise, and support.

The National Association of Girls and Women in Sports

The only national professional network devoted exclusively to opening up opportunities for female athletes is the National Association of Girls and Women in Sports (NAGWS) in Washington. Carol L. Thompson, executive director, explains that all board members of associations of professionals in the field of physical education are eligible to join. There are some 15,000 members who pay dues to the professional association that is NAGWS's umbrella group, the American Alliance for Health, Physical Education, Recreation, and Dance.

"The National Association doesn't deal with competitive sports as such," says Thompson. "We deal with the individual athlete. Our concern is more with the women who make up the teams than with the teams per se."

The structure of this national sports network is broad in range. It rates and trains officials for girls and women's sports. It has a national coaches council and gives up-to-date information on individual sports. If you want to learn to coach volleyball, you join its volleyball academy, for instance. Women's sports are promoted nationally and locally. NAGWS has an athletic training council that gives information and workshops for women who want to be trainers. It also sponsors in-service training of administrators of girls and women's programs at high schools and colleges; has a National Riding Commission, with clinics and rating centers for riders and teaching programs for women who want to become riding teachers; sponsors coaches conferences all over the United States every year; and is involved in career education, encouraging women to think of careers in sports.

This dedicated network published twenty-one guides for sports and writes all the rules that govern women's sports at the college level. Internationally, NAGWS sent eight women to play volleyball in Venezuela, using international rules compiled by NAGWS, and is working on a program to improve sports opportunities for women in Latin America.

The most important NAGWS commitment, Thompson says, is keeping women informed about sports. In connection with this, the network closely monitors Title IX of the Education Amendments of 1972, which requires equal treatment of women in sports and threatens to withhold federal funds from universities that fail to comply. The Department of Health, Education, and Welfare (HEW) is mandated by Congress to monitor Title IX, yet there is still a gross discrimination in funds allowed by high schools and colleges for women's sports as compared to men's—from supplying sneakers and paying for trips, to the actual facilities themselves. NAGWS has organized fifty-six groups nationally, in order to enforce Title IX and to keep a careful check on HEW rulings. The deadline has long since passed for schools to be in compliance, and that is not even close to happening yet.

Running Networks

One sport in which women have managed to break through enormous barriers is running. And networking has helped make that happen. "Networking breaks down the isolation of the woman runner," says Phoebe Jones, national coordinator of one of the largest running networks, the North American Network of Women Runners, formed in May, 1979, and based in Shaker Heights, Ohio. "You realize you're not alone. Otherwise, you think you're crazy when you feel the subtle putdowns at coed running clubs, and that's why a lot of women won't join them."

Jones is owner of Fitness, Inc., a consulting firm that sets up fitness programs and organizes races. She is dedicated to opportunity for women in sports and runs eight miles a day herself.

"If I'm the only one of a few women running at a club, I can't help but feel alone," says Jones. "Especially if I haven't developed as a runner. A lot of women are self-conscious about running. A lot of women won't even run in the daytime. Women have a tremendous lack of time and money, and that's the major deterrent, of course, even more than the psychological barrier."

The North American network tries to break down those barriers by serving as a means of communication for women runners. "When I started the network," Jones notes, "I thought there must be only two or three running clubs for women in the country. But I found out there are twelve—and more forming." The network is now international, with branches in Canada, and it is trying to make connection with women in other countries to get women's long-distance running as an event in the Olympics (a whole other track of sexism). The network is action-oriented and especially concerned with the issue of safety for women runners.

Phoebe Jones sees the political implications of running. "Running, for women, means taking back our bodies," she says. "It also means saying 'no' to weakness and 'yes' to individual time. 'No' to always being on demand at home and, ultimately, to housework. Men who say, 'Of course women have hours of time to run,' don't recognize the work women do at home."

Other women's running networks include Los Angeles Women Running, based in Santa Monica; the District of Columbia's Washington Runners in Alexandria, Virginia; Erie Runhers in Pennsylvania; the Goodyear Wingfoot Runners at the Goodyear plant in Akron; and the Happy Hoofers in Cheyenne, Wyoming—just to name a few.

Seaworthy Women

Women who want to learn sailing have found they are also intimidated by coed classes. "They are not encouraged to do well in classes with men, taught by men," says Jeannine Talley, who, with Ellen Power, operates a sailing instruction school in Santa Monica on weekends. Called Seaworthy Women, it was founded in 1976. The result: a network of women sailors, some 200 to 300 strong. Once again, women who go through instruction together and make it become a tightly knit network. Talley, a folklore and mythology instructor at UCLA, has a great love for the sea she wants other women to share.

"Sailing is an experience you can't have anywhere else but on the water," says Talley. "The peacefulness is so beautiful. And there's the satisfaction of knowing it's the one place in the world I'm completely on my own. There, I am completely self-sufficient."

Seaworthy Women owns two boats, *Sea Lass* and *Esperanza*. The crews are all-female and they take day sails, weekend cruises, and week-long cruises. "For many of the women who sail with us, the experience has changed their lives," says Talley. To spread that enjoyment around, Seaworthy Women is working to promote another network: Women at the Helm—Round the World. Women at the Helm has the ambitious project of developing the first all-women's circumnavigation of the world by sailboat. If all goes well, the three-year project will set sail in June, 1981.

The Great Outdoors Networks

For outdoor and water sports enthusiasts—previously the private domain of men only—there are such networks as Outdoor Learning Experiences (OLE!), a nonprofit, tax-exempt recreational network in Elk Grove, Illinois, which offers instruction in hunting, pistol shooting, skeet shooting, and the more traditional outdoor sports. On a local basis, the Heartland Healing Center in Berkeley, California, is a wilderness retreat with outdoor sports for women only. Woodswomen, in Minneapolis, has trips, rafting, and hikes in the woods for its members.

DOLLS (Dedicated Outdoor Lunker Lovers Society) gets together in Tulsa, Oklahoma, to fish, according to its president, Rose M. Ricklefs. Keep Listening in Sandy, Oregon, is a network of women who go on wilderness trips together. In Waltham, Massachusetts, the Infinite Odyssey arranges rafting and mountaineering trips for members. Camping Women provides trips for women in Sacramento, California.

Women in the Wilderness get together in the wilds of San Francisco. Earthwatch, in Belmont, Massachusetts, arranges scientific field trips specifically designed for those who are new to the ways of the wild. The International Women's Fishing Association casts bait in Palm Beach, Florida.

The National Women's Rowing Association has networks in Seattle, Washington, and Sunderland, Massachusetts. Women in the Water rafts in Berkeley. Lesbian Whitewater Rafting Weekends plans river trips in San Francisco. And a network with the right attitude is the Hot Flashers in San Anselmo, California. According to member Nancy Skinner, Hot Flashers is a network of mid-life women who start together to learn about the outdoors. And they stick together, too, developing the closeness that comes from besting the unknown together. Most of the members are single women, many of whom develop supportive friendships with each other and continue to socialize apart from network get-togethers.

Networks for the Net Set

Often, women athletes learn that if they don't arrange their own fun, their male counterparts will not arrange it for them. To ensure that the mature woman will have enough tennis—though no tennis player, regardless of age or gender, ever admits to having enough—the Senior Women's Tennis Association was formed. Based in Winter Park, Florida, this network is active in ensuring senior women enough tournaments to play in to be ranked. The categories are 35 years and over, 40, 45, 50, and 60. Because of the senior women's efforts, women's 35 and over is in the U.S. Open with a 16 draw and prize money of $10,000. Through its newsletter, it connects senior players nationally and keeps women informed of rankings and of dates and requirements of tournaments.

"The Senior Women's Tennis Association (SWTA) came into existence because the United States Tennis Association (USTA) did not offer equal attention to senior women's play," says Nancy Reed, president. "More senior women playing tennis are joining SWTA each year . . . and we will continue to strive for awareness and action for senior women by the USTA."

Game, set, match!

Everyone has heard of the international jet set, but some of the really Beautiful People are in the International Net Set. According to Jane Whitchurch, president, this network of women who love to play tennis was formed in 1967. At that time, a group of Chicago women were invited to

Mexico to play tennis by a woman who came each year from Mexico to bring her daughter to play in tournaments in the United States. Some forty women went to Mexico, stayed at the homes of women tennis players there, were wined and dined, and played in tournaments against their hostesses.

Since then, there has been an annual exchange, back and forth. In 1979, the International Net Set invited forty women from Toronto to come to Chicago, stay at their homes, and play tennis. This brings the membership up to more than 100. And next, the network is planning a tennis trip to Europe.

"Tennis has been very good to all the women," says Whitchurch. "Our families are entertained by our friends in Mexico when they visit. When children of friends come to the states, they stay in our homes. There are warm, reciprocal feelings that, without tennis, would have never happened."

Women's Rugby

Women who work hard and long to establish a new network form strong alliances that last a lifetime. An example of this is the Women's Rugby Football Network, which in 1978 came of age with its first national tournament. Rugby, which is described politely as a combination of soccer and football, and much more graphically as a street-corner brawl, had been traditionally a sport for men only. But in 1974, women got tired of watching men play, formed their own clubs, and now there are some 150 teams playing nationally.

One of the leaders of the rugby network, the woman who had a lot to do with making rugby *happen* for women in the United States, is Kathy Korse, who organized the first national tournament, held in a Chicago suburb. Teams representing Florida, Maine, Colorado, Wisconsin, Massachusetts, Texas, Georgia, and Illinois compete in the national classic. The women play hard and party hard, and a close network devoted to the best interests of women's rugby has formed.

It's also important to network with your competition, Kathy Korse points out. "I like to know everything about a new club," she says. "I want to know all about the better teams. When I see a successful team, I want to know how they condition, how they practice, and how often. The more information you have, the better a player you are, the better your team."

It took a long time for men to accept women rugby players—many still don't—but with the strong support they get from each other, the women rugby players are doing well in their struggles both on and off the field.

Women's Rodeo

Often networks are the only things that keep certain sports alive for women. Rodeo is one of these sports, and the Girls' Rodeo Association, a national network founded in 1948 to give women a chance to win prize money for barrel racing, running the calves, and roping, same as the men, is an example of the stick-to-itiveness of the sports networks. "Both my parents were in rodeo, so I was lucky," says founder Lydia Moore, a former trick rider. "My daughter's in it now. But not every girl has the opportunity."

Based in Spencer, Oklahoma, Moore's association puts women rodeo riders across the country in touch with one another. They learn where and how to learn the ropes of rodeo and are informed of prize-money races. And they all work together to get more events and more money for women in the sport. "Women still don't have a chance of earning anything like men do," says Moore. "The top male rider in 1979 earned more than $100,000. The top woman earned $24,000."

There are some 2,000 active members of the rodeo network, ranging in age from twelve to sixty-seven years. "We keep each other going," says Moore. "We are the closest friends with probably the greatest camaraderie you'll find among women in sports. We really help each other. We have to."

And, Moore says, her association is growing. "I'm not surprised," she says. "It's a marvelous way of life. Rodeo's hard to do, but it's fun to do, too."

The Message of Sports Networks: Be Self-Sufficient!

A network that has grown out of a tradition of self-sufficiency is the Artemis Institute in Medford, Massachusetts, devoted to the martial arts and to mountaineering. Its director is Dana Densmore, a computer systems designer. Densmore says the martial arts are a physical and philosophical study that result in "not feeling oppressed."

"We're interested in reducing the amount of violence in the world," she says. "By preparing ourselves physically and mentally, we are not seen as a victim. You learn to be in control of all situations."

Her course is informal but effective, teaching meditation, self-defense, and survival skills, both in the classroom and through rock climbing. "It is a calm approach to life," says Densmore, "a process that teaches self-belief. The longer you train, the more you are in control." Women who have studied with Densmore over the years remain close, a network of confidence and power.

"A woman not in control feels victimized," says Densmore. "She feels rage and anger. But she is not helpless. She can learn she is the equal to any situation that may arise."

Two wonderful by-products of sports networks are self-sufficiency and control over our bodies. Women, long excluded from games, have discovered sports are simply too much fun to miss out on. You will find it invigorating to join a sports network. And, if you decide you want to start your own, you'll find added pleasure in shaping it to be whatever you want it to be. Sports networks help women understand and enjoy the closeness of team sports, something men have known since they were very little boys. So, be a good sport!

6 | Political and Labor Networks

Look at me! Look at my arm! It's plowed and planted and gathered into barns
and no man could head me—and ain't I a woman?
—Sojourner Truth

I believe in equal rights but I'm not for women's lib. I enjoy being a lady.
—Marie Osmond

The gathering momentum of the women's movement of the past decade has
touched women everywhere, and as we begin to feel our power as a group in
business and the professions, the next step is inevitable: the creation of organizations to advance women in government and politics and in labor unions,
where policies are made that affect our everyday lives—and our future. The
avenue women are using to be included in government and union policy decisions is networking. And, even though women's direct input into these two
huge superstructures is quite new, results are already being felt, with women
like Sarah Weddington, presidential adviser, in top administrative posts and
positions of influence because of networking.

POLITICAL NETWORKS

Women in government and political organizations meet face to face with the
Old Boy Network every day—and it's often a frustrating experience. The
Old Boys work efficiently to get their friends named to important legislative
posts and sensitive government positions and to receive favorable political
decisions and treatment. In a democracy, however, we are *all* entitled to
equal treatment under the law, and women are forming networks to make
sure this happens.

The power of networking was proved in 1964, when women lobbied to
have the word "sex" included in Title 7 of the U.S. Civil Rights Act. The
Good Old Boys had gone blithely ahead, fully intending to leave women
out—again. But women made it happen, and that has made a difference for
millions of American women: "No discrimination because of sex." The magic
words have a powerful effect as a federal law, and networking by women,
for women, made it a law.

Women's political networks form in an effort to get informal forms of power and influence—access to key legislators, access to decision-makers, access to what's going on politically—for women too. Fateful decisions made in governmental bodies affect us all; women are asking to be included in the process.

Grass-roots networking has resulted in important federal laws that protect women, such as pregnancy disability and the inclusion of displaced homemakers as a category of disadvantaged workers (see chapter 4). The long struggle to be protected by the Constitution of the United States through the Equal Rights Amendment has galvanized thousands of women into action—and into networks.

How "Old Boys" Network in Politics

Among the Good Old Boys, there's a saying: "I'll walk it over." That saying is the response to other Good Old Boys who ask their contact to bring a request to the attention of a Very Important Person. "I'll walk it over" means just that. The Good Old Boy will personally put the paper in the hands of the V.I.P. making the decision. That's networking, of course, and now women are doing their own "walking." Women are networking at every government level to get appointments, to influence legislation, to be part of whatever wheels are turning.

How "Old Girls" Network in Politics

So noteworthy is the organization of political networks by women throughout the entire country that research into this "happening" is a special project of the Center for the American Woman and Politics, at Rutgers University in New Brunswick, New Jersey. Heading the study is Kathy Stanwick, research associate.

"What I've found is terribly exciting," says Stanwick, who got the research grant from the U.S. Department of Housing and Urban Development (HUD) through networking. "There has been a growth of political networks from 1978 to 1979. Women are organizing in their own interests, some within traditional organizations, and some on their own. More often, they overlap." California Elected Women, for instance, an important network, grew out of a meeting of the larger National League of Cities, which is for women and men. Today, California Elected Women is an independent network. Women in Municipal Government is another example. Stanwick counts some twenty-five to fifty formal political networks for women, and, there are also countless informal ones.

Getting into positions of power is critical for women, Stanwick finds. "We have to work from the inside and the outside," she says. "Women who have high positions *do* make a difference. Juanita M. Kreps, former secretary of the Department of Commerce; Patricia R. Harris, HEW secretary; and Eleanor Holmes Norton, EEOC [Equal Employment Opportunity Commission] head, selected women and minorities in more than 50 percent of their appointments, and they make their presence felt."

Why Women Need Political Networks

If you want to get an important local, state, or federal job, you know you can't do it alone. It will already have been claimed by someone on the inside before you ever get a chance to send in your résumé. Political networks help women find out in advance what's going on. The same is true of legislation. If a certain bill is important to you, only a network can help you have some input. That's exactly what a group of women in Lincoln, Nebraska, had in mind when they formed the Telephone Tree, a network to spread the word on important legislation.

Keeping in touch, getting to know one another, and making connections is a ritual men practice with ease and which women must learn. Through our political networks, and the savvy of the women who have already learned to wend their way through the political mazes (such as Patricia Harris, Sarah Weddington, Bella Abzug, Shirley Chisholm), women *are* catching on. This is a recent achievement, unfortunately: When the International Woman's Year (IWY) conference was held in Mexico City in 1975, thousands of women from all over the world attended, a moment in history. They came together and they left—with no precise record of who had been there. Yet a male conference on men's liberation, which attracted 400 men in St. Louis in 1977, had a computer printout of names and addresses for conference members to take home with them! That's Good Old Boy organization and political savvy, the kind women need to emulate.

Stanwick's research shows the feminist movement, the most popular kind of political network, is going strong. However, while the most effective political networks today *are* feminist, many political networks cut across ideology and political parties in their aim to advance women, such as the many women's networks working for the rights and recognition of displaced homemakers and those working for more political appointments for women.

"Men have always had the Old Boy Network to get the best political jobs," says Stanwick. "And we [women] always thought we had to have qualifications!"

The Washington Women's Network

One of the largest and most prestigious of all political networks—and growing in power every day—is the Washington Women's Network (WWN), located in the nation's capital, a city where, more than any other, women are daily confronted with the power of the Old Boy Network. It's not surprising that the Washington area has almost as many political networks, formal and informal, as there are members of Congress!

Membership

Though the WWN was formed by feminists, its large membership—some 1,000 active members and a mailing list of more than 2,500—is politically diversified and includes a politically "heavy" roster of names such as noted economist Alice Rivlin; Donna E. Shalala of HUD; Arvonne Fraser of the Agency for International Development; Patricia Harris of HEW; Betsey Wright of the National Women's Education Fund; Barbara Blum, deputy administrator of the Environmental Protection Agency; Irene Tinker of the Federation of Organizations of Professional Women; Sarah Weddington; Pat Dailey, Federal Trade Commissioner; Representative Barbara Mikulski (D-Md.); and Carol Bellamy, president of the New York City Council and member of the New York Women's Forum. Bellamy, even though she doesn't live in Washington, recognizes the importance to every woman in politics of strong Washington "connections." WWN has monthly meetings featuring important speakers and has a paid director to run the network for busy members.

WWN was conceived after Jimmy Carter was elected President in 1976 and was born in 1977, before his inauguration. "Right after the election, some of the women who were going to be in the Administration together began to think about ways to maintain links and conversations," says Betsey Wright. And Judy Lichtman, a charter member and executive director of the Women's Legal Defense Fund, says the founders "saw opportunities available for the first time. Strong feminists were in powerful positions in government. We wanted to seize that opportunity."

WWN Activities

WWN is incorporated as a not-for-profit organization, and, to maintain that status, may not endorse political candidates or lobby for or against specific legislation. Through the networking of individual members, however, WWN tries to ensure that women's perspectives get built into programs and that women's interests are brought to bear in new legislation. Its membership is kept informed and on the alert through the WWN mailing list, which circulates what's going on "on the Hill." So while the WWN itself takes no stands, its members have made concerted efforts on behalf of the extension of the ratification of the Equal Rights Amendment, the marriage tax bill, women's income, reproductive rights, displaced homemakers, child abuse, and Social Security provisions.

WWN also acts as a recruiting mechanism for Presidential appointments. Because of its commitment to filling government job openings with qualified women, WWN sends out notices of high-level government positions that have become available and distributes résumés of its members to other members. WWN network members pay $25 a year to belong, which also entitles them, at a discounted price, to a copy of the WWN directory, *Washington Women: A Directory of Women and Women's Organizations in the National Capital,* a potent handbook of powerful women.

When top openings occur, WWN alerts its members but does not lobby on their behalf. "We would not claim credit for placing a specific individual in a high-ranking job," says Arvonne Fraser of the Agency for International Development, a founder of WWN. "We would only say we helped put women in." And that, of course, is saying a lot in the heartland of the Good Old Boys.

"Our network is information sharing, with the benefit of an old boys' network—access to people," says Judy Lichtman. "I'm not sure the network wants to measure success in terms of people getting jobs. There's more than that. It's fun to see your friends in a social setting and it's nice to learn things from speakers that you would have no way to pick up during a regular work day. The network is also a place for making your views known, for supporting candidates. It provides members with a forum for our views from legislation to appointments."

Lichtman knows "a lot" of women in administration because of the WWN network, and that benefits her in her work with the Women's Legal Defense Fund. And, because it *is* a network, women in administration know Lichtman and her group and what they're thinking. Networks work so smoothly in political areas that Lichtman gives a hypothetical situation to show the difference they make: "Say, for example, there would be upcoming legislation to eliminate pregnancy benefits. I would very formally, at work, draft a letter of protest to Eleanor Holmes Norton, head of the Equal Employment Opportunity Commission, and have the president of the Defense Fund sign it. But say, instead, I would see Norton at a network meeting. I'd go up to her and say, 'Eleanor, are you crazy? The women's groups will be all over you if you let that kind of legislation through!' "

Feminist Networks

The political networks formed around feminist issues concerning women are apparent everywhere in the political scene. What is the philosophy underlying the proliferation of feminist networks? Gloria Steinem defines it this way: "A feminist network is made up of women who choose to make some functional connections with each other, in order to make some change in their status—and in the status of all women—for the better." And Nancy Stearns, an attorney with the Center for Constitutional Rights and a board member of the National Conference on Women and the Law, says feminist networks are spreading because women need them so much. "We get information through our networks that we can't get anywhere else," she observes.

The basis of political networks is women working for the betterment of all women. Thousands of women network through ERAmerica, to get the Constitutional amendment passed. The National Organization for Women (NOW), the nation's leading feminist organization, has given birth to scores of informal but very close-knit and effective networks among its members. Women's centers, in every major city of the United States, are feminist in orientation. Today, networks of women attorneys, psychologists, students, educators, and legislators are avowedly feminist.

There are national coalitions of women that are feminist networks, like the National Women's Agenda coalition. The Women's Action Alliance is another national network devoted to women's issues and programs. Getting women into public office is the goal of the National Women's Political Caucus, while HEW Feminist is a Washington network that tries to increase the number of feminists in that agency. The National Conference on Women and the Law is a network for feminist attorneys, law students, and women in allied fields. American Women in Psychology is also feminist; it's a clearinghouse, with international contacts, for women professionals in psychology. The National Women's Studies Association is a network of feminist educators who raise issues critical to feminist education. And on college campuses, women's centers help students learn to network for their own concerns.

The National Women's Agenda

This important national coalition links thirty-two national women's organizations, including the YWCA, American Association of University Women, National Gay Task Force, and National Women's Political Caucus. The coalition sponsors two influential networks, the Kentucky Women's Agenda and the Illinois Women's Agenda, which are on top of every women's issue in their states, sponsor candidate questionnaires on women's issues, and widely circulate the answers. The reason the National Women's Agenda has such an impact on proposed legislation and issues of importance to women is that many of its member groups also represent coalitions of smaller groups. The

Illinois Agenda, for instance, links more than forty women's organizations in the state.

The Women's Action Alliance

Firmly committed to full equality for all persons, regardless of sex, the Women's Action Alliance develops, coordinates, assists, and frequently administers programs to achieve this goal. Founded in 1971 and headquartered in New York, one of the net results of its forward-looking programs is networking. For instance, in 1979 the Alliance sponsored a special program, the Institute on Women's History, funded by the Lilly Endowment, with the cooperation of the Smithsonian Institution and the Women's History Program of Sarah Lawrence College. Forty-five women attended, representing the leadership of 37 national women's organizations and selected from among candidates nominated by more than 100 organizations. Among those present: National Alliance of Black Feminists, National Committee on Household Employment, Girls Clubs of America, Women Strike for Peace, National Council of Jewish Women, Comision Feminil Mexicana Nacional. The networking that has blossomed from the conference—in addition to the deeper understanding of women's largely unknown or forgotten accomplishments of the past—will grow and grow.

The National Women's Political Caucus

Getting women into public office and raising feminist issues in government is the goal of the National Women's Political Caucus (NWPC), founded in 1971. NWPC was formed by women who saw they "needed a political arm of the women's movement to address political issues," says Ellen Malcolm of NWPC. Today, NWPC has chapters in every state of the union; has gotten caucus members elected to important posts, such as representatives Pat Schroeder (D-Colo.), Martha Keyes (D-Mo.), and Millicent Fenwick (R-N.J.); has established a fund to help elect women to the U.S. Senate; and lobbies at the state and congressional level on such issues as the ERA and reproductive freedom.

The local and state NWPC units act as powerful networks, supporting women already declared as candidates; often, NWPC goes out looking for qualified women to run. Typical is the story of Sarah Weddington, Presidential adviser on women's issues, and her entrance into the political arena. Weddington, a lawyer, was working for the Texas Women's Political Caucus when it was first formed. The members got together and decided it would be important for one of them to run for the state legislature. Weddington was chosen as their candidate for the Texas House of Representatives. And she won, moving from there to important posts in the federal government.

Nationally, caucus members who are Republicans are outnumbered 4 to 1 by Democratic women, but in the past the disparity was greater. At its national meeting in Cincinnati in 1979, the gigantic network geared itself up for the 1980 Presidential election, brainstorming methods to achieve representation for women among delegates to both parties' conventions. Iris Mitgang of Orinda, California, was elected NWPC president by the membership, which now numbers more than 30,000 women.

One of the NWPC network's major tasks is to have women appointed judges, from the district court to the U.S. Supreme Court. NWPC lobbying has resulted in quadrupling the number of women on the federal bench, from 1 percent in 1977 to 5 percent in 1979—still not a significant amount, but a move forward. Susan Ness, a 1974 graduate of Boston College Law School, heads the Legal Support Caucus, a unit of the NWPC formed by women lawyers. Until the network-within-a-network was formed, U.S. presidents asked only the American Bar Association to screen candidates for judicial posts. Now, at NWPC's suggestion, the Federation of Women Lawyers also screens nominees. Judge Shirley Hufstedler, secretary of the new Department of Education, is a product of NWPC networking. Many predict she will be the first woman appointed to the United States Supreme Court.

National Conference on Women and the Law

Working together on feminist issues at workshops and panel discussions, the National Conference on Women and the Law is a feminist legal network that helps attorneys of similar beliefs get acquainted. "Except for major urban areas," says Nancy Stearns, attorney with the Center for Constitutional Rights, "women lawyers are isolated from each other—and even in major urban areas, we are sometimes *still* isolated. At the conferences, I have contact with other women lawyers I wouldn't otherwise ever get to meet. And that is a joy."

Helping themselves, they help all women. "It's important to share my own thinking and research," says Stearns. "I did work recently in the area of sterilization of women. I can share material on sterilization abuse that I wouldn't otherwise be able to share. And people share *their* research with me. We're all on both the giving and taking end of this kind of thing."

American Women in Psychology

Like feminist attorneys, feminist psychologists have joined forces to make sure their beliefs are reflected in their profession. American Women in Psychology (AWP) has no officers but is ruled by committees that feed information to the general body. Each year, it awards a feminist research prize, and, according to AWP member Cindy Villis, this is an important statement by the group, for even though AWP makes only one or two grants annually, the research prize helps counterbalance some of the many research grants that go to men. Through its newsletter, AWP alerts members to jobs, feminist issues in psychology, and current research.

The newsletter, which carries job announcements, has a creative approach to so-called "equal opportunity" employers. "AWP receives job notices daily," says P. Kay Coleman, women's career administrator of Ashland Oil Company, Ashland, Kentucky. "For the ones we know to be genuine searches for women, we use informal contacts as well as newsletters to spread the news. Announcements that are just for affirmative action purposes, we print in the newsletter—and charge them for the printing!" Politically, AWP is a group known to speak up on issues of importance to all women. Bogus research that could have a disastrous effect on women is fought by AWP members, galvanized by telephone calls from one end of the country to the other. AWP is a politically active feminist force in this country.

The National Women's Studies Association

A recurring issue in networks is the relationship between the network and politics. Often, a political stance cannot be avoided, even if the original purpose was only to find out about job openings and to exchange information. The National Women's Studies Association (NWSA) is a network of feminist educators; it raises issues critical to feminist education. At the group's 1979 conference, representatives of the Agency for International Development (AID) had an exhibit on international women's studies and it was quickly apparent to NWSA members that AID is active in areas inconsistent with feminist principles, such as its involvement in the support of individuals and institutions attempting to control the reproductive lives of Third World women.

NWSA was stuck by its lack of knowledge about the agency, and this led to the raising of other political issues: the involvement of women's studies with the women's liberation movement, and the accountability of feminist educators to nonacademic feminists and to Third World, poor, and working-class women. According to a report on the conference published by Northeastern Illinois University's Women's Studies Program, a large segment of the conference participants is concerned about the "add women and stir" focus of the women's studies movement. This recognition of what is happening in the world and how it affects women personally and as a group is resulting in more and more political networks.

Campus Women's Centers

On many campuses, women's centers complement the work of women's studies programs. All are centers of feminist activism, reports Lisa Cronin Wohl in *Ms*. The National Women's Centers Training Project of the University of Massachusetts at Amherst surveyed 348 centers across the country. At Brooklyn College Women's Center, Women's Clearinghouse, an information and referral network, handles some 8,000 calls a year on subjects ranging from health care, battered women, and rape crisis to feminist and community activities. Women college students network for protection from rape and for nonjudgmental medical treatment at campus health clinics, especially on such matters as pregnancy and venereal disease. It's also interesting to note that a recent study shows that many younger college women are not politically active; instead, political networks on campuses are often initiated by the mature woman returning to school to complete her degree.

Other Political Networks

Feminism is not the only belief women's networks form around. In addition, there is often a coalition among women of many political persuasions who work together to get women named to politically sensitive jobs, to pass legislation, and to find out what's going on. In Washington, where men are Presidents and women are supposedly invisible, fifty women's organizations joined to form the Ad Hoc Coalition for Women's Appointments. Jane O'Reilly reports in *Savvy* magazine that the coalition makes up cross-referenced lists of jobs and thousands of women to fill them—then "girds its collective loins" to get the jobs for women. Also politically active in Washington are the national Women in Muncipal Government, Congresswomen's Caucus, and—never underestimate their power—Congressional Wives Task Force.

Networks of Women as Decision-Makers

Outside the nation's capital, women are networking to get the bills passed that matter to them. And women legislators increasingly see the need to caucus together. The Telephone Tree of the Nebraska Coalition for Women alerts members when an important issue is up for vote, according to Ada Munson of Lincoln. "We call one another, and then we call our legislator, to make sure our views are represented," she says. Also in Lincoln is the Women's Legislative Network, made up of twenty women's organizations who stay on top of current bills before the state legislature. Politically aware Lincoln has still another network that operates smoothly and effectively: The

Nebraska Legislative Task Force on Displaced Homemakers assigns one or more women to communicate directly with one legislator about displaced homemaker bills, establishing a contact. This setup works so well that now some legislators have two women assigned to them, which can only work well for displaced homemakers. The president of the task force is Ina Mae Rouse, a displaced homemaker who works as a volunteer in the office of the Nebraska Commission on the Status of Women.

Networks of Women Politicians

A Group of Women Legislators is a network of pols in Storrs, Connecticut, headed by State Senator Audrey Beck. The Maryland Association of Elected Women is headquartered in Annapolis; the Texas Association of Elected Women is in Austin. In Springfield, Illinois, Paula Johnson, a lobbyist for the Illinois Education Association, has organized "Statehouse Women," a network of lobbyists and of members of the Conference of Women Legislators (COWL). "Don't forget the 'l' in COWL!" cautions State Representative Susan Catania. COWL selects issues of interest—teenage pregnancy has been named its top priority issue—and puts their combined forces together to bring about change. The group starts its efforts to solve problems by holding public hearings in legislative districts.

Networks Concerned with Political Issues

In Fort Lauderdale, Florida, the National Task Force on Prostitution launched a Kiss and Tell campaign to expose the hypocrisy of those against prostitution by exposing the names of the men who use prostitutes' services. The Ad Hoc Religious Committee for ERA is a network in Vienna, Virginia. Mormons for ERA are in Sterling, Virginia, headed by Sonia Johnson, excommunicated from her church for her ERA activity. The Wisconsin Task Force on Women is a network concerned with the political issues of marital property and inheritance tax reform.

Networks on State and Local Politics

Women into Public Leadership is a Kansas City, Missouri, network of local officials. The Women's Coalition of Howard County, Maryland, lobbies the county government on issues related to women's rights. New Jersey Women Elected Officials meets in Newark and is made up of councilwomen of East Orange and Essex counties and of Essex County freeholders. The Women's Network of the National Conference of State Legislators is headed by Andrea Wollock of Denver. And, on the West Coast, the California Women-Elected Association in Berkeley is chaired by Sue Hone, vice-mayor of

Berkeley. Another political network, this one in Los Angeles, has the right idea for a name: Women in Power was created from a joint effort of members of the state Status of Women Commission, women on advisory boards, women in the judiciary and legislature, and community women. The thrust of the network is women as decision-makers, according to Vicki Kellinski, acting executive secretary. "We organized to get together some women with power who can help other women get power," she says. The network focuses on the power structure and decision-making bodies.

Networks for Political Appointments and Jobs

Government jobs are such a nitty-gritty concern for women that some business and professional networks have political advancement as their goals, too. Martha McKay, a politically savvy woman who is president of McKay and Associates, a management consultant firm for women, is director of Affirmative Action for the State of North Carolina. A professor in the school of management at Duke University, she is an organizer and founder of the Women's Forum of North Carolina, patterned after the New York Women's Forum. The network has these aims: to increase the number of women in the state legislature, to secure passage of the ERA, and to develop leadership among women in the state. There are some eighty women in the forum, which is run by an executive director.

"We had no illusions about running this thing in our spare time," comments McKay. "We had no illusions about having spare time. No one has spare time."

The forum has a commitment to women's issues and is concerned about power. "Women who've achieved do not have the power and the leverage of men who've achieved," says McKay. The network is statewide. Recently the forum was able to place a woman with her doctorate in sociology in an important state post. "She wrote to us," says McKay, "because she knew we are involved in women's issues. We made some phone calls and she got a job."

Grace Rohrer, a forum member, was in the cabinet of the state's last Republican administration. When the administration went out, the top men were taken care of. They had offers because of the Old Boy Network. But Rohrer didn't fall heiress to that, and the kinds of offers made to the men were not forthcoming to her. Through the forum, though, she made contact with Duke University and is working there now.

Informal Political Networks—They Work, Too!

In Sacramento, California, when Jerry Brown started looking around for a new superintendent of banks, an Old Girl network went to work. Carl In-

gram of the *Los Angeles Times* reports that through phone calls, active recruiting, and a great deal of networking, an informal network of women in
banking and government came up with a name of a qualified woman and
put her in touch with Governor Brown. Today, Mary Ann Graves, who is
now keeper of the state's purse at a salary of $54,693, is the new superinten-
dent of banks for the State of California. When the vacancy occurred, she
was a vice-president of the Bank of America. Graves has the No. 2 spot in
the state's executive branch. "It's great to know that the Old Girl Network
works," she says.

Networks of Minority Women

Though black, Hispanic, and other minority women are active in a variety of
networks, many ethnic groups feel their self-interest is best served by forming their own political networks. One of the largest minority networks is the
National Hook-up of Black Women, which was organized in 1975 to provide
a communications network for the millions of black women dedicated to action, to bettering the status of the black community in general and of black
women in particular. "We need a network of black women to achieve positive change in our society," says Dr. Arnita Y. Boswell, founder and national
president. "We need a network to deal with issues relevant to black women
today."

That's exactly what the National Hook-up is—an effort to hook up, to
network with black women. The network grew out of the Black Women's
Agenda, which grew out of the International Women's Year. "We're not a
status organization," she says. "We are a working network of black women.
We want to link talents."

The network supports the Congressional Black Caucus; it tries to reach
the broad spectrum of black women by creating and implementing an agenda that is acceptable to and answers the needs of the diversity of its membership. The National Hook-up works for the passage of the Equal Rights
Amendment and is a national support base for all black women activists.
From a few hundred members, the network has grown to more than 1,000,
representing some 150 organizations of black women; it has monthly regional
meetings and yearly national conferences and has opened a national office in
Washington to coordinate an effective structure for the network.

"Our big question has been, how do we bring all black women together,
when there is so much fragmentation?" says Dr. Boswell. "How do we hook
up with one another?" The answer, Dr. Boswell believes, is networking.

Latina women also are forming their own political action groups and
demanding political rights for Mexican and Spanish-speaking women, such

as Chicago's Mujeres Latinas en Accion. Many of these networks, however, do not work exclusively for the rights of women. Most are involved in trying to save their communities from the crimes of bad schools, arson, unemployment, and indifference. Many are networks of women *and* men and are not, therefore, *women's* networks.

How Grass-Roots Networks Grow

Working at the grass-roots level to speak out against prejudice, ethnic hatreds, sexism, and segregation is a big assignment, but Brownie Ledbetter of Little Rock, Arkansas, has been doing that successfully since 1963. She heads an organization of speakers, supporters, and colleagues called the Panel of American Women. But they could not be so effective in raising these issues if the panel were not based on the strong support and networking of a larger group of women, battle-scarred activists, who have been together for almost two decades, fighting the good fight.

"The desegregation crisis was the beginning of our group," says Ledbetter. "A group of us thought if women—'Mommies'—went out and talked to other 'Mommies,' talked personally, no one would feel threatened. We went out in teams: a black woman, a Jewish woman, and a white majority woman. The whole community was so polarized that we were forced into political action. We did a lot of talking then. We still do."

Ledbetter says she and her network became involved in different crises as they arose: anti-Vietnam, the women's movement, and, always, racial prejudice. Last year, her panel teams made more than 200 appearances throughout the state, giving talks, letting people see them face to face, equipped with audiovisual aids and other instructional material. Today, the Panel of American Women receives $98,000 in federal funds for in-service training on how to deal with prejudice.

"We learned on those panels that you *can* diffuse hostile remarks and still confront the issues," says the panel's director. Ledbetter has been a political activist for years, was the first political action chair of the National Women's Political Caucus in 1973, and was appointed by President Carter to his Advisory Commission on Women. Ledbetter led the walkout of commission members when Carter summarily fired its chair, Bella Abzug. The panel now has 2,000 members who give talks, monitor some educational presentations, and visit classrooms through the state.

Ledbetter networks because she has to. "We struggle every year," she says. In her studies of the history of Arkansas, she found that her state was the headquarters for the National Women of the Ku Klux Klan back in the twenties. Today, Arkansas has the highest incidence of reported rape in the nation. "When our governor was asked why is rape so high in Arkansas," says Ledbetter, "he replied that women in Arkansas are prettier. That is what we are up against."

Wisconsin Women's Networks: The Grass Roots Are Strong!

Brownie Ledbetter has a national reputation for being in touch with what is going on politically, for making things happen. Another woman with this same deserved respect and reputation is Kay Clarenbach, who was the first in the nation to help organize a state Governor's Commission on the Status of Women. Her state is Wisconsin, and through her efforts, Wisconsin became a pacesetter nationally as a leader in the women's movement. Clarenbach was the first chair of the board of the National Organization for Women (NOW) and took a major role in the IWY meeting in Houston. And then along came a new governor of Wisconsin, Lee Dreyfus, who abolished the State Commission on the Status of Women, leaving Clarenbach without a home base. She has lost her posts on important committees that hinged on her commission connection, but even without portfolio temporarily she remains an active political networker.

A reaction to the demolition of the Commission on the Status of Women in Wisconsin was the formation late in 1979 of the Wisconsin Women's Network, which, according to its paid legislative coordinator, Helen Casper, is "definitely political." Wisconsin's network is based in Madison but is statewide, consisting of twenty-one organizations—from the Junior League to the National Organization for Women—and an initial 250 members. Members pay $20 annually; organizations, $100. There have been short-lived coalitions in Wisconsin previously, organized around ERA laws, divorce reforms, homemakers' rights, farm women, older women, minority women, and inheritance tax. But this is the first statewide network to work on these issues together. Though the group is made up of the leaders deposed by Governor Dreyfus—Clarenbach, chair of the Women's Education Resources department of the University of Wisconsin Extension, is an organizer and board member—the governor attended the network's first meeting in September, 1979, to wish it luck! Therein, once again, lies the power of networking: The governor *had* to be there.

Grass-Roots Networks Against Pornography

A network that dramatically crosses political affiliations is New York's Women Against Pornography, with members from the far right to the far left, each of whom agrees pornography is violence against women. More than 20,000 women marched through Times Square in New York City—where there is more pornography per inch than in any other part of the country—in protest against this abuse of women. Says Susan Brownmiller, author of *Against Our Will*, a study of rape: "The objection to pornography is based on our belief that it represents hatred of women, that pornography's intent is to degrade and dehumanize the female body for the purpose of erotic stimulation and pleasure. We are unalterably opposed to the presentation of the female body being stripped, bound, raped, tortured, mutilated, and murdered in the name of entertainment and free speech."

The network of Women Against Pornography unites women who have never before worked together but who share in common a sense of revulsion when they pass a newsstand. The network is taking on a multimillion dollar porn industry, including films and magazines such as *Hustler, Penthouse,* and *Playboy*. It is an example of how political networking might mean survival for women individually and for all women as a class.

A National Grass-Roots Network for All Women

Women USA, organized by Bella Abzug, reaches out to all women with no previous affiliation. Abzug, an attorney and former New York congresswoman, explains, "We want to put together a vehicle to communicate with people all over the country who are not now involved. Through direct mail, we'll disperse information to our members on issues of importance, especially legislative ones. We'll have an answer sheet, and we will try to make sure the views of the members of the network are reflected in Congress."

Organizers of Women USA include Yvonne Brathwaite Burke, Patsy Mink, Gloria Steinem, and Brownie Ledbetter. Abzug says the network, based on input from members, will put together women interested in diversified areas—working women, consumers, club women, homemakers—who previously have not made their views known. Women USA will be a lobby for women, a network that could organize an action in a local supermarket on a consumer issue or mount a letter-writing campaign in protest of some practice. Whatever is done, it is done in the name of a group that represents thousands of American women. Grass-roots women. Voters. Concerned women. That structure makes all the difference politically, both in approach and in results.

"I think the concept of a network is a good one in all fields of endeavor," says Jane Byrne, mayor of Chicago. "I can understand it especially well after my experiences in the two recent elections. The comparison between my efforts without the Democratic organization during the primary and then with their support in the general election showed me that, while an organization cannot make you a success, it can certainly lighten your burden!"

LABOR NETWORKS

Women seeking both to "lighten the burden" of their work and to increase work opportunities were the backbone of the American labor union movement. These same union activists are the organizers of many of the labor networks in existence in the country today. Unlike union organizers, women's labor networks don't specifically work for better jobs or safer working conditions, though those issues are important concerns. What labor networks do is try to get women into important positions in the union itself, such as the Coalition of Labor Union Women; to break into apprenticeship programs for the high-paying jobs now controlled by men, such as the Coal Employment Project and Women Working in Construction; and to get recognition, respect, and compensation for work all women do, such as Wages for Housework networks.

The Coalition of Labor Union Women

One of the most vigorous labor networks in the country is the Coalition of Labor Union Women (CLUW), founded in 1974 to bring together trade-union women. CLUW is an offshoot of the larger, male-dominated labor unions, where women are now insisting that they be heard.

There was no visible contingent of labor union women at the time," says Addie Wyatt, a founder and executive vice-president of CLUW. "Everyone else was organizing—churchwomen, the National Women's Political Caucus, businesswomen—so nine women active in the trade union movement and in the women's movement decided to form our own coalition."

As in every field of endeavor, women active in unions weren't visible and did not know each other. "We didn't know how many of us there were," recalls Wyatt. "We had a Midwest meeting first and we expected about ninety people. Two hundred came. We had another meeting and this time we expected fifteen hundred. Instead, thirty-two hundred women showed up. There was such spirit, such joy and excitement in all of us. It was unique, historic. We didn't have enough food for that second meeting. We decided to split the sweet rolls in half and let the sisters share, like Jesus did with the loaves of bread and the fish!"

Wyatt says the specific requirements to CLUW include membership in a collective bargaining union *plus* being a woman. "Otherwise, men would join," she notes wryly. Today, CLUW has some 6,000 members—with a potential of 6 million, Wyatt adds. She herself is an example of the importance of networking. When CLUW was founded, Wyatt was director of development of Women's Affairs for the meatcutters union. Today, she is international vice-president of the union, which has been renamed United Food and Commercial Workers, AFL-CIO.

CLUW networks to get women into leadership positions in unions. It does this by encouraging women to make a bid for an important post and supporting them when they get it. One CLUW "success" is Alice Peurala, a mechanical-equipment tester, who is president of Local 65 of the United Steelworkers in Chicago, representing 7,500 employees, the first woman in production in the industry to head a major local. CLUW presses unions to include women at all levels, as speakers in programs and as representatives to meetings with government, public officials, and other unions. Wyatt says in 1979 alone she addressed some sixty major conferences as a representative of trade unionism.

Political Activities of Labor Networks

CLUW pushed for the AFL-CIO endorsement of the ERA—and got it. It works for affirmative action in the workplace and collective bargaining. CLUW urges its membership to take political action, to participate in the legislative process. And it's working. "It's an idea whose time has come," Wyatt observes. "It was not always easy. There was strong resistance at first to women getting together. But we have come together and we have clout in togetherness. We're breaking down the barriers to women's full participation in the labor market. Women are speaking for themselves."

Organizing Boycotts

Union women know the importance of sticking together, and CLUW has taken a political stand supporting J. P. Stevens Company workers, a struggle taking place in the southern textile industry between the Amalgamated Clothing and Textile Workers Union and Stevens. A national network was formed by the National Women's Committee to Support J. P. Stevens Workers, headquartered in New York. The network has organized a nationwide boycott against the company, keeps the issue before the public, and supports the striking workers, most of whom are women.

Organizing Clerical Workers

A new area of networking is among clerical workers, who sometimes find attempts to network in their own offices are perilous to their jobs. So a network is imperative for protection. An innovative attempt to reach clerical workers is being made by a national network of thirteen organizations, loosely affiliated as the National Association of Working Women (NAWW). Ann Crittenden reports in the *New York Times* that the network has a total of about 8,000 women, including such groups as Nine to Five in Boston, Women Office Workers in New York, Women Employed in Chicago, Cleveland Working Women, and 60 Words per Minute in Washington. The network has been able to challenge a number of employers and has chosen the nation's banks as its target.

Other groups working in employment include Twelve to One in Amherst, Massachusetts, where secretaries meet at noon to discuss job problems, and Seattle Working Women, a network in the state of Washington. Wider Opportunities for Women in Washington, D.C., has as its project the forming of an employment network of white-collar workers. Unorganized workers, according to the Bureau of Labor Statistics, earn 30 percent less than those who are organized.

Apprenticeship Programs

As difficult as it is for women white-collar workers to get decent wages, work conditions and hours are not usually overwhelming problems. But women who go into blue-collar work, which is predominantly male, find actual work obstacles beyond what would be expected in other fields. This is especially true in apprenticeship programs, in which women are insisting on being included, on being given a chance, like men, to have high-paying jobs.

There are some seventy agencies in the United States which train women specifically for blue-collar jobs, says Muriel Lederer, author of *Blue Collar Jobs for Women,* and the push to get into apprenticeships is a common problem. In some states, it's almost impossible for women to find out what the basic entrance requirements of apprenticeship programs are. Other states—through networks—are breaking that barrier, says Lederer. Fostering the effort are Wider Opportunities for Women in Washington; Women in the Trades, New York; the YWCA of Portland, Oregon; the Women's Apprenticeship Outreach Service, Milwaukee; the Southern California Area Construction Opportunities, Santa Ana; and the Boston YWCA, which trains women in building and maintenance skills.

"There's an increasing number of job openings," notes Lederer. "But," she adds, "the hardest thing is to get *in* apprentice programs and get training in the first place. Many women need coaching or tutoring to pass the entrance exams for training programs, and that's where networking comes in."

In Wisconsin, an informal network of "Women in Apprenticeships" was initiated and has spread throughout the nation, involving the establishment of skilled training programs and information resources that lead women to apprenticeship jobs. In Little Rock, Arkansas, a network called Women

Working in Construction tries to help other women get started in the building trades. In Wichita, Kansas, where women construction workers are something new, Work Options for Women networks to open jobs for women.

"The first few days, I thought I'd die," Kathy Brown of Wichita told R. C. Longworth in the *Chicago Tribune*. But I'm used to it now. My muscles are built up." Brown, twenty-four, divorced mother of two, works for Utility Contractors, largely through the efforts of the Wichita network. A former waitress, Brown started as a laborer, worked up to a job greasing the company's equipment, and hopes to become a heavy equipment operator— where the pay is *really* good.

Women Coal Miners: A Breakthrough for Women

With the panic over energy shortages, coal mines are reopening throughout the United States. In most states, men have the jobs. In a few states, however, women are making a breakthrough.

"You have to have forty hours of mine safety training before you can even go into the mines," says Connie Farmer of the Coal Employment Project in Oak Ridge, Tennessee. The project trains women sixteen years and older, in groups of twenty.

The groups "keep in real close contact," according to Farmer. "Coal companies aren't up for women getting jobs. Yet here, the only place you can work and make a decent living is in the mines or TVA. We all work together to help one another."

The Oak Ridge group networks with women in Wyoming, New Mexico, West Virginia, and Illinois. "Mining is a dirty job," says Farmer, "but physically and mentally, it's not as hard as some other jobs women do."

A recent graduate of the project, Sandy Brown, twenty-two, is divorced and has two children. She had been unemployed, but after her training she was hired by the Pemco Mine at an entry-level job, shoveling coal but not yet operating machinery. The salary: $65 a day. "We're real proud of ourselves!" exults Farmer.

Household Workers

Some of the hardest work there is involves household employment: cleaning and scrubbing and moving furniture around. To upgrade household employment, scores of national networks of household workers have been formed. Household Technicians of America, for example, headquartered in Warren, Ohio, has twenty-one chapters which try to find jobs for women, give support to household workers, and push for better working conditions and for Social Security coverage. The National Committee on Household Employment has some 10,000 members. Caroline Reed of New York says the network operates in forty-one cities and through statewide affiliates to improve working conditions for its members. In the Bronx, New York, is an active network of Household Technicians, trying to upgrade this highly underrated profession. Though most business entrepreneurs who own maid services are anti-union, Coralee Kern, owner of Maid-to-Order in Chicago, wants to see maids unionized. She also believes strongly in the importance of networking and has formed her own business network.

Wages for Housework

Household workers are generally looked upon as an unimportant source of labor because the work they do is considered "women's work" and therefore trivial. Not only does this evaluation hurt the household workers, it hurts all women workers. The hurt is in the pocketbook. Even when women do the same job as men, they still are paid an average of 40 percent less. It is critical that the ideal of "women's work" be respected, that the homemaker, the basis of the employment structure of all women, be recognized as someone who performs labor of great economic value.

The value of a homemaker is placed at about $25,000 a year—without vacation, time off, or sick leave. Because homemakers deserve respect—and money is the commonly accepted measure of respect for work done—a strong international network called Wages for Housework has formed. Wages for Housework has chapters, vocal and active, in Brooklyn, Philadelphia, Cleveland, Chicago, Los Angeles, San Francisco, London, and Toronto.

Since 1974, the network has made gains, most important of these being the recognition of housework as work. "Hardly anyone disputes that anymore," says Phoebe Jones, an active housework networker. Jones feels that if housework were paid for by the government, funded by taxes on corporations which benefit from those who stay home, raise children, prepare meals, and clean the house, it would make our system of welfare unnecessary. "Wages for housework, paid by the government, makes sense," she says. "The work women do, unpaid, benefits the government and business. Why should there be charity instead of payment for hard work done well?" she asks. "We demand more than charity."

The Wages for Housework network is important because it breaks down the division that separates women who work at outside paying jobs and women who "don't work." Homemakers *do* work. "Every woman is a husband away from welfare," says Jones, "unless we get paid."

Even affluent women are suing in divorce courts for "back wages." They haven't won yet, but the issue is raised and treated seriously. During her divorce, Claire Gallagher asked that her former husband, John F. Gallagher, a Sears executive who earns $200,000 a year, be made to pay her on an hourly basis for each "job" she did during their marriage of some thirty years, years in which she helped him to gain success in the business world. She was denied her calculation of $40,823 a year due her. But the divorce court *was* influenced—she was granted a $750,000 settlement. And the country is now aware that at least some women will stand up in court and proclaim housework as a vocation worthy of pay.

With the premise that all women are housewives, the network's branches proliferate: Black Women for Wages for Housework (Brooklyn); Wages Due Lesbians (Philadelphia); Black Women for Wages for Housework (England); London Wages for Housework Committee; Toronto Wages for Housework Committee; and chapters in Greece, Finland, Italy, Iceland, China, the Philippines, Poland, and France.

"Without women, no one else can work and the whole economy stops dead," says Jones. The theme of the international network is: "Every woman's a housewife, and all of us mothers."

The organizing of housewives is a massive networking project, but already the impact of Wages for Housework is being felt.

If you are interested in politics, have some pet cause you want to see succeed, or want to work actively, at some level, to bring about needed positive change for women in politics and in labor and in employment, you can join networks that are active nationally or locally. You will find the networks informative, supportive, and effective. Through them, you will have an opportunity to participate in the decision-making policies that determine the realities of your life. And that's a good feeling!

7 Artistic Networks:

Painting, Sculpture, Music, Writing, Radio, Television, Theater

> The struggle to bring this piece ["The Dinner Party"] into fruition has given birth
> to a community—one which is centered on creating art that can affect the world
> and help change its values.
> —Judy Chicago in *The Dinner Party*

Artists work alone. The act of creating a work of art is more often than not a
solitary one, and artists like it that way; they need the "space" to create. But
women artists—sculptors, painters, writers, craftswomen, publishers, editors,
musicians, actresses, dancers, composers—need each other too, for a support
community and to bring their work to the public. To answer this need, artistic networks of support groups, where women artists are learning the value
and necessity of helping other women artists, are not part of the American
scene.

The Isolation of the Artist and the Birth of Networks

How important are networks to women artists? Writer Judith Barnard, in a
memorial to Judith Wax, the journalist, author, and poet who was killed in
an airplane crash near O'Hare Airport in 1979, starts her tribute in *Chicago
Magazine* by saying, "Judy Wax and I met at a gathering sponsored by a
group of women who called themselves, with conscious irony, 'The Old Girls
Network.'" Though Barnard and Wax had lived in the same city for years,
they had never met. Barnard continues, "Later, at lunches, we speculated on
a writer's place in such a network of executive women who helped each other in their fields of law, medicine, banking, business, industry, labor unions,
and the media."

Like many artists, Wax, before her death, was concerned about her time
and energy. The artist's dilemma has always been the burning need to communicate versus the equally burning need to be alone to create. The isolation, whether by choice or geographic reality, is something all women artists
must deal with, from the most sophisticated painters and sculptors to rural
craftswomen. "The women we know," say Nancy Raven and Maya Miller in
the introduction to their directory, *Craftswoman's Catalogue*, "work in their
kitchens and spare rooms—too often isolated from each other and those of us

who might want to buy." So the two San Marcos, California, women attempt to help "women make their own links to one another" through their catalogue, a form of networking. Yet, artists are often the most reluctant group of women to join networks—this is true even among women gallery owners—because they are fiercely individualistic.

"The Dinner Party"—An Example of Why Women Artists Need Networks

Artist Judy Chicago's sculpture "The Dinner Party" is a tribute to the hundreds of women, real and mythical, in western civilization who shaped women's lives. "The Dinner Party" cost $200,000 to create, and some four hundred other artists, mostly women, participated in its creation. During the years it took to produce the sculpture, Chicago had to reconcile her own need for a private "art-making" life with her need for help from hundreds of other artists. And when the work was completed, she quickly discovered she still needed the help of other women, artists and art supporters, to make sure her work was *seen*. For despite its successful showing at the San Francisco Museum in 1971, "The Dinner Party" had to be dismantled and crated because no other museum wanted to exhibit it—even though 1,000 people a day had come to see it in San Francisco.

At this point, networking began by women throughout the United States who were determined to bring the treasure to their own cities. In New York, Rochester, Boston, Philadelphia, Chicago, Houston, Seattle, and St. Louis, women challenged their city museums to present the show and formed groups to try to raise enough money to present it themselves. One of the most successful was the Texas Art and Cultural Organization (TACO), headed by Mary Ross Taylor in Houston. Because of TACO, "The Dinner Party" opened in Houston in March, 1980, at the University of Houston. Grass-roots campaigns throughout the country formed to finance slide exhibits or trips to Houston, such as the Chicago Committee to Exhibit "The Dinner Party," which worked with the Midwest Women's Center to organize fund-raising parties, discussions, and slide exhibits, and persistently negotiated with local museums and colleges to show the work in the Midwest. The result: It will be shown in Chicago in 1981. Networks are keeping "The Dinner Party" alive.

The Goals of Artistic Networks

Getting artistic works seen and heard is one of the most important targets of artistic networks, such as the annual Women's Jazz Festival in Kansas City; Fairfield 8, an informal network that plans art exhibits and shares information among its Westport, Connecticut, members, and Olivia Records in Oakland, a music network that produces record albums by women.

Many artistic networks act as *facilitators*: Sophie's Parlor in Washington, D.C., for example, which produces music programs for public affairs and women's-issue shows that network members create. Woman Image Now (win), a network of women in Tempe, Arizona, who want to expand the image of women in the world of arts, and the Woman's Building in Los Angeles, a public center for women's culture and all art forms, do the same. And in Watertown, Massachusetts, Pomegranate Productions is a lesbian collective that focuses on development of a strong woman's culture in the United States.

The day-to-day goal, however, of artistic networks is support, aid, and encouragement to break through all the barriers women face in making a commitment to art, a reality brilliantly delineated by author Germaine Greer in her study of women artists, *The Obstacle Race: The Fortunes of Women Painters and Their Work*. A Rose by Any Other Name is a support group of women in the visual, literary, and performing arts in Philadelphia. Women Drawing Women in San Francisco is a sketching and support group; the women meet weekly in each other's homes and draw each other. The Community of Women Artists in St. Louis meets in members' studios and gives each other encouragement and support. A group of twenty-two artists in Brooklyn, called Where We At Black Women Artists, is also a support network. So is New Mexico Women in the Arts, in Albuquerque. There are scores of support networks for artists, and the reason they exist is because women recognize the need for them.

Another form of artistic support that is gathering momentum in such networks as American Women in Radio and Television is the bringing along of professional writers, publishers, broadcasters, and other women in the media into positions of importance, so that they can themselves be more creative and at the same time open doors for other women. Two of the oldest of these networks are the Women's National Book Association, founded in 1917, and Women in Communications, Inc., founded in 1919. More recently, women in the Public Broadcasting System have formed strong networks to influence public radio and television, such as the WGBH Women's Caucus in Boston. And Thelma Norris of Women in Music in Chicago produces all-female commercial musicals and plays that give women the opportunity to be in the cast, production crew, and administrative staff.

Because it is apparent to most women in the arts that you cannot get where you want to go alone, the initial resistance many women artists felt to networking is being overcome by a healthy respect for the power of networking, and women are learning to combine the need for privacy to create with the need for public attention. And the extra bonus for you as an artist who networks is the sense of joy and pride in giving support to *other* women artists, too.

The Range and Variety of Artists' Networks

There are more networks of women in traditional art forms than any other kind of artistic networks, and just a list of the names gives a good idea of their wide variety and scope. Front Range Women meets once a month in Boulder, Colorado, at members' homes, to display artwork to each other. Organized in 1954, the network of thirty active members is composed of former University of Colorado graduate students in the arts. The Studio Group of Wilmington, Delaware, has seventy-five members who paint together and give each other support.

In Fresno, California, Gallery 25 began as a feminist art class of twenty-five women college art teachers and graduate students; today the network has its own gallery. In other cities, the Washington (D.C.) Women's Art Center is a meeting place for women artists, and the Baltimore Women's Art Community has ongoing artistic activities for its members. In Chicago, ARC Gallery is an alternative cooperative whose member artists are women. A dozen women belong to the Custer Art Colony in South Dakota, which meets twice a month and sponsors exhibits, with the month of July devoted to major artistic events. And only six women belong to the Feminist Art Co-op in Seattle, which is based on the feminist concept that small is beautiful.

On a national and international scale, Women in the Arts, an outgrowth of International Women's Year that is headed by Ellouise Schoettler, networks for women everywhere out of Chevy Chase, Maryland. The National Association of Women Artists is headquartered in New York. And Women's Caucus for Art, founded in 1972, is made up of two thousand women who are artists, historians, educators, and museum professionals. Lee Anne Miller, of the art department at Wayne State University in Detroit, an active network member, says her group's chapters meet monthly, and a national conference of the caucus is held annually. And the Coalition of Women's Art Organizations, representing ninety women's groups, galleries, and arts publications, is located in Chevy Chase.

Minority and Regional Women in Artistic Networks

Needlepoint, patchwork, quilting, and other crafts are the artistic outlet and contribution of many creative women. Society in general tends to consider these works "domestic" and, therefore, trivial, but their richness and discipline are worthy of true artistic recognition. To help these artists be accepted into the mainstream of artistic life, networks are forming. Traditional mountain crafts, for instance, are the basis of a network among Appalachian women in David, Kentucky. The women, who do patchwork and quilting, have banded together for business, economic, and artistic development, says Mary Pineau, and in order to market their work. They are called David Appalachian Crafts and work out of St. Vincent's Mission.

Networks of Women in Music

Women are almost invisible as performers, composers, and concert-givers. As in other areas, women musicians are joining forces to become an integral part of the music scene. Bay Area Women in Music is an active network of musicians in San Francisco. American Women Composers, of Washington, D.C., formed its network in 1976 to assist women in getting works published and performed. Also in Washington is the National Congress of Women in Music. And a musical network happening is the National Women's Musical Festival in Champaig·ı, which holds impressive concerts each June at the University of Illinois campus.

We Want the Music is a national collective based in Mount Pleasant, Michigan, which promotes and supports all forms of music created by its members. The Arlington Street Women's Caucus in Massachusetts is a network of some twenty women who have written music and who perform extensively for women's groups. The caucus has cut two records and has published a songbook and a book of poetry, reports member Ruth Evans.

Networks of Women in the Theater

All the world's a stage, and women want to be part of that world, not only as performers, but as playwrights, producers, directors, and stage crew. There is also a strong commitment among women in theater networks to communicate to the rest of the world what women's lives really are, as seen and interpreted by women. In Berkeley, a support system for visual artists, dancers, and women in the theater is named Motion. In Minneapolis, two active and popular theater networks are Circle of the Witch collective and At the Foot of the Mountain collective. Another theater network is Women's Coffee Coven in the state of Washington. A lesbian theater network in Atlanta has the gentle name Womansong. Chicago Women's Theatre Group, founded by Marilyn Kollath, meets monthly to read plays. The network has established its own women's theater and is producing its own plays, too. And a theater network that makes important social and political statements through puppet shows is Las Cucarachas in San Francisco.

Networks of Women Film Makers

Lights, camera, network! Hollywood is still mostly a man's world, says Jan Haag, founder of the film workshop that taught women like Joanne Woodward, Dyan Cannon, and Anne Bancroft to become film directors. "There's no question about it," Haag told the *Christian Science Monitor,* "the studios are controlled by men." As a result, Women in Film is an active, energetic network. It has 200 members who hold monthly meetings in Los Angeles, provides a support group and no-risk setting in which to explore new ideas, and tries to be a positive influence to eliminate racism, sexism, and elitism in films. In the network are producers, directors, and entertainment attorneys. New Mexico Feminist Film Makers has similar goals, meeting in Santa Fe to promote its art. And Chicago Women's Video Group holds discussions and critiques and also produces film strips.

Women in the Media Networks

Women on newspapers and in radio and television are concerned about the male-dominated and owned media, in which women, individually, have very little input. A group of people, media women have discovered, *can* make a difference, and networks have been established with that goal in mind. Women's Media Resource Center is in Santa Monica, California, and a women's social art network, Ariadne, meets monthly in Venice, California. Ariadne is predominantly a study group concerned with women's political issues and the image of women in the media.

It is as important for women writers and other women in the media to get together and connect now as it was some sixty years ago when Theta Sigma Phi, made up of women journalists, was formed. Today, as Women in Communications, the network's national chapters offer support services and the sharing of job openings, among them free-lance referrals, "job vine" employment, and workshops in skills and professional development. The network keeps a roster of speakers of national significance in communications.

The so-called power of the press can be wielded by women journalists, too, when they get together to use it. A dramatic example is the Women's Media Group of New York, a network made up of eighty women in communications who conceived the idea that eventually became the "ERA July Project." Through the group's efforts, thirty-five magazines published articles on the ERA in the same month in 1978, and one of the results of this networking was the time extension for ERA as a proposed Constitutional amendment. In November, 1979, the same network once again published articles in various member magazines, encouraging ERA ratification. Two more media networks that actively work for women's rights are the National Federation of Press Women and the D.C. Feminist Writers Guild, both in Washington, D.C. Also in Washington is *Media Report to Women,* a newsletter that is an effective networking tool. A publication of the Women's Institute for Freedom of the Press, it's edited by Dr. Donna Allen, with Martha Leslie Allen as associate editor. The report is devoted to "what women are doing and thinking about the communications media" and does a thorough, professional, and important job.

Women's Networks in Radio

There are so many enthusiastic network members in radio they are radio-active! The Feminist Radio Network in Washington, D.C., produces and distributes feminist radio programs and acts as a clearinghouse for jobs. American Women in Radio and Television (AWRT) networks on a national scale. AWRT has sixty chapters in seven geographical areas, and, according to Dee Bradley, director of the network's public relations, conferences are carefully planned in various geographical areas to provide a setting so that members can get to know each other, what's going on, and where the job opportunities are—the basics of networking. AWRT has 2,800 members and thirty college affiliate chapters. Television personality Jessica Savitch was a recent conference speaker, as was Ann Jones, commissioner of the Federal Communications Commission. One winner of AWRT's Silver Satellite Award was Joan Ganz Cooney, the creative and influential producer of "Sesame Street."

Some Outstanding Artistic Networks That Really Work

Some of the networks for women artists have caught on, grown, spread, and have had direct positive results not only for members but for the cultural life of all women. Some of the advances achieved by women book publishers, women in public broadcasting, women music producers, and women-owned record companies are inspiring.

The Women's National Book Association

There are some 1,100 members in eleven chapters of the Women's National Book Association, made up of women book publishers, editors, and sellers. President Ann Heidbreder Eastman of Blacksburg, Virginia, says the chapters vary in size from 30 women in Grand Rapids to 250 women in New York. "The Association works as a highly effective network, mostly on an informal basis," says Eastman. "Two of the chapters—New York and Los Angeles—have a 'Network Directory.' We're making a special effort now to help younger women in publishing get a start, so they don't have to begin as secretaries, which was once the only route."

Traditionally, explains Eastman, women in the book industry were confined to "public relations and children's books," and to break out of that mold takes a group effort. Today, more than 60 percent of all employees in the world of publishing are female, a survey made by Women in Publishing in 1973 shows. "If all the women stayed home, they couldn't publish a book," Eastman says.

Networks of Women in the Corporation for Public Broadcasting (CPB)

"Women are more likely than men to experience professional isolation at any job level in any organization, and those who have tried it say networking can be especially rewarding for women," says deWolf Smith in *Equal Access*, a newsletter for women in public telecommunications, published by CPB in Washington. The result is that women in public broadcasting are forming strong alliances to help move one another ahead. In Boston, Hershey, Pennsylvania, and Washington, D.C., women at the local affiliates have tailored basic networking to meet their specific needs.

Some fifty women belong to Boston's WGBH's Women's Caucus, which is investigating pension discrimination against women by insurance companies and child care arrangements for working mothers at the station. It also monitors its own television station for programs that may be racist or sexist. Caroline Collins, caucus president, says members know how to work as a group to effect change. "Several years ago, we might have drafted memos demanding things," she says.

At WITF in Hershey, station women meet every payday for a "working lunch," according to program director Kay Walker. "Knowing others are aware and understanding . . . has given people the courage to fight for themselves," says Walker in *Equal Access*. And at CPB in Washington, the women's network zeroes in on job opportunities, program content, and career development.

The Women's Jazz Festival Network—It's a Blast!

In the world of jazz, exciting things are happening for women, and the catalyst, the new ingredient that is making the difference for women jazz musicians who have been long-ignored, is networking.

The Women's Jazz Festival in Kansas City has succeeded in identifying female jazz musicians throughout the United States and putting them in touch with one another. The jazz network publishes a directory of all available women in jazz, at no charge for a listing. Dianne Gregg, president, says the first directory, published in 1979, listed 153 names from twenty-nine states and Canada. The 1980 directory had more than 300 names from thirty-six states, Canada, and Holland. The group's newsletter is published every six weeks and sent to some 1,200 individuals and organizations.

"Without meaning to, we've become a clearinghouse for people interested in women and jazz," says Gregg, "because there is no place else to go for this kind of information." Gregg and Carol Comer, executive director of the Women's Jazz Festival, attend many jazz festivals and are bothered by the lack of women as featured performers. Their annual festival is a year-round network that helps women jazz musicians be seen and heard. Gregg, former radio producer for jazz programs, now works for the festival full-time, and Comer, former jazz singer, is a correspondent for *Downbeat* magazine.

Through the Jazz Festival, women musicians meet each other—and things happen. At the March, 1979, Festival, six women from New York who had never before met each other got in touch through the directory, put a group together, named it "Aeriel," and entered the festival's jazz combo contest. They won. Soon after, their first record was made on Inner City Records, a top jazz label. They were also the first all-women's jazz group to play at the Newport Jazz Festival.

The festival networks for newcomers and for veteran women jazz musicians, too. Melba Liston, trombone player and arranger, and the only woman with the distinction of having played with Count Basie's band, was in professional retirement for several years, confining herself to teaching and arranging. But the Women's Jazz Festival talked her out of retirement to play at the 1979 Festival. After the Festival, she left teaching to perform again full-time.

In response to the Jazz Festival, other women's jazz festivals have formed. "We get called all the time for information on how to start a festival," says Gregg, who is happy to receive the calls. "There's a need for networking. There's a need to know who's out there, and what they're doing. It's good to have support, to know you're not the only jazz musician who's a woman."

The Olivia Records Network

Women who are tired of hearing music that relates women's lives only in terms of men—and, more often than not, tired of hearing songs about who-he-is and how-bad-you-feel and how-you-miss-him and how-bad-he-was-to-you—are turning away from songs and performances by male composers and singers and making their own music. "Our concept of women's music is speaking about women in a positive way," says Judith Dlugacz of Olivia Records in Oakland. Olivia is a music network, born out of a collective started in 1973 that is instrumental in creating a new cultural movement, an underground word-of-mouth network that makes beautiful music for and by women.

"The network is composed of women producers of concerts, musicians, independent album makers, and distribution companies run totally by women throughout the United States," says Dlugacz. "We sort of act as a central point for information about women's music: how it's made, the technical aspects, and distribution."

Officially, because of the network, Olivia itself has become a successful record company, producing nine albums on its own label, such as "The Changer and the Changed," by Cris Williamson, singer, pianist, and composer, and numbering sales in the millions. Olivia has also produced more than twenty other independent women's albums and songbooks.

The underground has changed to overground, as often happens with networking, especially around artistic themes. Olivia started as a commune. "We had an idea," says Dlugacz. "No money, no experience in recording, but an idea. We were offended by the themes of the music we heard on records, the way they depicted women." Five women started with a good idea, a lot of support from women, and a record they wanted to make, "I Know You Know." They only had a $12,000 budget, accumulated from small donations, from 50 cents to $5. "We pressed 5,000 records," says Dlugacz. "We thought that was a likely amount. But in the first six months we sold well over 30,000 copies." Olivia was on its way.

Today, Olivia arranges concert tours to big cities like Birmingham and small towns such as Eureka Springs, Arkansas. "Women are isolated from other women," says Dlugacz. "We reach each other through networks. Our concerts help to develop those networks." Olivia also assists women who want to set up their own production and distribution networks, many of which are informal but still income-producing for the independent woman distributor. In music circles, distribution and production is generally controlled by men—as the music reflects. But Olivia is making a few inroads. "We have a very strong network of record distributors, both of our label and others," says Dlugacz. "Each individual woman has her own territory. The network is called WILD—Women Independent Label Distributors."

Olivia, whom many women musicians turn to in order to get a foot in the door of the music business, has an overall view of it. "The growth of women's bookstores and record shops is an outgrowth of networking, too," says Dlugacz. "They are very necessary in the process of getting women's music to women. Traditional radio stations and record stores don't promote or sell women's music."

If you are an artist and feel the need for close connections with women, you can probably find the right network for you, one made up of supportive and talented women who are serious about their work. Hundreds of women artists are forming their own networks today, instead of continuing to isolate themselves from one another. They're making things happen for themselves and for other women.

And that's networking really working.

8 | Informal Networks That Work

If you can't help somebody, something's wrong with you.
—Karolyn Rose

Helping others comes easy to Karolyn Rose, former wife of baseball player Pete Rose of the Philadelphia Phillies. Karolyn has known for many years how hard, lonely, and difficult it is to be a baseball player's wife. She has automatically reached out to other baseball player's wives over the years, helping, listening, advising, comforting, and being comforted.

"You're in this game like the rest," says Karolyn Rose. "It's not just your husband on the team. It's the whole family. At first, when you're coming up as a rookie, it's hard to break into a new club. It's hard to find your way around in a new town. I think it's important to help other wives find a good doctor, a good baby doctor, and a nice apartment. Little things like that."

What Informal Networks Are All About

The "little things" like listening, being there, helping out, giving support and comfort are the basis of many informal networks. Informal networks are made up of friends who love and care about you, and who come through for you when you need them simply because you ask them to. Informal networks are made up of women who will help you when you are depressed, who will spend special time with you because you are lonely; of women who share common health problems and really understand what you are going through; and of women who will go out and have a good time with you, to help forget the worries of the day.

Informal networks, like Tish Sommers's Cancer Support Group in Oakland and Mother's Morning Out, North, in Boston, are made up of your friends, who are willing to be there for the good times, and the bad. "What does it take to make time to listen to somebody else?" asks Karolyn Rose. Not much time is involved, but what matters is the commitment, and informal networks are a commitment to help to make life better for another woman— and therefore for yourself. "When you listen to someone's problems and really try to help, it makes them smile," Rose observes.

Informal Networks: A Guaranteed Personal Support Group

Informal networks are the oldest form of networking. Women have always reached out this way instinctively. Homemakers, young mothers, know what it means to have an informal network. "They're very special women," says a suburban housewife, mother of four children under six. "They are the kind of people that when you're talking to them on the phone and you yell at the kids, you don't have to put your hand over the receiver. They understand!" She relies on her network of a few friends who will help out when her kids are sick, with car pools, food shopping, errands. Informal networks have no weekly meetings, dues, or set of bylaws. They are purely and simply women helping women.

Informal Networks at Work

Everyone knows about the grapevine. Where would we be without one in the business office, for instance? Informal networks operate just as powerfully for women as the grapevine does for both sexes, because informal networks are not gossip being passed on, they deal with information that is helpful to *you*. "Informal networks help when one needs information on strategies for an administrative or political action," says Arlene Kaplan Daniels, sociologist.

Smart women use informal networks wisely in the work world. Informal networks are created to start letter-writing campaigns in support of issues, in protest, to recommend someone for a job—or to try to keep a job for someone about to be fired. Business confidences are entrusted to small, select groups of dependable friends. "We really respect each other," a middle-management woman says of the four women in her company at her level who share problems and insights. "When there's trouble, we give advice. It doesn't mean anyone has to take it. But they know they have a friend. You've got to have a friend."

Why Top-Ranking Women Have Informal Networks of Their Own

Every woman needs a friend, even those who are so successful professionally you would think there is nothing they lack. "It's so simple—I just felt isolated," explains Toni Dewey, vice-president of the corporate staff of Motorola Inc., and director of public relations and advertising. Dewey formed her own network in 1978. "I found I'm the highest female out there and I wanted to talk to other women professionals and executives. I wanted that communication." So she called her old friends and they began to meet on an informal basis. Dewey feels good about her friends, and they feel the same about her. "We're happy for each other when nice things happen," she says. And that is one of the rewards of networking—you feel great about yourself as a woman.

The Variety of Informal Networks

Networks without names and titles are at work informally everywhere. There are networks of women in housing projects; the networks have no formal structure but the women need desperately to communicate with one another. Women therapists network informally to refer women to nonsexist therapists, regardless of gender. Home economists have formal associations; their informal networking is powerful, too, in exchanging job information, industry news—even recipes. One network of concerned women is trying to establish a nursing home for feminists, where those who need it can spend a week in surroundings that physically and emotionally nuture them back to health; another network is setting up a retirement home for feminists. Rape victims have informal networks. Women in seminars frequently form informal support groups as outgrowths of their shared intellectual experience and growth in the classroom. Alumnae groups, especially of women's colleges, network energetically for their sister alumnae. "I always have a place to stay if I visit a city where another Vassar graduate lives," says one woman. "It's almost automatic. We *expect* the grads to stay with us, even if we hardly knew them back then or weren't even that friendly at school."

A typical informal network is Spring Friedlander's Creative Mundanes in Oakland, a group of friends who barter and exchange skills, tasks, and knowledge on an equal-time basis. Women who want to do informal sports such as backpacking, canoeing, cross-country skiing—just for fun—get in touch with each other through the Midwest Women's Expedition Exchange in Chicago. And Friends of the Rag, a group of costume designers in Seattle, share resources and job information informally. Right up front about their purposes are the Professionals in Social Sciences Support Group of Arlington, Virginia; the Women's Support Group of Hendrix College in Conway, Arkansas; and the Ph.D. Candidates Support Group of the University of Washington. Informally, the women get together to exchange feedback on doctoral research.

Individual Informal Networks: We Care About Each Other

Thousands of individual women feel a commitment to other women, to let them know what's going on, to keep them in touch with women they need to know. Mary Jo Walsh of Detroit, part-owner of New Options Personnel, has her own informal network going. Interviewed in *Newsweek*, Walsh has contacts in government that tell her which industries are under compliance to hire women, and she has also lined up Junior League wives to report openings in their husbands' companies—so a woman can have a shot at the job before an Old Boy gets it.

Another highly committed woman who takes her responsibilities to help other women most seriously is Ilana Rovner, assistant deputy governor of the State of Illinois. "I am a network," says Rovner, who works tirelessly to hire qualified women, to let women know what jobs are available or are opening up, and particularly to assist women who, in turn, will also help other women. In every city and town there are women like Rovner who network automatically.

Networks That Help You Get Through the Day

A touching article about a helpful support group appeared in *Ms.* magazine in June, 1979. Karen Lindsey, free-lance journalist and poet, tells about a network of friends who helped her survive periods of intense depression, friends she could call and ask for help. "My therapist was a help," she says, "but what made the experience bearable is the large and amorphous group . . . who created an informal network of support. . . . They probably saved my life." Lindsey is not the only one to learn the secret of such a network. I, too, am on the receiving end of similar phone calls as part of an informal network a friend of mine uses to help get her through depressions. She asked my permission first—timidly: Could she call me when she was down? It was usually in the early mornings, she said, and if she could just get through the mornings, she could make it through the rest of the day. She wouldn't call often, she said. (She hasn't.) And she has a long list of other friends whom she can call and who help her. When she does call, my heart sinks for her, but I listen and tell her how wonderful I think she is, which I do. She tells me I cheer her up, and that makes *me* feel good.

A Cancer Support Network That Helps

It is more than folklore that those who fight back against tragedy and disease do better than those who do not, that those who heed Dylan Thomas's advice to "rage, rage against the dying of the light" often get longer reprieves from illness. Five women who know this have formed an informal cancer support group in Oakland. One of them is Tish Sommers, who works hard to help older women in general and displaced homemakers in particular (see chapter 4). Sommers, now in her sixties, had a mastectomy two decades ago. In July,

1979, cancer cells appeared in another place in her body. It was then she formed the support group, she says, because "we recognize that the medical profession doesn't have all the answers."

One of the women in the network was told she had three months to live. "She's not accepting it and we're not letting her accept it," says Sommers. The woman has already lived more than the "allotted" three months. "Feisty women live longer," observes Sommers, quoting a study conducted recently at Johns Hopkins Hospital. In the study, women diagnosed as terminally ill who were demanding of their physicians and refused to accept the fatality of their situation lived an average of 22.8 months longer. Those who were passive lived 8.6 months. "In other words, fight back," says Sommers.

Another woman in the network had had a considerable amount of surgery, and when she suddenly had to go back to the hospital again—to the emergency room—she called her network friends and they rushed to the hospital to be with her. She had to have an emergency operation, but it was made somewhat easier by the presence of loving, caring friends. When she was released from the hospital, the woman was in good spirits and immediately took off for a Gray Panthers convention.

"We recognize the disease we have is incurable," says Sommers, "but so are many other diseases. People learn to live with them, and in many cases people can learn to live with cancer." The women in her support group and in others like it *are* learning.

Networks That Let You Gripe and Complain All You Want

Some working women find it's fun to get together informally after a hard day's work and openly cry in their beer. Thursday's Child, who had far to go, is a drinking group in Birmingham, Alabama, that meets every Thursday night at Beefeater's Tavern. Actually, the drinking is incidental to the real purpose: the airing of problems. Thursday's Child is for women only, and all women are welcome. Everyone gets a chance to speak out about the many injustices of life, and everyone feels much better about their jobs after the weekly meetings, which are strategically planned to give an extra added boost because the next day is Friday!

MAD (Men Are Dumb) is another informal and enthusiastic group which meets every Wednesday at 5 P.M. in a bar or restaurant in the nation's capital. It's an informal network, mostly of women who work for the Corporation for Public Broadcasting (CPB). The group first lifted its glasses in 1979 when women from CPB and other professional offices nearby were feeling as if they'd "had it." "We usually meet at a bar where there is a woman bartender," says Denise Oliver of CPB. "One wonderful bartender is named Ingrid. She doesn't treat us like little girls. She takes us seriously as businesswomen. She also mixes good drinks."

What happens at MAD is wonderfully therapeutic. "You cry over your daiquiri or white wine," says Oliver. "We help each other in many ways. We give each other hints about how to deal with the boss. Some days, you just feel like quitting."

Every once in a while, men are invited. "We let them get the cheese and crackers," says Oliver. MAD members say they get enough strength from their drinking group to go back and beard MCPs (Male Chauvinist Pigs) in their dens.

Informal Networks That Grow Out of Formal Ones

Women in networks interweave and intertwine so closely they never forget one another. Permanent loyalties are formed, and even if the official network is disbanded, the informal network of women that remains is often as strong and binding as the one that brought them together in the first place.

Mother's Morning Out, North, made up of women from traditional Italian-American backgrounds in the North End of Boston, is one such network that continues, operating unofficially. Mother's Morning Out was formed in 1972 by Maria Anastasi, who was a counselor at a neighborhood health center, the North End Community Health Center, and a member of the National Congress of Neighborhood Women, based in Brooklyn, New York. Anastasi was born and raised in the neighborhood she worked in. "The women's movement was making a lot of noise that year," recalls Anastasi. "But the women in this neighborhood couldn't buy it. Culturally, it was totally foreign to them."

Whether they understood the women's movement or not, some of the issues raised in those days about women's lives were manifesting themselves, even there, in the North End of Boston. "At the health center, doctors reported that young women were coming in frequently, reporting headaches and backaches," says the counselor. "Lots of them. It was clear that these were not solely medical problems. Their lives were rigid, and they felt trapped in them."

Because she was not an outsider but was known and trusted, Anastasi was specially qualified to help these women. "I put an ad in the local stores, where I knew it would be read," says Anastasi. "I named the group Mother's Morning Out, North. I invited women to come with their kids. It would be an educational group for both women and kids. That way, they wouldn't feel guilty about taking time for themselves, because the children would benefit too." Some twenty-five young women—and their children—showed up for the first meeting. Anastasi persuaded the local university to staff a day care center and provide a good program for the kids.

For two hours a week, the women met with the counselor while their children had excellent day care. "We served coffee and cake and we talked," says Anastasi. "The women at first wanted to discuss their kids, husbands, and families. Slowly, the concept evolved that these two hours a week belonged to them, the mothers. It was theirs. They could do anything they wanted. It was then the network took off!"

The group met from September, 1972, until June, 1973, when it recessed for the summer months. In September, 1973, when Mother's Morning Out, North, resumed, all the women came back to renew their discussions.

"But I made some changes," says Anastasi. "There would be no free baby-sitting that year. If they wanted to belong to the group, they'd have to hire their own baby-sitters. I helped them find sitters; they helped one another. They didn't hesitate to get sitters, as they would have a year earlier. They were already committed to the idea that Mondays were theirs."

The women met on that basis for five years. "It was as if they were starving," says Anastasi. "They wanted to learn and do everything. You name it, we did it."

After that, the group began to diminish in size. Some women went back to school. Others found jobs. By 1977, there were only nine members left and Anastasi disbanded the formal group. But each year there are "alumnae" meetings, and almost each day one of the women is in touch with another of the members or with Anastasi. What has evolved is an informal network, a personal support group the women can depend on.

Informal support networks form every day, brought into existence by women strong enough to ask, "Please be there for me." Their flexibility and their ability to grow and change to fit needs is their advantage. They are not structured enough to have that familiar necessity clout, nor to develop power as a group. Instead, informal networks strengthen their individual members so they can cope with daily reality.

Informal networks are around only long enough to help you, as needed. And that is everything.

9 | How to Set Up Your Own Network

Women have got to think of women and recommend women for jobs, and encourage our mothers, aunts, and daughters, because we've got to lick this. Remember the good old girl network.
—Lynda Bird Robb

I want to be able to solve all my business problems with three phone calls.
—Jean Allard, attorney

Women's networks are exploding throughout the United States because they give you a chance to make things happen. Networks let you in on some of the secrets of the business world; they include *you* as a decision-maker in matters of health, sports, politics, and the arts. And what's more, networks are fun. They make you feel great! Ask the woman who runs or owns one. In fact, why not *be* the woman who runs one? Setting up your own network, tailored to your own specific needs, may be one of the most rewarding experiences of your life.

SETTING UP YOUR OWN NETWORK

Setting up a network is not complicated because there are so many women eager to join, enthusiastic about the idea of networking. If your group is small, setting up a network may take only a few hours; larger, more complicated networks take more time and energy. But whatever size, once networks start, they keep going of their own momentum. The point is to get one started. To help you set up the best network for you in the easiest way possible, here is a list of ten checkpoints to follow:

✔ 1. Should Your Network Be Small or Large?

What you want to do will determine the size; or, as a member of an artistic network puts it, "Let the content determine the form." Ten women in a network of clergymen's wives, for instance, is the right number for intimacy, trust, and support. On the other hand, 1,000 active members of the Washington Women's Network is actually the minimum number necessary to have an impact in the nation's capital. Business networks tend to have more members on a local basis than other forms of networks. The Women's Forum of Colorado has a membership limit of 125; in Los Angeles, Women in Business has 250 members; Women Entrepreneurs in San Francisco has 400. If you prefer direct one-to-one contacts and strong personal friendships, the smaller the network the more comfortable you will be. But if your aim is to effect change, to find out about a variety of job opportunities, to inspire other women, the larger the network, the more effective it will be. You may want to start small at first, feel your way around, and then increase membership. Or, if your membership gets too large, it may break up into smaller networks based on geographical location of members, such as Boston's Women's Lunch Group, which now has offshoots in several surrounding suburbs.

✔ 2. Should Members All Share the Same Interest or Should You Have a Diverse Group?

Some networks work best because all members are in the same profession or interest group and share exactly the same concerns, such as Women in Research, Seaworthy Women, and Displaced Homemakers networks. Networks of women runners, painters, gourmet cooks, and education administrators are also successful because all members are part of a specific interest group. On the other hand, many business groups find they do best when they include women in a *variety* of professions, such as the New York's Women's Forum, New Girl Network of Winston-Salem, and Women Can Win. Women in Business in Los Angeles takes in new members twice yearly and makes sure that its members reflect a broad career mix. Denver's Women's Forum also insists on diversity, preferring members who are not only high-caliber businesswomen but who are also active in civic and community life. You may find there are simply not enough women in your chosen field to make an effective network; in that case, you will have to branch out to include women in other fields. *The only important thing members must have in common for networks to work is a shared commitment to women helping women.*

✔ 3. How Do You Select Members for Your Group?

Since it is your network, you will be the one making important decisions, and who should be included is one of the most critical and sensitive of these. If you want to start a network of women who have had Cesarean deliveries, it is pretty clear that all women who have undergone this surgery are welcome as members. So is everyone who wants to play rugby, distributes women's record albums, or is a feminist therapist, if those particular interests are the basis of your network.

If you form a business network, however, where there are often thousands of potential members, you may have to establish some ground rules, some specific entry requirements, in order to be effective. "I don't like this aspect of it, but if you want power, what are you going to do?" asks Martha McKay, a member of the Women's Forum of North Carolina and director of affirmative action for the state.

Another way of looking at it is this: "If you can't do something for the other women in the network, they don't need you," says one new member of a business network. The selection process can be a matter of inviting all women with the same title or responsibilities. Or, as in the most prestigious business networks, it can be a very complicated process. Denver's Women's Forum has a membership committee that judges applicants on a scale of 1 to 100. In New York's Women's Forum, four sponsors and the approval of both the membership committee and the board are necessary. Membership in the Professional Women's Alliance of San Francisco is by invitation only, and the woman must have three sponsors who are active PWA members. The nominee meets with the membership committee and fills out forms. This is the way PWA maintains its composition of the most important women in the area, including Mayor Dianne Feinstein.

Sometimes basic ground rules result in the exact membership composition you want. The Philadelphia Forum for Executive Women has no requirements as such for membership, but the one condition that has to be met is that potential members have management jobs paying at least $25,000 a year, or who *should* be getting that sum for the work they do. Under this umbrella, the Forum has seventy active members.

Of course, it is much easier and often more comfortable to form a network where everyone is invited; a range of success, interests, and careers are a stimulating mix. Martha Fleer, director of the New Girl Network, has opted for a more informal, open network. It is a cross-section of the working population, including secretaries and professional women. Its relaxed atmosphere permits women who may never have gotten together to enjoy each other's company. "This works well for the upwardly mobile woman," she says, "but it lacks the elitism that goes with being chosen. You tend to lose higher-level management women who know the 'real' job openings. It reaches a point where there's nothing in it for upper-level women." Still, Fleer's network is a strong support group and a vital organization for its members, and as the New Girls move up in management, they do not forget the ties and links they have with their network.

✔ 4. How Do You Contact Potential Members?

When women want to get something done, they get on the telephone and get to work. Sometimes, that's all it takes to get a network started, especially the smaller, more informal ones. Some groups send out mimeographed letters explaining what the network is all about. Those with more money have invitations printed, stating their purpose, founding members, and dues. Fleer's New Girl Network started by getting names from women in seminars Fleer gives, sending out letters, and advertising meetings in the local paper. Judy von Seldeneck, who runs a placement service in Philadelphia, contacted potential Forum members by putting together a luncheon based on her mailing list of about sixty-five women, handing out a questionnaire to measure interest, and forming a nucleus out of those who were.

If you belong to a seminar or workshop group that especially interests you, you may already have the members for a network among your classmates; Doctor's Wives began this way. If you belong to a professional organization or to a union that seems to you far more interested in male goals and perspectives, form a woman's network from among the females in the group. This is how many legislative and municipal networks for women have begun, as well as one of the most important labor networks of all, the Coalition of Labor Union Women.

The one thing you can count on in your efforts to contact potential members is that good things have a way of snowballing. Women's networks are a good thing, so don't be surprised when many women come to you and ask for more information about joining. At that point, you'll know you're on your way.

✔ 5. How Do You Get People to Attend Network Meetings?

Most people *want* to attend network meetings, but a little hype doesn't hurt. Some networks, especially business and professional ones, feature speakers women want to hear. Others offer concrete workshops and seminars in subjects of vital interest to network members, such as the Women in Health Science Conference, the National Women's Studies Association, and the National Women and the Law Conference. Some networks attract attendance by having individual members—especially high-ranking ones—lead group discussions. Or, you could take a cue from Coralee Smith Kern, founder of WOMAN, the new woman's network of Chicago, who mailed tickets for chances along with information about the network to ensure a good turnout for the first meeting in June, 1979. The door prizes were: (1) a business in-a-kit computerized financial planner, (2) 200 printed-to-order business cards, (3) Norelco Burger Cooker, and (4) two annual memberships in WOMAN. The network also had a speaker, Shawn McGuinness of Merrill Lynch Pierce Fenner & Smith. The result: some fifty new members.

Since you are the organizer of your network, it is also helpful to make some phone calls the day of the meeting to encourage people to come and to get some estimate of the attendance. Your own personal enthusiasm and excitement in the network will generate interest by itself.

✔ 6. When, Where, and How Often Should You Have Meetings?

Some network members network every day by telephone and face-to-face discussions. At the other end of the spectrum, some of the large national networks only meet once a year, such as the Women's Jazz Festival. The majority of other networks fall somewhere in between in frequency of meetings. The Boston Women's Health Book Collective and Gourmet Exchange meet once a week; most business and professional groups meet once a month; and some of the more prestigious groups, whose members are extremely busy women, meet three or four times a year. Meetings held once a month seem to be the most practical and productive.

When to meet is an important decision because it determines whether the majority of your network members will be able to attend. While businessmen are known for their clubby breakfasts, they are not known for preparing breakfast for their families. But most women do, so few women's networks meet at breakfast. Lunches are a popular time because even the busiest women eat lunch, and you have the chance of a larger turnout in the middle of the day rather than at night or on weekends. Lunch meetings, of necessity, fall into rigid time limits, but this is also an advantage because it creates a very businesslike atmosphere. Evening meetings, with outstanding speakers, are the general fare of the most informal and the most formalized networks. The latter have wine, cheese, a long cocktail hour, and dinner; the former usually meet for cake and coffee after dinner. You will have to decide what is best and most convenient for your network, aiming for optimum membership attendance.

Where to meet is another strategic decision. Informal networks enjoy meetings at members' homes. Many business and professional networks, on the other hand, view the living room as counterproductive to the image they're trying to achieve, so they meet in downtown clubs and restaurants. You may start out with meetings at home and then decide to have more formal arrangements. For networks involving busy women, it is often important to have meetings in close geographic convenience for a majority of members. Unless you're able to walk from your office to a networking meeting— whether at lunch or dinner—many of your members may not show up. Try to make it easy, in every way, for network members to attend meetings.

✔ 7. *Should You Have Dues or Should Membership Be Free?*

Some of the smaller networks have no membership fees or dues, such as the Creative Mundanes. But it is a reality of today's world that it costs money to run things. The Custer Art Colony, for instance, only charges $1 for membership, but that takes care of mailings. The Women's Building in Los Angeles charges $15 a year to be included on its mailing list. Some networks charge according to ability to pay, such as woman, where memberships are $25, $35, and $45, keyed to income; and women who can't pay anything do volunteer work instead.

National networks have annual dues of from $15 to $25. Most networks try not to price themselves out of existence but to reach a happy medium, such as the $75 the Women's Forum of Colorado charges annually to cover speakers, transportation, food, and administrative costs. One of the highest membership fees is charged by The Chicago Women's Network, but the $200 annual fee includes the cost of five dinner meetings.

✔ 8. *Should You Have Officers, Directors, and Bylaws?*

Most women belong to clubs and organizations that are highly structured, run by Robert's Rules of Order, and with iron-clad goals and aims—all in writing. Women who join networks don't want more of the same. So your best bet for an effective network is the old maxim that she governs best who governs least. It is wise to keep all but the most general rules and procedures to a minimum. Some of the best networks, like the National Women's Health Network, run by committee. Since you are the one organizing the network, *you* choose your own board of directors, if one is necessary. And *you* pick the officers too, if they are needed to run the network. Don't be shy about naming yourself president of the group, either. Officers of networks are *named*, not elected, because, in the beginning at least, they are such a reflection of the person or persons organizing them.

Paid Staff

Some networks need a full-time or part-time director. "We have a full-time executive director to do the things we don't want to do," says Colorado's Ingraham. "We don't want to volunteer time to the organization or to ask anyone else to do so. We volunteer enough." The Washington Women's Network has a part-time director. The job of the director is to plan meetings, arrange for speakers, and supply information to members. Some networks have telephone answering services. Others, such as the Bay Area Executive

Women's Forum, hire agencies to handle phone calls and details, plan meetings, and do promotion.

Bylaws

If you do charge dues or fees, you may have to incorporate in your state as a not-for-profit organization. The same charter that grants you tax immunity also forbids political activity, an important thing to remember.

You will find that most women do not object to paying a fair membership fee when they get the results they are looking for. And since networks *work*, right from day one, you will find your members have very few complaints about the cost.

✔ 9. Should You Have Programs for Network Meetings?

In general, you don't have to worry about having a program, because the initial "shoulder-rubbing" at your meetings where members meet face to face—many for the very first time—is what networking is all about. The contacts made during these informal times are the nitty-gritty of networks. So that members can follow up, it is important to have a *printed list* with *names, titles, addresses,* and *phone numbers of members*. The list should be distributed at the very first meeting, whether there are six women present or 400. What the list says is: "Here is my name. Here is my phone number. Call me." And the smart businesswoman will bring her business cards with her to every network meeting.

Women who join networks to discuss how to be effective politically, in business, or in consumer and community matters rarely discuss a lack of baby-sitters, traffic problems, or domestic troubles. You will find your members really want to get down to the business of the day, either in general discussions or one-to-one conversations. They are not there to be entertained either, but good speakers, seminars, and workshops may help your members achieve their goals.

"Many referral and customer contacts are traded at our meetings," says Mary Constantaras, vice-president of Women in Real Estate (WIRE). "Our regular meetings serve as a social meeting place as well as a business forum." This exchange suits perfectly the needs of the two hundred members of this Chicago-area professional group.

Remember that the *real* program of networks is to "solve all problems with three phone calls."

✔ 10. Should You Try to Keep in Touch Between Meetings?

Most network members keep in touch by phone, but the large networks, with larger budgets and greater impact, have newsletters that go out to the membership and help tie them together. There are hundreds of such newsletters, like *Broomsticks*, by Options for Women over 40, and *Equal Access*, by the Corporation for Public Broadcasting in Washington.

Directories

Professional and business women need information, and some networks answer this need by publishing annual directories, such as the National Association of Women Business Owners' various regional chapters are doing. Oregon Women in Education Administration publishes a directory of administration candidates and sends the directories to school districts looking for candidates. This listing of qualified personnel is also networking. Maintaining a listing and location of members and potential members is an effective means of communication among members who are looking for jobs. One example of such identification is a roster being compiled by the Office of Women in Higher Education of the American Council of Education. There are now forty-one states feeding information to the network, with the goal of increasing the number of women prominent in higher education.

You may find you will be able to get as much done between meetings as you do at the meetings themselves because, if you put your network together wisely and carefully, you will find network members are there for you to rely on every day, whenever needed, not just on specific occasions. That is one of the rewards when your network gets off the ground.

TWO EXAMPLES OF HOW A NETWORK IS FORMED: ONE SMALL, ONE LARGE

The Pillsbury Bake-Off Girls

A small network of about a dozen women can be an exciting happening, a source of joy. Back in November, 1975, three Sioux City women sent a mimeographed letter to a dozen of their friends. Here are excerpts from the initial correspondence that ultimately developed into the Pillsbury Bake-Off Girls and, later, Women in Transition.

> There are a handful of us who would like to encourage some growth and support which can happen when women can share their experiences, their failures, and successes. . . . None of us belongs to a group organized around women's issues, and we don't want to start a new group in a formal sense. . . . There are smaller groups of women who have found that by bringing a personal or professional situation to the attention of two or three close friends, a solution has been found simply because one of the others had an experience and found a successful way to deal with it.
>
> We want to suggest getting together. . . . We don't want charters, bylaws, dues,

scheduled meetings, or votes of group goals. We would like the growth and stimulation that can come about through genuine sisterhood—by women sharing. . . . Are you interested? Please let us know your wishes.

The women did reply, they did want to get together, and the first meeting was planned. Members were invited to a meeting at the home of one of the organizers, 7:30 P.M., Tuesday, January 6, 1976. Specific driving directions were given, once again on a mimeographed sheet of paper that was mailed to the membership. And then this followed the time, place, and directions:

Be on time . . . because . . . 13 awards, totaling $81,000 in cash prizes, will be given for the best recipes!

Also on the mimeographed sheet was a review of a movie that could only offend thinking women in every way, filled with racism, sexism, and prejudice. The tone was set for the new network: light and humorous in approach, serious subjects to be discussed. And if new members wondered what the meeting was going to be like, their curiosity and interest stimulated by the invitation, they'd have to show up to find out.

Getting to Know You

The group spent months getting to know each other, both in meetings and outside of them. After it became Women in Transition, a mimeographed memo suggested, "It is hoped everyone who has never spent time outside the group with any particular member of WIT will make an effort to do so: Take a WIT to lunch!"

And so the network keeps on keeping on, providing a comfortable home base for its members. And the members keep expanding their possibilities, advancing in their jobs, improving their personal lives. "The way I judge whom I choose as friends has nothing to do with age but with whether they are growing," one Pillsbury Bake-Off Girl says proudly. The Sioux Falls network is one of the simplest and most informal. Yet it still takes planning to make it happen and to keep it going. "There's a special sense of knowing each other," a member says, summing up the strong ties among the women this network has precipitated.

The Chicago Network, Inc.

Early in 1978, five high-ranking Chicago women got together to plan a Chicago network of highly qualified women, the ranking women of Chicago in art, science, labor, social services, management, and the media. The same women had participated a year earlier in a one-shot meeting of "The Old

Girl Network," at which fifty women got together, introduced themselves, talked, and went home with a list of names and phone numbers of those at the meeting. And that was the end of that, though other women held similar network meetings in various communities.

Now these leading business and professional women wanted something ongoing, a group of peers that could and would help one another, merely because they had finally met and now belonged to the same organization. But who were the women, and how to find them?

The Challenge: Finding High-Ranking Women

Diann DeWeese Smith was asked to locate and identify Chicago's highest-ranking women. She was an excellent choice because she was the one person in the city who knew all the women who were doing things. Smith had been executive director of the Loop Center YWCA and had turned it into a vital center for women helping women. She had helped organize rape support groups, a crisis center, help for abused women, abortion counseling, Women Employed, the Gray Panthers. Using her list of 500 names accumulated during ten years at the YWCA, Smith began to target women on their way up. Her research was also an amalgam of everybody's knowledge.

"Over the years I had often been asked to organize important business-women," says Smith, "but at the time I wasn't interested. The exclusivity part had bothered me. But later, when I went into the business world, I saw the need. Organizing ranking women, I realized, would help all women. It is just another special interest group, and I have certainly organized many of those."

The choices were arbitrary. "Selections were not based on whether we liked the women or not," says Smith. "And just having a title was not a qualification. In fact, we sifted through twenty-five bank vice-presidents to end up with three or four for the network. There is no one in the network in education who isn't president of a college or university. There is no one in law who isn't a full partner in a prestigious firm. Members have both prestige and expertise."

Her assignment, Smith says, took thousands of phone calls. It was hard work and took *eighteen months* to do. "I knew it would be hard when I accepted the job," says Smith, who was paid $4,000 for the work and is now paid director of The Chicago Network, Inc. "It was my final big organizing dues. I suppose I'm just like an old firehorse when it comes to organizing: I smell women organizing, I go!"

Though ranking women helped identify the qualified women in their fields, it was clear from the beginning that prestigious businesswomen did not know each other as prestigious businessmen do. Ranking women comp-trolers did not know high-powered women in banking; bank women didn't know women in securities. Often women with high titles in government have no measurable power, and The Chicago Network had to sift that out, too, to find out who really does what.

The organizers also studied executives in social service, a profession more difficult to assess. There, too, however, no one below executive director was invited, and their agencies had to have budgets of at least $2 million. Women in the media had to head their departments or have national impor-tance. The more she researched, the more convinced Smith became of the vi-tal importance of networking for top-level women. "They have rights, too," she says. "They have the right to be named to boards of corporations. They also have the right to know each other."

Smith accumulated hundreds of names and ran them by the group's or-ganizers. Next, twenty prestigious Chicago women were asked to be on the board. All accepted. And then the job began of winnowing membership pos-sibilities down to a manageable number. Finally, the group emerged with 113 women. Engraved invitations were sent out. They read:

The Chicago Network has been established to bring together women distin-guished by their achievements in business, the professions, and the arts in the Chicago metropolitan area. By its existence, The Network will demonstrate the substantial number of women who have attained a high level of accomplishment.

The Network will hold five dinner meetings annually in a private Loop setting with speakers both from within the group and the national arena. The cost of the din-ners will be included in the $200 annual membership fee.

Initially, approximately 100 women of outstanding status have been identified for prospective founding membership in The Chicago Network. You are among them and we take pleasure in extending an invitation to join this peer group. A response is requested no later than June 6, 1979.

Out of those originally invited, 97 accepted. Three more women were invit-ed and accepted. And The Chicago Network was on its way.

A Statement of Purpose

For tax purposes, The Chicago Network decided to incorporate. The officers of incorporation were Jean Allard, Eleanor Peterson, and Sheli Z. Rosenberg. In the papers, in which the network is established as a not-for-profit organi-zation, this statement was made: "The object of the Network shall be to aid in the creation and expression of enlightened public opinion on the impor-tant economic and social questions of the day and to demonstrate by its existence the substantial number of women who have attained a high level of achievement."

A Sound Budget

Part of the network's instant success was due to the sound start-up budget, which might be helpful for other beginning networks to look at:

Chicago Network, Inc. Fiscal Year June 1, 1979 to May 31, 1980

Summary of fiscal proceedings: Dues from members will be collected before June, 1979. Funds will be disbursed June 1 in payment of start-up expenses. Combination checking/saving account will be established in May, 1979, to maximize interest on cash flow, with $10,000 put in 6-month Treasury Rate Certificate. Checks require two signers.

Income-Expense Statement

Income: Membership dues—100 members at $200/yr. $20,000

Expense:

Start-up period

Repayment of loan for research	$ 750
April 17 meeting	80
Clerical expense	40
Professional salary	1,500
Subtotal	$ 2,370

First-year budget

Dinner meetings: 100 people at $20 each 5 times a year	$10,000
Speakers' honoraria/expenses	2,300
Professional salaries, paid quarterly	4,000
Clerical/printing for 5 meetings	880
Stationery	250
Phone, miscellaneous	200
Subtotal	$17,630
TOTAL EXPENSES	$20,000

Financial Notes: a. Full and partial scholarships expected to be offered to a small number of women by the board of directors.

b. The founding board recommends to the duly constituted board of directors that, given excess funds at year end, a bonus be voted for D. Smith as professional staff in light of the low compensation for her start-up efforts.

The job of putting together The Chicago Network was well done!

Where Networks Are Going

Where networks will go next is the next question asked by those women who are quick to see the power and momentum of the groups they belong to. There is a move to form national networks out of local ones, and many groups, from the National Women's Education Fund in Washington to WOMAN in Chicago, are putting out feelers in that direction.

An alliance of professional women—"professional" being used in the larger context of "businesslike, competent, knowledgeable," not just meaning professional occupations—is being formed. It's called the National Alliance of Professional Women's Networks (NAPWN). Several meetings have been held at a national level, according to Ann Peterson, executive director of All the Good Old Girls (AGOG) of Minneapolis, an NAPWN member. NAPWN has asked for seeding funds of $200 from each interested network to get the alliance started.

The creation of national networks does lead to the birth of many local networks. The Good Old Girls, for instance, has been asked for help and advice on establishing new networks, not connected with theirs, in Albany, Georgia; Tacoma, Washington; and Dallas, Texas. Using the National Alliance of Professional Women's Networks as an umbrella, more and more networks will continue to proliferate with the help and advice of the "old-timers."

National Impact of Networks: Growing Every Day!

Some business networks are making efforts for national impact by trying to get corporations to name more women to boards of directors. Some networks are submitting names to boards—names they cannot ignore. Whether networks become political remains to be seen. Early women's groups in the nineteenth and twentieth centuries that started out as service organizations quickly became politicized over such issues as slavery and the right of women to vote. Volunteers at settlement houses soon banded together to name women to various city boards so they would have the power to change things, not only to suggest. Self-interest and group interest may lead networks in this direction, too.

The truth is, no one knows where networks may go but everyone acknowledges their force and power. These are the early years of networks and everyone in them is, therefore, an innovator.

"*The beauty of networks is that all options are open*," says Colleen Dishon, a member of The Chicago Network. "*They can go anywhere.*"

10 Listings

National, State, and Local Networks in the United States

There are more than fourteen hundred networks in this listing, representing thousands of women who have joined together to help each other and themselves. The networks are listed by state and then topic. Look them over carefully. Find out what they're all about and what they hope to do. Because of the nature of networking, many networks do not have formal names or formal addresses or meeting places. So if there are no networks presently formed around the issue you are concerned with, you can still get in touch with people in your locale to find out how they solved problems that might arise for you. And while you're doing that, you'll be networking.

For though this is the first complete compilation ever of networks of women exclusively devoted to issues concerning women, the real goal of these listings is to encourage *you* to join a network, to urge you to be part of something very important that is happening for women, and that women just like you are making happen.

NATIONAL

Abortion

Abortion Rights Movement
1212 Pennsylvania Avenue, Southeast
Washington, D.C. 20003
(800) 424-4985

Catholics for a Free Choice
201 Massachusetts Avenue, Northeast
Washington, D.C. 20002
(202) 546-4523

National Abortion Rights Action
League
825 15th Street, Northwest
Washington, D.C. 20005
(202) 347-7774

Religious Coalition for Abortion Rights
100 Maryland Avenue, Northeast
Washington, D.C. 20002
(202) 543-7032

Reproductive Rights National Network
c/o Meredith Tax, CARASA
P.O. Box 124, Cathedral Station
New York, New York 10025
(212) 866-9596

Architecture, Landscape

Committee for Women in Landscape
  Architecture
American Society of Landscape
  Architects
1750 Old Meadow Road
McLean, Virginia 22101

Art

Coalition of Women's Art
  Organizations
c/o Ellouise Schoettler, Executive
  Director
9112 Brierly Road
Chevy Chase, Maryland 20015
(307) 652-3811
  Joyce Aiken, President

National Association of Women Artists
41 Union Square West
New York, New York 10003
(212) 675-1616

Women in Arts IWY Caucus
c/o Ellouise Schoettler
9112 Brierly Road
Chevy Chase, Maryland 20015

Women's Caucus for Art
c/o Lee Anne Miller, President
Department of Art and Art History
Wayne State University
Detroit, Michigan 48202
(313) 577-2986

Baby and Child Care

The Cesarean Clearinghouse
P.O. Box 11
Westmont, Illinois 60509

La Leche League International, Inc.
9616 Minneapolis Street
Franklin Park, Illinois 60131
(312) 455-7730

Banking

National Association of Bank Women
111 East Wacker Drive
Chicago, Illinois 60601
(312) 644-6610
  Sharon Pierce

Battered Women

National Coalition Against Sexual
  Assault
c/o Pam Klein
Rape and Sexual Assault Care Center
Box 154
Southern Illinois University
Edwardsville, Illinois 62026

National Center of Volunteers Against
  Violence
c/o Domestic Violence Project, Inc.
1917 Washtenaw Avenue
Ann Arbor, Michigan 48104
(323) 955-5460

Business and Management

Business and Professional Women's
  Foundation
2012 Massachusetts Avenue, Northwest
Washington, D.C. 20036
(202) 293-1200
  Katherine Selden

International Association of Personnel
  Women
P.O. Box 3057, Grand Central Station
New York, New York 10017

National Association for Female
  Executives
160 East 65th Street
New York, New York 10022
(212) 371-8086
  Wendy Rue, Executive Director

National Association of Negro Business
  and Professional Women's Clubs
1806 New Hampshire Avenue,
  Northwest
Washington, D.C. 20009
(202) 483-4880

The National Federation of Business
and Professional Women's Clubs,
Inc.
2012 Massachusetts Avenue, Northwest
Washington, D.C. 20036
(202) 293-1100

Women Leaders Round Table
1922 F Street, Northwest
Washington, D.C. 20006
(202) 331-6049
    Margaret E. Upson, President

WILD (Women's Independent Label
    Distribution Network)
c/o Terry Grant
736 Shiawassee Street
Lansing, Michigan 48915
(517) 321-0679

Business Owners and Entrepreneurs

National Association of Women
    Business Owners
2000 P Street, Northwest, Suite 410
Washington, D.C. 20036
(202) 338-4321
    Donna O'Bannon, President

Civic and Cultural Groups

Association of Junior Leagues, Inc.
825 3rd Avenue
New York, New York 10022
(212) 355-4380

Daughters of the American Revolution
1776 D Street, Northwest
Washington, D.C. 20006
(202) 628-1776

General Federation of Women's Clubs
1734 N Street, Northwest
Washington, D.C. 20036
(202) 347-3168

Women in Community Service
1730 Rhode Island Avenue, Northwest
Washington, D.C. 20036
(202) 293-1343
    Arlene K. Schindler

Women in Development Coalition
c/o Maxine Hitchcock
1500 Mariposa Street
Boulder, Colorado 80302

Communications and the Media

American Newspaper Women's Clubs
1607 22nd Street, Northwest
Washington, D.C. 20008
(202) 332-6770

American Women in Radio and
    Television, Inc.
1321 Connecticut Avenue, Northwest
Washington, D.C. 20016
(202) 296-0009
    Francine P. Proulx, Executive
    Director

National Association of Media Women
157 West 126th Street
New York, New York 10027
(212) 666-1320

National Federation of Press Women
721 Massachusetts Avenue, Northeast
Washington, D.C. 20002

National League of American Pen
    Women
Pen-Arts Building
1300 17th Street, Northwest
Washington, D.C. 20036
(202) 785-1997

Women in Communications, Inc.
Box 9561
Austin, Texas 78766
(512) 345-8922
    Mary E. Utting

Women's Institute for Freedom of the
    Press
3306 Ross Place, Northwest
Washington, D.C. 20008
(202) 966-7783
    Dr. Donna Allen

Women's National Book Association
c/o Ann Heidbreder Eastman
716 Burrus Drive, Northwest
Blacksburg, Virginia 24060
(703) 951-4770

Computer Science

Feminist Computer Technology
    Project
c/o Helen Eisen-Rotkopf, Coordinator
4407-C Normandy Trace Drive
St. Louis, Missouri 63121

Construction

Women in Construction
P.O. Box 3045
Washington, D.C. 20010
(202) 434-2995

Divorced Women

National Association of Divorced
    Women
Pan Am Building
200 Park Avenue, Room 303E
New York, New York 10017

Education

American Association of University
    Women
2401 Virginia Avenue, Northwest
Washington, D.C. 20035
(202) 785-7700

National Association for Women
    Deans, Administrators, and
    Counselors
1028 Connecticut Avenue, Northwest
Washington, D.C. 20036
(202) 659-9330
    Joan McCall, Executive Director

National Council of Administrative
    Women in Education
c/o Josephine P. Coiner
1815 Fort Myer Drive North
Arlington, Virginia 22209
(703) 528-6111

National Identification Program for
    the Advancement of Women in
    Higher Education Administration
c/o American Council on Education/
    Office of Women in Higher
    Education
One Dupont Circle, Northwest, Room
    829
Washington, D.C. 20036
(202) 833-4692

Neylan Conference
c/o Sr. Martha Jacob, Executive
    Director
3105 Lexington Road
Louisville, Kentucky 40206
(502) 895-0695

The Women's College Coalition
1725 K Street, Northwest, Suite 1003
Washington, D.C. 20006
(202) 466-5430
    Marcia Sharp, Director

Women in Business Education
c/o Suzanne Atwood
107 Vance Hall
University of Pennsylvania
Philadelphia, Pennsylvania 19104

Employment

National Women's Employment
    Project
1609 Connecticut Avenue, Northwest
Washington, D.C. 20036
(202) 797-1384
    Jane Pinsky

Women in the Economy Project
    Conference on State and Local
    Policies
1901 Q Street, Northwest
Washington, D.C. 20009
(202) 234-7014

Engineering

Society of Women Engineers
United Engineering Center
345 East 47th Street
(212) 644-7855
  Inez Van Vranken, Executive
  Director

Ethnic and Minority Women

Asian-Pacific Women's IWY Caucus
c/o Tin Myaing Thein
17422 Matinal Drive
San Diego, California 92127

Black Women's Community
  Development Foundation
1028 Connecticut Avenue, Northwest,
  Suite 1020
Washington, D.C. 20036

Black Women's IWY Caucus
c/o Dorothy I. Height
National Council of Negro Women
10 Waterside Place, Room 33F
New York, New York 10010

Ethnic Women's IWY Caucus
c/o Christine Noschese
31 Crosby Street
New York, New York 10013

Hispanic Women's IWY Caucus
c/o Sandra Serrano Sewell
1245 Sinaloa Avenue
Pasadena, California 91104

Mexican American Women's National
  Association
P.O. Box 23656 L'Enfant Plaza,
  Southwest
Washington, D.C. 20024
(202) 245-9180

National Alliance of Black Feminists
202 South State Street, Suite 1024
Chicago, Illinois 60604
(312) 939-0107

National Conference of Puerto Rican
  Women, Inc.

P.O. Box 4804, Cleveland Park Station
Washington, D.C. 20008
(202) 244-2974 or 365-0339

National Congress of Neighborhood
  Women
1129 Catherine Street
Brooklyn, New York 11211
(212) 388-6666
  Roni Haggarty

National Council of Negro Women
  Black Women's Agenda
1346 Connecticut Avenue, Northwest
Washington, D.C. 20036
(202) 293-3902

National Hook-up of Black Women
2021 K Street, Northwest, Room 305
Washington, D.C. 20006
(202) 882-5244

Native American Women's IWY
  Caucus
c/o Billie Nave Masters
Office of Technical Education
SST 443, University of California
Irvine, California 92717

Organization of Chinese American
  Women
1443 Rhode Island Avenue, Northwest,
  Room 6
Washington, D.C. 20005
(202) 232-3971

Organization of Pan Asian American
  Women
719 Fern Place
Washington, D.C. 20012

Ukranian National Women's League
108 Second Avenue
New York, New York 10003

Farm and Rural Women

Farm Woman
930 National Press Building
Washington, D.C. 20045
(202) 347-2776
  Nedra Bayne Carpel

Rural American Women
1522 K Street, Northwest, Suite 700
Washington, D.C. 20005
(202) 785-4701
  Jane Threat

Rural Women's IWY Caucus
c/o Marianne Bruesehoff
Route 2
Watkins, Minnesota 55389

Health

DES Action/National
Long Island Jewish Hillside Medical
  Center
New Hyde Park, New York 11040
  Fran Fishbane, President

National Women's Health Network
2025 I Street, Northwest, Suite 105
Washington, D.C. 20006
(202) 223-6886
  Belita Cowan

Women and Health Roundtable
Federation of Organizations for
  Professional Women
2000 P Street, Northwest, Suite 403
Washington, D.C. 20036
(202) 466-3545
  Ilene Wolcott, Program Director

Homemakers and Domestic
  Workers

HERA (Homemakers Equal Rights
  Association)
c/o Anne Follis
Rural Route 3
Urbana, Illinois 61801
(217) 684-2422

Household Technicians of America
c/o Geneva Reid, President
2719 Duke Street, Southeast
Warren, Ohio 44484
(216) 369-6552

National Committee on Household
  Employment
500 East 62nd Street

New York, New York 10021
(212) 644-6699
  Caroline Reed

Labor Movement

Coalition of Labor Union Women
c/o Gloria Johnson
I.U.E.
1126 16th Street, Northwest
Washington, D.C. 20036
(202) 296-1200

Labor Women's IWY Caucus
c/o Joyce Miller
15 Union Square
New York, New York 10003

National Association of Office Workers
1258 Euclid Avenue
Cleveland, Ohio 44115
(216) 566-8511
  Karen Nussbaum

National Women's Committee to
  Support J. P. Stevens Workers
770 Broadway, 13th Floor
New York, New York 10003

Women's Bureau Constituents
c/o Women's Bureau
Department of Labor
200 Constitution Avenue, Northwest
Washington, D.C. 20210
(202) 523-6611
  Evelyn Farber

Women's Workforce
c/o Wider Opportunities for Women
1649 K Street, Northwest
Washington, D.C. 20006
(202) 638-4868
  Betsy Cooley

Law

Federation of Women Lawyers'
  Judicial Screening Panel
c/o Lynn Hecht Schafran
36 West 44th Street, Suite 415
New York, New York 10036
(212) 354-1225

National Association of Women
    Lawyers
American Bar Association
1155 East 60th Street
Chicago, Illinois 60637
(312) 947-2549 or 947-4000

National Association of Black Women
    Attorneys
1343 H. Street, Northwest, Suite 602
Washington, D.C. 20005

National Conference on Women and
    the Law
Golden Gate University School of Law
536 Mission Street
San Francisco, California 94105
(415) 442-7000
    Judy Bloomberg, Coordinator

Medicine

American Association of Women
    Dentists
c/o American Dental Association
211 East Chicago Avenue
Chicago, Illinois 60611
(312) 642-7538

American Medical Women's
    Association
c/o Claudine Gay, M.D.
403 East Capitol Street
Washington, D.C. 20003
(202) 547-2277

American Nurses Association
2420 Pershing Road
Kansas City, Missouri 64108
(816) 474-5720

Gay Nurses Alliance
c/o American Nurses Association
2420 Pershing Road
Kansas City, Missouri 64108
(816) 474-5720

National Feminist Therapists
    Association
c/o Center for Women's Studies and
    Services

P.O Box 1302
San Diego, California 92112
(714) 233-8984

The National Midwives Association
P.O. Box 163
Princeton, New Jersey 08540
(609) 924-1448
    Shari Daniels, President

Music

American Women Composers, Inc.
6192 Oxon Hill Road, Suite 406
Washington, D.C. 20021
(202) 567-4490

League of Women Composers
c/o Marga Richter
3 Bay View Lane
Huntington, New York 11743
(516) 421-1532

National Congress of Women in Music
c/o Jeannie G. Pool
P.O. Box 436, Ansonia Station
New York, New York 10023

National Women's Music Festival
P.O. Box 2721, Station A
Champaign, Illinois 61820
(217) 333-6443

We Want the Music Collective
1501 Lyons Street
Mt. Pleasant, Michigan 48858
(517) 772-0582

Women's Jazz Festival, Inc.
P.O. Box 22321
Kansas City, Missouri
(816) 361-1901

Older Women

Older Women's IWY Caucus
c/o Joanne Turner
40 East Stokes Road
Willingboro, New Jersey 08046

The National Action Forum for Older
Women
c/o Nancy King
Center on Aging
University of Maryland
College Park, Maryland 20742
(301) 454-5856

Politics and Government

Federal Women's IWY Task Force
c/o Joan Biordi
4917 42nd Street, Northwest
Washington, D.C. 20016

Federally Employed Women (FEW)
National Press Building, Room 485
Washington, D.C. 20045
(202) 638-4404
    Daisy B. Fields, Executive Director

Women in Municipal Government
c/o National League of Cities
1620 I Street, Northwest
Washington, D.C. 20006
(202) 293-7310
    Carol Patrylick and Debbie White

Women Officials in NACO
c/o National Association of Counties
1735 New York Avenue, Northwest
Washington, D.C. 20006
(202) 785-9577
    Cindy Kenny

Professional Women

Federation of Organizations for
    Professional Women
2000 P Street, Northwest, Suite 403
Washington, D.C. 20036
(202) 466-3547

Religious Groups

Church Women United
475 Riverside Drive
New York, New York 10027
(212) 870-2355

Committee on Women and Society
United Church of Christ

132 West 31st Street
New York, New York 10010

Council on Women and the Church
United Presbyterian Church in the
    USA
475 Riverside Drive, Room 1149
New York, New York 10027
(212) 870-2019
    Dr. Elizabeth H. Verdesi

Episcopal Women's Caucus
935 East Avenue
Rochester, New York 14607

Jewish Women's IWY Caucus
c/o Betty Shapiro
3001 Veazey Terrace, Northwest,
    #1604
Washington, D.C. 20008

Leadership Conference for Women
    Religious of the U.S.A.
1302 18th Street, Northwest, Suite 701
Washington, D.C. 20036
(202) 293-1483

National Assembly of Women
    Religious
1307 South Wabash Avenue
Chicago, Illinois 60605
(312) 663-1980

National Coalition of American Nuns
1307 South Wabash Avenue
Chicago, Illinois 60605
(312) 341-9159

National Council of Jewish Women
1346 Connecticut Avenue, Northwest
Washington, D.C. 20036
(202) 296-2588

National Council of Catholic Women
1312 Massachusetts Avenue, Northwest
Washington, D.C. 20005
(202) 638-6050

United Methodist Church Women's
    Division
475 Riverside Drive
New York, New York 10027

Women's Ordination Conference
P.O. Box 4597
Washington, D.C. 20017

YWCA National Board
600 Lexington Avenue
New York, New York 10022
(212) 753-4700

Science

Association for Women in Science
1346 Connecticut Avenue, Northwest,
  Room 1122
Washington, D.C. 20036
(202) 833-1998

Social Science

American Women in Psychology
c/o Diane L. Simpson
555 Main Street
51802 Roosevelt Island
New York, New York 10044
(212) 751-6164

Sociologists for Women in Society
1243 Linden Place, Northeast
Washington, D.C. 20002
(202) 396-0777

Sports and Leisure

Association for Intercollegiate Athletics
  for Women (AIAW)
1201 16th Street, Northwest
Washington, D.C. 20036
(202) 833-5485 or 833-5558

Girls Rodeo Association
8909 Northeast 25th Street
Spencer, Oklahoma 73084
(405) 769-5322

National Association for Girls and
  Women in Sports
1201 16th Street, Northwest
Washington, D.C. 20036
(202) 833-5540
  Carol Thompson, Executive Director

North American Network of Women
  Runners
P.O. Box 924
Shaker Heights, Ohio 44120
(216) 566-9873
  Phoebe Jones, National Coordinator

Task Force on Outreach to Women
Sierra Club
530 Bush Street
San Francisco, California 94108
(415) 981-8634
  Judith Kanofsky

Women in Sports IWY Caucus
c/o Carol Oglesby
6012 Green Street
Philadelphia, Pennsylvania 19144

Women's International Bowling
  Congress
4301 South 75th Street
Greendale, Wisconsin 53129
(414) 421-9000

Women's Olympic Distance
  Committee
c/o Henley Roughton, Chair
8208 East Boulevard Drive
Alexandria, Virginia 22308
(703) 768-0444

Women's Sports Foundation
195 Moulton Street
San Francisco, California 94123
(415) 563-6266
  Barbara Fox, Research Director

Support

Displaced Homemaker's Network, Inc.
755 Eighth Street, Northwest
Washington, D.C. 20001
(202) 347-0522

Women's Rights and Political Issues

Center of Concern—Women's Project
3200 13th Street, Northwest
Washington, D.C. 20017
(202) 635-2757

Center for Law & Social Policy
Women's Rights Project
1751 N Street, Northwest
Washington, D.C. 20036
(202) 877-0670

Clearinghouse on Women's Issues
1346 Connecticut Avenue, Northwest,
    Suite 924
Washington, D.C. 20036
(202) 466-3429

Coalition for Women's Appointments
c/o Ann Kolker
National Women's Political Caucus
1411 K Street, Northwest, Room 1110
Washington, D.C. 20005
(202) 347-4456

Congressional Clearinghouse on
    Women's Rights
722 House Annex Building No. 1
Washington, D.C. 20515
(202) 255-2947

Continuing Committee of the National
    Women's Conference
c/o Anne B. Turpeau, Co-chair
1909 19th Street, Northwest
Washington, D.C. 20009
(202) 254-8420

Disabled Women's IWY Caucus
c/o Ann Attar
1340 East 9th Street, Room E-4
Brooklyn, New York 11230

ERAmerica
1525 M Street, Northwest
Washington, D.C. 20005
(202) 833-4354

Human Rights for Women
1128 National Press Building
Washington, D.C. 20004

Judicial Appointments Project
c/o National Women's Political
    Caucus
1411 K Street, Northwest, Room 1110
Washington, D.C. 20005
(202) 347-4456

League of Women Voters
1730 M Street, Northwest
Washington, D.C. 20036
(202) 296-1170

Lesbian Women's IWY Caucus
c/o Frances Doughty
192 St. John's Place
Brooklyn, New York 11217

National Coalition for Women in
    Defense
805 15th Street, Northwest, Suite 822
Washington, D.C. 20005
(202) 638-1961
    Carol Parr

National Communication Network for
    the Elimination of Violence
    Against Women
4520 44th Avenue South
Minneapolis, Minnesota 55406

NOW (National Organization for
    Women)
425 13th Street, Northwest, Suite 1001
Washington, D.C. 20004
(202) 347-2279

National Women's Agenda
c/o National Women's Action
370 Lexington Avenue
New York, New York 10017
(212) 532-8330

National Women's Centers Training
    Project
University of Massachusetts at Amherst
Amherst, Massachusetts 01003
(413) 545-0111
    Kathryn Girard and Joan Sweeney

National Woman's Party
144 Constitution Avenue, Northeast
Washington, D.C. 20002
(202) 546-1210
    Elizabeth Chittick

National Women's Political Caucus
1411 K Street, Northwest, Room 1110
Washington, D.C. 20005
(202) 347-4456

Religious Advocates for Equality
c/o National Council of Churches
110 Maryland Avenue, Northeast
Washington, D.C. 20002
(202) 544-2350
  Gail Lambers

Republican Women's Task Force
National Women's Political Caucus
5022 V Street, Northwest
Washington, D.C. 20007
(202) 225-0580

SPRINT
Women's Equity Action League Fund
805 15th Street, Northwest, Suite 822
Washington, D.C. 20005
(800) 424-5162
  Betty Garrett

Women USA
c/o Bella Abzug
76 Beaver Street
New York, New York 10005
(212) 422-1414

Women, Welfare, and Poverty IWY
  Caucus
c/o Joan Guernsey
10107 Dupont Avenue
Bloomington, Minnesota 55431

Women's Action Alliance
370 Lexington Avenue
New York, New York 10017
(212) 532-8330

Women's Equity Action League
805 15th Street, Northwest
Washington, D.C. 20005
(202) 638-4560

Women's Lobby
201 Massachusetts Avenue, Northeast
Washington, D.C. 20002

Women's Network of NCSL
National Conference of State
  Legislators
1405 Curtis Street, 23rd Floor
Denver, Colorado 80202
(303) 623-6600
  Andrea J. Wollock

Women Strike for Peace
145 South 13th Street, Room 407
Philadelphia, Pennsylvania 19107
(215) 923-0861

Youth IWY Caucus
c/o Sharon Talbot
132 Glenwood Avenue
Portland, Maine 04102

Women's Studies and Education

Coalition for Women in International
  Development
c/o Overseas Education Fund
2101 L Street, Northwest, Suite 916
Washington, D.C. 20037

National Coalition for Women and
  Girls in Education
One Dupont Circle, Northwest
Washington, D.C. 20036
(202) 296-1770

National Women's Education Fund
1410 Q Street, Northwest
Washington, D.C. 20009
(202) 462-8606
  Betsey Wright, Director

National Women's Studies Association
c/o Elaine Reuben, Coordinator
University of Maryland
College Park, Maryland 20742
(301) 454-3757

ALABAMA

Art

Women's Caucus for Art
c/o Janice Ross
437 Wrights Mill Road
Auburn, Alabama 36830

Business and Management

The Breakfast Club
c/o Susan Reeves
2027 First Avenue North
Birmingham, Alabama 35203
(205) 322-6631

Community Centers

Birmingham Jefferson Women's
  Center
11th Avenue Methodist Church
1200 11th Avenue
Birmingham, Alabama 35228
(205) 325-5611
  Diane McEwen

Sports and Leisure

Thursday's Child at Beefeater's Tavern
1318 20th Street South
Birmingham, Alabama 35234
(205) 870-7740
  Millie Cox

ALASKA

Baby and Child Care

BABE (Better Alaskan Birth
  Experiences)
c/o Peg Newman
Prince of Peace Drive
Eagle River, Alaska 99577
(907) 694-9050

Education

The Alaska Council of Administrative
  Women in Education
Department of Education, State of
  Alaska
Pouch F, State Office Building

Juneau, Alaska 99811
(907) 465-2800
  Gladys Tinney

Ethnic and Minority Women

North America Indian Women's
  Association
807 River View Drive
Fairbanks, Alaska 99701

Women's Rights and Political Issues

Anchorage Women's Liberation
7801 Peck Avenue
Anchorage, Alaska 99504

ARIZONA

Art

Women's Caucus for Art
c/o Betsy Benjamin Murray
3511 North Miller Road
Scottsdale, Arizona 85251

Womankraft
Box 4694
Tucson, Arizona 85719

Business and Management

The Executive Women's Council of
Southern Arizona
c/o Carolyn Lucz
2700 East Speedway Boulevard
Tucson, Arizona 85716
(602) 326-2739

Community Centers

Flagstaff Women's Resource Center
3 North Leroux Street, Room 201
Flagstaff, Arizona 86001
(602) 774-1008

Sojourner Center
c/o Suzanne Vilmain
P.O. Box 2649
Phoenix, Arizona 85002

Women's Center
333 East McDowell Street
Phoenix, Arizona 85004
(602) 258-9227

Employment

PHASE (Project for Homemakers in
Arizona Searching for
Employment)
Continuing Education for Women
1717 East Speedway Boulevard, Room
3212
Tucson, Arizona 85719
(602) 626-3902
Lynn O'Hern, Coordinator

Medicine

American Medical Women's
Association
Professional Resources Research
Center
Speedway Professional Building, Suite
206A
2302 East Speedway Boulevard
Tucson, Arizona 85719
(602) 795-2677

Arizona School of Midwifery
114 East Mohave Road
Tucson, Arizona 85705
(602) 325-3978

Rape

Center Against Sexual Assault
P.O. Box 3786
Phoenix, Arizona 85030
(602) 279-9824

Sports and Leisure

Women's Cycling Union
P.O. Box 12746
Tucson, Arizona 85732
(602) 296-9524

Women's Rights and Political Issues

Tucson Women's Collective
243 West 33rd Street
Tucson, Arizona 85713
(602) 792-1929

WIN (Woman Image Now)
Department of Art
Arizona State University
Tempe, Arizona 85281
(602) 965-3525
Muriel Magenta

Women's Studies and Education

SWIROW (Southwest Institute for
Research on Women in the
Western Frontier)
Women's Studies Program
University of Arizona
Tucson, Arizona 85721
(602) 626-4470
Dr. Myra Dinnerstein

ARKANSAS

Baby and Child Care

Better Births
Women's Center
207 Razorback Road
Fayetteville, Arkansas 72701
(501) 443-4998

Battered Women

Northwest Arkansas Project for
    Battered Women and Their
    Families
Washington County EDA
P.O. Box 1168
Fayetteville, Arkansas 72701

Community Centers

Pine Bluff Women's Center
P.O. Box 5832
Pine Bluff, Arkansas 71601
    Becky Kilmer

Women's Center
207 Razorback Road
Fayetteville, Arkansas 72701
(501) 443-4998

Communications and the Media

Arkansas Press Women
c/o Carol Griffee
2610 North Taylor Street
Little Rock, Arkansas 72207
(501) 666-6425

Women of the Ozarks Radio
    Collective
Women's Center
207 Razorback Road
Fayetteville, Arkansas 72701
(501) 443-4998

Construction

Women Working in Construction
c/o Suzanne Rasmussen
402 East 9th Street
Little Rock, Arkansas 72201

Education

Women in Higher Education
UALR Commission on the Status of
    Women
33rd and University Streets
Little Rock, Arkansas 72204
    Mary Alice Orahood

Health

Fayetteville Women's Health
    Collective
210 Locust Street
Fayetteville, Arkansas 72701

Mari Spehar Health Collective
P.O. Box 545
Fayetteville, Arkansas 72701

Support Groups

Women's Support Group
c/o Cynthia Greer
Hendrix College
607 Fourth Street
Conway, Arkansas 72032

Women's Rights and Political Issues

Arkansas Women's Rights
P.O. Box 2843
Little Rock, Arkansas 72203
    Edith Cox

ERArkansas
c/o Alice Glover
78 West Windsor Drive
Little Rock, Arkansas 72209
(501) 565-7388

Panel of American Women
2200 Main Street
Little Rock, Arkansas 72205
(501) 376-7913
    Brownie Ledbetter

CALIFORNIA

Architecture

Association of Women in Architecture
4511 Finley Avenue
Los Angeles, California 90027

Organization of Women Architects/
    Design Professionals
Box 26570
San Francisco, California 94126

Art

Artists in Prison
13248 Chalom Road
Los Angeles, California 90049
(213) 879-1905
    Susan Loewenberg

Crane Mountain Abbey
P.O. Box 717
Fairfax, California 94930

Emma's Place
P.O. Box 717
Grover City, California 93433

Gallery 25
1936 Echo Street
Fresno, California 93704
(209) 266-6244

San Francisco Women Artists
1407 Gough Street
San Francisco, California 94109
    Maureen Marshall

Santa Barbara Women Artists Group
c/o The Women's Center
University of California
Santa Barbara, California 93106
(805) 961-3778
    Melinda Louise, Coordinator

The Woman's Building
1727 North Spring Street
Los Angeles, California 90012
(213) 221-6161
    Ruth Iskin and Arlene Raven

Women Drawing Women
c/o Trisha Womon
620 Guerrero Street, Apt. 10
San Francisco, California 94110

Women's Caucus for Art
c/o Kathleen Kenyon
1870 North Van Ness Avenue
Hollywood, California 90028
(213) 469-4344

Women's Caucus for Art
c/o Janice Cox
3025 Arizona Street
Oakland, California 94602

Women's Sonic Collective
c/o Ellen Robinson
2214 McGee Street
San Francisco, California 94703
(415) 845-1622

Baby and Child Care

Association for Childbirth at Home
16705 Monte Cristo Street
Cerritos, California 90701

Holistic Childbirth Institute
1627 10th Avenue
San Francisco, California 94112
(415) 664-4900

Battered Women

Western States Shelters Network
c/o San Francisco Neighborhood Legal
    Assistance Foundation
Women's Litigation Unit
870 Market Street
San Francisco, California 94103
(415) 433-2535

Business and Management

Bay Area Executive Women's Forum
4095 17th Street
San Francisco, California 94114
(415) 431-8740
  Laura Talmus

Bay Area Professional Women's
  Network
55 Sutter Street, Room 329
San Francisco, California 94104
(415) 391-9197
  Cynthia Blanton, President

Interconnections
c/o Patricia Schroeder
123 Pearl Alley
Santa Cruz, California 95060
(408) 426-1317

Orange Coast Network
c/o Dorothy Doan
1501 West Cliff Drive
Newport Beach, California 92660

Organization of Women Executives
c/o Judy Miller
Director of Public Relations
Suntory International
612 South Flower Street
Los Angeles, California 90017
(213) 627-5761

Professional Women's Alliance
1804 Bush Street
San Francisco, California 94109
(415) 563-5600
  Nancy Honig, President

Western Women's Business Association
c/o Kandra S. Driggs, Drisem
  Associates
Legasti Towers
500 Airport Boulevard
Burlingame, California 94140
(415) 342-0199

Women Can Win
c/o Judi Hochman

8383 Wilshire Boulevard, Suite 517
Beverly Hills, California 90211
(213) 653-5991

Women in Business
c/o Ruth Crack
5900 Wilshire Boulevard
Los Angeles, California 90036
(213) 933-7330

Business Owners and Entrepreneurs

California Women Entrepreneurs
  Trade Mission
c/o Contemporary Management
  Consultants
1333 Howe Avenue, Suite 100
Sacramento, California 95825
(916) 920-2272

Los Angeles Association of Women
  Business Owners
c/o Carol Filderman, President
Dean, Witter and Reynolds
10899 Wilshire Boulevard
Los Angeles, California 90024
(213) 477-4541

Small Business Women Owners'
  Association
c/o Darlene Faucher
432 F Street
San Diego, California 92101
(714) 233-0928

Women Entrepreneurs
P.O. Box 26738
San Francisco, California 94126
(415) 788-4430
  Virginia Littlejohn, Program
  Coordinator

Women Entrepreneurs of Napa Valley
c/o Helen Ballou, Representative
Moon Tree Business Assistance for
  Women
1041 Jefferson Street
Napa, California 94558
(707) 253-2344

Women Entrepreneurs of Santa Clara
c/o Sharon Hermasillo, Esq.,
    Representative
Galloway, Thomson, Kilduff and
    Hermasillo
900 LaFayette Street, Room 600
Santa Clara, California 95959
(408) 984-1200

Communications and the Media

Ariadne
c/o Suzanne Lacy
28 Avenue 27
Venice, California 90291

Feminist Writers' Guild (FWG)
Box 9396
Berkeley, California 94709

Women's Communication Coalition
c/o Robin Citrin
Communication Arts Department
San Francisco State University
1600 Holloway Avenue
San Francisco, California 94132
(415) 469-1787

Women's Media Resource Center
P.O. Box 5595
Santa Monica, California 90405

Community Centers

River Queen Women's Center
P.O. Box 726
Monte Rio, California 95462

San Francisco Women's Center
63 Brady Street
San Francisco, California 94103
(415) 431-1180

San Luis Obispo Women's Resource
    Center
738D Higuera Street
San Luis Obispo, California 93401
(805) 544-9313

Computer Science

The Network of Feminist Computer
    Professionals
P.O. Box 626
Talmage, California 95481
(707) 462-7962
    Anne Gould

Design

Women in Design
P.O. Box 2607
San Francisco, California 94126

Women in Design
Box 747
Venice, California 90291
(213) 399-5310
    Nikki Deal

Doctors' Wives

Doctors' Wives Support Group
c/o Margaret Harris
5604 Dorothy Way
San Diego, California 92115
(714) 583-1584

Employment

WOE (Women Organized for
    Employment)
127 Montgomery Street
San Francisco, California 94104
(415) 982-8963
    Kathleen Connolly

Ethnic and Minority Women

Black Women Organized for Action
P.O. Box 15072
San Francisco, California 94115
(415) 861-5334

Chicano Service Action Center
2244 Beverly Boulevard
Los Angeles, California 90057
(213) 381-7261

Comision Feminil Mexicana Nacional
279 South Loma Drive
Los Angeles, California 90803

Committee Concerned with Asian
    Wives
c/o Bok-Lin C. Kim
964 La Jolla Rancho Road
La Jolla, California 92037

Puerto Rican Organization for Women
c/o Elba Montez
3067 24th Street
San Francisco, California 94110
(415) 648-4031

Film

West Coast Women Filmmakers
The Woman's Building
1727 North Spring Street
Los Angeles, California 90012

Women in Film
8489 Third Street
Los Angeles, California 90068
(213) 651-3680
    Gloria Goldsmith

Health

Alcoholism Center for Women
1147 South Alvarado Street
Los Angeles, California 90006
(213) 381-7805

Berkeley Women's Health Collective
2908 Ellsworth Street
Berkeley, California 94705
    Cindy Medrano

Common Women's Force
Everywoman's Clinic
2600 Park Avenue, Room 106
Concord, California 94520
(415) 825-7900

DES Action/Northern California
4079A 24th Street
San Francisco, California 94114

DES Action/Southern California
c/o Thea Rahmani
2210 3rd Street, Apt. 206
Santa Monica, California 90405

Everywoman's Clinic
2600 Park Avenue
Concord, California 94520

Feminist Health/Mental Health
    Project
American Friends Service Committee
2160 Lake Street
San Francisco, California 94121

Feminist Women's Health Center
330 Flume Street
Chico, California 95926
(916) 488-7591

Feminist Women's Health Center
1112 South Crenshaw Street
Los Angeles, California 90019
(213) 936-6293
    Carol Downer, Director

The Heartland Healing Center
c/o Hogie Wyckoff
2843 Fulton Street
Berkeley, California 94705
(415) 549-1811

The Marin County Women's Health
    Collective
YWCA
1618 Mission Avenue
San Rafael, California 94901

Network Against Psychiatric Assault
2150 Market Street
San Francisco, California 94114

Nevada City Women's Health
    Collective
12585 Jones Bar Road
Nevada City, California 94949

Oakland Feminist Women's Health
    Center
2930 McClure Street
Oakland, California 94609
(415) 444-5676

Orange County Feminist Women's
   Health Center
429 South Sycamore Street
Santa Ana, California 92701
(714) 836-1941

Palo Alto Self-Help Collective
270 Grant Street
Palo Alto, California 94306

San Francisco Women's Health Center
3789 24th Street
San Francisco, California 94114
(415) 282-6999

Santa Cruz Women's Health Center
250 Locust Street
Santa Cruz, California 95060
(408) 427-3500

Sonoma Women's Health Collective
103 7th Street
Santa Rosa, California 95401
(707) 542-HEAL

Westside Women's Health Care
   Project
1711 Ocean Park Boulevard
Santa Monica, California 90405

Womancare—A Feminist Women's
   Health Center
424 Pennsylvania Avenue
San Diego, California 92103
(714) 298-9352

Womankind Health Services
250 Locust Street
Santa Cruz, California 95060
(408) 427-3500

Women Helping Women
1334 Haight Street
San Francisco, California 94117
(415) 861-1302

Women's Alcohol Coalition
69 Brady Street
San Francisco, California 94103
(415) 626-2170

Women's Community Clinic
696 East Santa Clara Street

San Jose, California 95112
(408) 287-4322

Women's Health Collective
Humboldt Open Door Clinic
10th and H Streets
Arcata, California 95521

Women's Need Center
Haight Ashbury Free Medical Clinic
558 Clayton Street
San Francisco, California 94117

Homemakers and Domestic
   Workers

Creative Mundanes
c/o Spring Friedlander
434 66th Street
Oakland, California 94609
(415) 653-1017

Wages for Housework
P.O. Box 14512
San Francisco, California 94114
(415) 681-4667

Wages for Housework
P.O. Box 26325, Edendale Station
Los Angeles, California 90026
(213) 661-0095

Labor Movement

Los Angeles Working Women
304 South Broadway, Suite 534
Los Angeles, California 90013
(213) 628-8080
   Lydia Baca

Medicine

GNA West (Gay Nurses Alliance)
Box 1793
San Diego, California 94112

Program for Women in Health
   Sciences
University of California/San Francisco
1343 Third Avenue
San Francisco, California 94143

Music

Bay Area Women in Music
829 Folsom Street
San Francisco, California 94107
(415) 546-6466

Olivia Records
4400 Market Street
Oakland, California 94608
(415) 655-0364

Older Women

Fat, Female, and Forty
Options
63 Brady Street
San Francisco, California 94103
(415) 431-6944

Hot Flashers
c/o Nancy Skinner
180 Oak Springs Drive
San Anselmo, California 94960

Jobs for Older Women Action Project
3102 Telegraph Avenue
Berkeley, California 94705
(415) 849-0332

owl (Older Women's League)
235 Hill Street
Santa Monica, California 90405
(213) 399-9813

Older Women's League Educational
    Fund
3800 Harrison Street
Oakland, California 94611
(415) 653-1435 or 658-8700
    Tish Sommers and Laurie Shields

Options for Women over Forty
c/o Dovre Hall
3543 18th Street
San Francisco, California 94110
(415) 431-6944

Politics and Government

California Women-Elected Association
c/o Sue Hone, Vice-Mayor

2180 Melvia Street
Berkeley, California 94704
(415) 644-6243

Women in Power
c/o Vicki Kellinski, Acting Executive
    Secretary
Los Angeles Commission on the Status
    of Women
Room 1701, City Hall
200 North Spring Street
Los Angeles, California 90012
(213) 485-6533

Prostitutes

CAT (California Advocates for
    Trollops)
8730 Wilshire Boulevard, Apt. 5E
Beverly Hills, California 90022
(213) 657-1738

COYOTE (Call Off Your Old Tired
    Ethics)
P.O. Box 26354
San Francisco, California 94126
(415) 957-1610

Rape

Bay Area Women Against Rape
P.O. Box 240
Berkeley, California 94701
(415) 845-RAPE

Sports and Leisure

Camping Women
2720 Armstrong Drive, Department A
Sacramento, California 95825
(916) 488-1297

Gourmet Exchange
c/o Spring Friedlander
434 66th Street
Oakland, California 94609
(415) 653-1017

Lesbian Whitewater Rafting
    Weekends
c/o 81A Sanchez Street
San Francisco, California 94114

Los Angeles Women Running
c/o Sylvia Gentile
1001 B Pier Avenue
Santa Monica, California 90405
(213) 396-7146

Seaworthy Women
2210 Wilshire Boulevard, Suite 254
Santa Monica, California 90403
(213) 397-7728

Task Force on Outreach to Women
c/o Sierra Club
530 Bush Street
San Francisco, California 94108
(415) 981-8634
    Judith Kanofsky

Women in the Water
2901 Piedmont Avenue
Berkeley, California 94705
(415) 848-1611

Women in the Wilderness
13 Columbus Avenue
San Francisco, California 94111
(415) 981-8634

Women's Rugby Groups
c/o Helen Marcus
344 Noe Street
San Francisco, California 94114

Women's Sports Foundation
195 Moulton Street
San Francisco, California 94123
(415) 563-6266
    Barbara Fox, Research Director

Support Groups

Cancer Support Group
3800 Harrison Street
Oakland, California 94617
(415) 653-1435
    Tish Sommers

Disabled Women's Coalition
607 Eshleman Hall
University of California
Berkeley, California 94720

Theater and Performing Arts

Las Cucarachas (Puppets and Politics)
c/o Dorinda Moreno
Concillio Mujeres
725 Rhode Island Street
San Francisco, California 94107
(415) 826-1530

Motion
1148 High Court Drive
Berkeley, California 94708
(415) 626-3439
    Judith Barry

The Performing Woman
c/o Janice Dinneen
26910 Grand View Street
Hayward, California 94542
(415) 881-1423

Women's Conference Committee
Screen Actors Guild
1750 Sunset Boulevard
Hollywood, California 90046

Trucking

American Association of Women
    Truck Drivers
P.O. Box 248
La Puente, California 91744
    Kristy Cook

Women's Rights and Political Issues

Advocates for Women
256 Sutter Street
San Francisco, California 94108
(415) 391-4870

Coalition for the Medical Rights of
    Women
3543 18th Street
San Francisco, California 94110
(415) 621-8030

Equal Rights Advocates, Inc.
c/o Judith Kurtz
433 Turk Street
San Francisco, California 94102
(415) 441-2618

WATCH (Women Acting Together to
   Combat Harassment)
c/o Feminist Women's Health Center
1112 Crenshaw Boulevard
Los Angeles, California 90019

Women Against Violence in
   Pornography and Media
Berkeley Women's Center
2112 Channing Way
Berkeley, California 94704

Women's Studies and Education

The Math Science Network
c/o Joanne Koltnow, Coordinator
Math Science Resource Center
Mills College
Oakland, California 94613

Women's Educational Equity
   Communications Network
1855 Folsom Street
San Francisco, California 94103

COLORADO

Baby and Child Care

Informed Home Birth Group
P.O. Box 788
Boulder, Colorado 80306
(303) 484-8337
   Marianne Schroeder

Business and Management

Women's Forum of Colorado
6051 Eldorado Avenue
Denver, Colorado 80222
(303) 779-4070

Clergymen's Wives

Clergymen's Wives Support Group
c/o Virginia E. Pike
2268 Tiffany Drive
Grand Junction, Colorado 81501
(303) 245-6624

Community Centers

Boulder County Women's Resource
   Center
1406 Pine Street
Boulder, Colorado 80302
(303) 447-9670

Womanspace
938 Pearl Street
Boulder, Colorado 80302
(303) 449-1362

Farm and Rural Women

WIFE (Women Involved in Farm
   Economy)
Box 172
Crook, Colorado 80726

Health

Fort Collins Self-Help Clinic for
   Women
629 South Hawes Street
Fort Collins, Colorado 80521

Women's Health Services of Colorado
   Springs
1703 North Weber Street
Colorado Springs, Colorado 80907

Theater and Performing Arts

Boulder Feminist Theatre Collective
2043 Pine Street
Boulder, Colorado 80302
(303) 449-5319

Colorado Women in the Arts
299 Green Rock Drive
Boulder, Colorado 80302
(303) 449-7534 or 494-9156
  Cecille Sirotkin

Front Range Women/in the Visual
  Arts
c/o Sally Elliot
Valley Vista Lane
Jamestown Star Route
Boulder, Colorado 80302
(303) 443-6224

CONNECTICUT

Art

Fairfield 8
c/o Ann Chernow
2 Gorham Avenue
Westport, Connecticut 06880

Connecticut Women Artists
c/o Mollie Bornstein
105 Orchard Court
West Hartford, Connecticut 06117
(203) 521-9480

Battered Women

New Haven Project for Battered
  Women
P.O. Box 1329
New Haven, Connecticut 06505

Community Centers

Hartford Women's Center
57 Pratt Street, Suite 301
Hartford, Connecticut 06103

Prudence Crandall Center for Women
37 Bassett Street
New Britain, Connecticut 06051
(203) 225-6357

Women's Center
110 Broad Street
New London, Connecticut 06320
(203) 447-0366

Women's Center of Ridgefield
P.O. Box 112
Ridgefield, Connecticut 06877
(203) 438-9339

Women's Center of Southeastern
  Connecticut
Neighborhood Center
120 Broad Street
New London, Connecticut 06320
(203) 443-1425

Women's Place
73 Marshall Ridge Road
New Canaan, Connecticut 06840

Health

Grace Hirsch Self-Help Clinic
2 Hemlock Drive
Stamford, Connecticut 06902

Hartford Women's Health Co-op
c/o Mary Palmer
92 Rowe Avenue
Hartford, Connecticut 06106
(203) 233-7346

Therapy Rights Committee
215 Park Street
New Haven, Connecticut 06511

Office and Clerical Workers

Hartford Office Workers
57 Pratt Street
Hartford, Connecticut 06103
(203) 527-5773
  Janet Waggoner

Office Workers of New Haven
148 Orange Street
New Haven, Connecticut 06510

Politics and Government

A Group of Women Legislators
c/o Audrey P. Beck, State Senator
100 Dunham Pond Road
Storrs, Connecticut 06268

DELAWARE

Art

Studio Group
1305 North Franklin Street
Wilmington, Delaware 19806
  Constance Nichols, President

Ethnic and Minority Women

National Council of Negro Women/
  Delaware Chapter

c/o Mrs. Hazel Showell
Route 1, Box 73A
Fredrica, Delaware 19946

Rape

Rape Crisis Center of Wilmington
P.O. Box 1507
Wilmington, Delaware 19889
(302) 658-5011

DISTRICT OF COLUMBIA

Architecture

Washington Women in Architecture
Box 32074
Washington, D.C. 20007
  Linda Spottswood

Art

Adhibit Committee
c/o Rosemary Wright
6911 Fifth Street, Northwest
Washington, D.C. 20012

Foundry Gallery Cooperative
2121 P Street, Northwest
Washington, D.C. 20036

Local 1734 Art Collective
1734 Conneticut Avenue, Northwest
Washington, D.C. 20008

P Street Paper Works Collective
1743 Conneticut Avenue, Northwest
Washington, D.C. 20008
(202) 797-9264

Washington Women's Art Center
1821 Q Street, Northwest
Washington, D.C. 20009
(202) 332-2121

Womanspace
Marvin Center, Room 430
800 21st Street, Northwest
Washington, D.C. 20052
(202) 676-7554

Baby and Child Care

HOME (Home Oriented Maternity
   Experience)
Tacoma Park
511 New York Avenue
Washington, D.C. 20012

Business and Management

Interdepartmental Task Force on
   Women
1111 20th Street, Northwest, Suite
   3050
Washington, D.C. 20036
(202) 653-5406

The Network
c/o Lynne D. Finney
Director of Industry Development
Federal Home Loan Bank Board
1700 G Street, Northwest, 4th floor
Washington, D.C. 20552
(202) 377-6707

Women Managers
c/o Carol Parr
Women's Equity Action League
805 15th Street, Northwest
Washington, D.C. 20036

Washington Association of Women
   Business Owners
c/o Edie Fraser
Fraser Associates
1800 K Street, Northwest
Washington, D.C. 20006
(202) 452-1188

Communications and the Media

D.C. Feminist Writers Guild
c/o Michele Mager
8802 Plymouth Street, Apt. 5
Silver Springs, Maryland 20901
(301) 587-4042

Feminist Radio Network
Box 5537
Washington, D.C. 20016
(202) 244-2331
   Lynn Chadwick

Sophie's Parlor
1532 Varnum Street, Northwest
Washington, D.C. 20011

Washington, D.C., Women in Cable
c/o S. B. Craig
3406 Macomb Street, Northwest
Washington, D.C. 20016

Computer Science

Association for Women in Computing,
   Inc.
c/o Elizabeth Adams
Math/Statistics Computer Science
   Department
American University
Massachusetts and Nebraska Avenues,
   Northwest
Washington, D.C. 20016
(202) 686-2000

Ethnic and Minority Women

Inter-Agency Task Force on American
   Indian Women
c/o Mary Notani
Women's Bureau, Department of
   Labor
200 Constitution Avenue, Northwest
Washington, D.C. 20210
(202) 523-6642

Health

DES Action/Washington
P.O. Box 5311
Rockville, Maryland 20851
(301) 468-2170

Law

National Association of Black Women
   Attorneys
Charlotte Ray Chapter
805 Florida Avenue, Northwest
Washington, D.C. 20001
(202) 638-5110

Office and Clerical Workers

60 Words Per Minute
1346 Connecticut Avenue, Northwest
Washington, D.C. 20036
(202) 797-1384

Politics and Government

Congresswomen's Caucus
2471 Rayburn Building
Washington, D.C. 20515
(202) 225-6740
   Betty Dooley, Executive Director

Federal Women's Inter-Agency Board
451 17th Street, Southwest, Suite 3232
Washington, D.C. 20420

Women in Government
c/o Roberta Severo
BP North America, Inc.
1730 M Street, Northwest, Suite 901
Washington, D.C. 20036

Professional Wives

Congressional Wives Task Force
U.S. House of Representatives
Washington, D.C. 20515

Prostitutes

Spread Eagles
135 11th Street, Northwest
Washington, D.C. 20001
(202) 833-2634

Rape

Feminist Alliance Against Rape
Box 21033
Washington, D.C. 20009

Religious Groups

D.C. Women's Clergy Association
624 17th Street, Northeast
Washington, D.C. 20009
(202) 397-7209

Sports and Leisure

MAD (Men Are Dumb)
c/o Betsy Dirnberger
Corporation for Public Broadcasting
1111 Sixteenth Street, Northwest
Washington, D.C. 20036

Washington Runhers
c/o Caroline Hahn
4633 Seminary Road, Apt. 104
Alexandria, Virginia 22304

Theater and Performing Arts

Theatre of Sorts
3106 18th Street, Northwest
Washington, D.C. 20010
(202) 367-8677

Women's Rights and Political Issues

Capitol Hill Women's Political Caucus
319 Cannon House Office Building
Washington, D.C. 20515
(202) 225-2836

The Feminist Connection
c/o Mary Hilton, Deputy Director
Women's Bureau, Department of
   Labor
200 Constitution Avenue, Northwest
Washington, D.C. 20210
(202) 523-6612

HEW Feminist Network
c/o Cheryl Yakamoto
Hubert Humphrey Building
200 Independence Avenue, Southwest,
   Room 624D
Washington, D.C. 20201
(202) 245-8454

Washington Women's Network
1410 Q Street, Northwest
Washington, D.C. 20009
(202) 462-8606
   Gail Kelleher, Coordinator

FLORIDA

Art

Women's Caucus for Art
c/o Arlene Sierra
19420 Royal Birdale Drive
Miami, Florida 33015

Baby and Child Care

Birthplace, Inc.
635 Northeast First Street
Gainesville, Florida 32601
(904) 372-4784
　Judy Levy

Battered Women and Violence

Domestic Assault Shelter
c/o YWCA
901 South Olive Avenue
West Palm Beach, Florida 33401
(305) 833-2439

WATCH (Women Acting Together to
　Combat Harassment)
c/o Feminist Women's Health Center
1017 Thomasville Road
Tallahassee, Florida 32303

Business and Management

Florida Women's Network
c/o Nancy Ford
234 East Davis Boulevard
Tampa, Florida 33606

Miami Association of Women Business
　Owners
c/o Rita Boerst
Caribbean Title Insurance
10871 Caribbean Boulevard, Suite 204
Miami, Florida 33189
(305) 251-1447

Community Centers

The Women's Center of Tampa
1200 West Platt Street
Tampa, Florida 33606
(813) 251-4089

Health

ABCDE (Association for Breast Cancer
　Detection Earlier)
1110 South Dixie Highway
Coral Gables, Florida 33146

Feminist Women's Health Center
1017 Thomasville Road
Tallahassee, Florida 32303
(904) 224-9600
　Ann Haskell

Women's Center Health Group
Box 1350
Tampa, Florida 33601

Motherhood

MOTHER (Mothers of the Whole Earth
　Revolt)
c/o Feminist Women's Health Center
1017 Thomasville Road
Tallahassee, Florida 32303
(904) 224-9600

Prostitutes

Florida COYOTE
Box 22762
Fort Lauderdale, Florida 33335
(305) 462-5522

National Task Force on Prostitution
"Kiss and Tell" Campaign
c/o Darlene Lashman
Box 22762
Fort Lauderdale, Florida 33335
(305) 462-5522

Sports and Leisure

International Women's Fishing
Association
P.O. Box 2025
Palm Beach, Florida 33480

Senior Women's Tennis Association,
Inc.
First One In, Ltd.
112 Park Avenue, South
Winter Park, Florida 32789
(305) 644-0702

GEORGIA

Art

Atlanta Women's Art Collective
1759 Indiana Avenue, Northeast
Atlanta, Georgia 30307
(404) 881-1729
Callahan McDonough, Coordinator

Business and Management

Achievement for Women
c/o Diannacy Taylor
Suite 306B, Northside Tower
6065 Rosewell Road, Northeast
Atlanta, Georgia 30328

Film

Women in Film
Box 52726
Atlanta, Georgia 30355
Betty Jo Taylor, President

Health

Feminist Women's Health Center
580 14th Street, Northwest
Atlanta, Georgia 30318
(404) 874-7551

Law

Women Law Students Association
University of Georgia Law School
Athens, Georgia 30602
(404) 542-7669

Sports and Leisure

Women's Rugby Groups
c/o Bobbie McCracken
801 Michaels Street, Northeast
Atlanta, Georgia 30329

Theater and Performing Arts

Womansong
Box 15462
Atlanta, Georgia 30333

Women's Rights and Political Issues

Feminist Action Alliance
P.O. Box 54717, Civic Center Station
Atlanta, Georgia 30308
(404) 525-5138

HAWAII

Baby and Child Care

Informed Home Birth Group
c/o Annette Kaapana
45-342 Lilipuna, Apt. 202
Kaneohe, Hawaii 96744

Health

Women's Health Center
319 Paoakalani

Honolulu, Hawaii 96815
(808) 946-8844

Community Centers

University YWCA Women's Center
1820 University Avenue
Honolulu, Hawaii 96822
(808) 947-3351

IDAHO

Baby and Child Care

IDAHOMEBIRTHS
1815 West Washington Street
Boise, Idaho 83702

Business and Management

New Women Council
c/o Louise Jones
2309 Mountainview Drive
Boise, Idaho 83706
(208) 344-3263

Community Centers

Women's Center
University of Idaho
Moscow, Idaho 83843

Women's Resource Center
720 West Washington Street
Boise, Idaho 83669
(208) 243-3688

ILLINOIS

Advertising

Women's Advertising Club
c/o Jane Ellen Murray
J. Walter Thompson Company
875 North Michigan Avenue
Chicago, Illinois 60611
(312) 263-2215

Architecture

Chicago Women in Architecture
c/o Gunduz Dagdelen Ast
1750 North Clark Street, Warehouse
    Level 2
Chicago, Illinois 60614
(312) 642-6900

Art

Artist Residents of Chicago (ARC)
6 West Hubbard Street
Chicago, Illinois 60610
(312) 266-7607

Artemesia Gallery/Fund
9 West Hubbard Street
Chicago, Illinois 60610
(312) 751-2016

Women's Graphic Collective
1226 West Grace Street
Chicago, Illinois 60613
(312) 477-6070

Baby and Child Care

CHILD
c/o Mary Smith
40 North Lorel Street
Chicago, Illinois 60644

C-Section Experience
2908 West Greenleaf Street
Chicago, Illinois 60645
(312) 274-8777

Cesarean Support of Fox Valley
c/o Susy Stone
148 Long Beach Road
Aurora, Illinois 60538

Cesarean Support of the Western
    Suburbs
14 East 60th Street
Downers Grove, Illinois 60515
(312) 852-2042

Day Care Home Operators Association
of Illinois
c/o Betty J. Wisniewski
6832 Beckwith Road
Morton Grove, Illinois
(312) 966-4657

Springfield Area Day Care Home
Operators
4500 South Sixth Street
Springfield, Illinois 62706
(217) 786-6840

Battered Women

Battered Women's Support Group
Loop Center YWCA
37 South Wabash Avenue
Chicago, Illinois 60603
(312) 372-6600

Business and Management

American Business Women's
Association, Chicago Chapter
957 Montana Street
Chicago, Illinois 60614
(312) 947-3502

Bloomington/Normal Women's
Network
c/o Marie E. Grimmius
1311 Holiday Lane
Bloomington, Illinois 61701
(309) 662-5506

Chicago Finance Exchange
P.O. Box 49252
Chicago, Illinois 60649

The Chicago Network, Inc.
c/o Diann Smith
417 Roslyn Place
Chicago, Illinois 60614
(312) 929-3551

DuPage Women's Forum
c/o Focus on Women
College of DuPage
Glen Ellyn, Illinois 60137
(312) 858-2800, ext. 2519

Illinois Federation of Business and
Professional Women's Clubs
610 East Vine Street
Springfield, Illinois 62703
(217) 528-8985

International Association of Personnel
Women/Chicago Chapter
c/o Mildred Emery
Kemper Insurance
Long Grove, Illinois 60049
(312) 540-2193

International Organization of Women
Executives
1800 North 78th Court
Elmwood Park, Illinois 60635
(312) 456-1852

New Girl Network
42 East Superior Street
Chicago, Illinois 60611
(312) 266-9572

WOMAN (Woman, Owner, Manager,
Administrator, Networking)
c/o Coralee Kern
2520 North Lincoln Avenue, #60
Chicago, Illinois 60614
(312) 472-8116

Women in Management
1301 West 22nd Street, Suite 501
Oak Brook, Illinois 60531
(312) 968-8044

Women in Management
8845 Bronx Avenue
Skokie, Illinois 60077
(312) 967-5120, ext. 350

Women in Organizational
Development
c/o Nancy Miller
Women, Inc.
15 Spinning Wheel Road, Suite 14
Hinsdale, Illinois 60521
(312) 325-9770

The Women's Forum of Chicago
c/o Loop Center YWCA
37 South Wabash Avenue
Chicago, Illinois 60603
(312) 726-1194
    Rosemary Aitken

Business Owners and Entrepreneurs

Chicago Association of Women
    Business Owners
520 North Michigan Avenue
Chicago, Illinois 60611
(312) 467-0295
    Joan Buegen, President

Communications and the Media

Chicago Women in Broadcasting
c/o Sharon LeMaire
566 Central Street
Woodale, Illinois 60191

American Women in Radio and
    Television, Chicago Chapter
c/o Annette Minkalis
Association Films, Inc.
875 North Michigan Avenue
Chicago, Illinois 60611
(312) 266-8625

Women in Communications, Inc.
c/o Norma Green
Advertising Age
740 North Rush Street
Chicago, Illinois 60611
(312) 649-5266

Woman's Production Club
c/o Joan Luttge, President
D' Arcy-McManus & Massius, Inc.
200 East Randolph Street
Chicago, Illinois 60601
(312) 861-5000

Community Centers

McCambridge House Women's Center
c/o Mary Camp
723 Fifth Street
Springfield, Illinois 62703
(217) 544-8751

Midwest Women's Center
53 West Jackson Boulevard, Room 623
Chicago, Illinois 60604
(312) 663-4163
    Rebecca Sive-Tomashefsky,
        Executive Director

Quad Cities Women's Center
c/o Reba Stewart
400 16th Street
Rock Island, Illinois 61201
(309) 793-4095

Southwest Women Working Together
    (SWWT)
3201 West 63rd Street
Chicago, Illinois 60629
(312) 436-0550

Spoon River Book Co-operative
1131 South Grand Avenue, East
Springfield, Illinois 62702
(217) 523-5357

A Woman's Place
505 West Green Street
Urbana, Illinois 61801
(217) 384-4390

Women for Alternatives
306 North Cuyler Street
Oak Park, Illinois 60302
(312) 386-7165

Women's Center/Carbondale
408 West Freeman Street
Carbondale, Illinois 62901
(618) 529-2324

Crisis Centers

Crisis Advocates
c/o YWCA
220 East Chicago Street
Elgin, Illinois 60120
(312) 742-7930

Sojourn Women's Crisis Center, Inc.
915 North Seventh Street
Springfield, Illinois 62702
(217) 544-2484

Engineering

Society of Women Engineers
c/o Eleanor Bast
2 North 514 Valewood Road
West Chicago, Illinois 60185
(312) 231-3861

Ethnic and Minority Women

Alpha Kappa Alpha Sorority
c/o Anne Mitchem Davis
5211 South Greenwood Avenue
Chicago, Illinois 60615
(312) 684-1282

Lakeview Women's Programs
c/o Iris Bruno
Universidad Popular
3225 North Sheffield Street
Chicago, Illinois 60657
(312) 549-7550

League of Black Women
c/o Darlene L. Paris
4800 Chicago Beach Drive
Chicago, Illinois 60615

Mexican-American Women of Illinois
3618 West 26th Street
Chicago, Illinois 60623
(312) 521-7300

Mujeres Latinas en Accion
1823 West 17th Street
Chicago, Illinois 60616
(312) 226-1544

National Alliance of Black Feminists
202 South State Street, Suite 1024
Chicago, Illinois 60604
(312) 939-0107

National Hook-up of Black Women
c/o Arnita Boswell
University of Chicago
969 East 60th Street
Chicago, Illinois 60637
(312) 667-7693

Ukranian National Women's League
of America, Inc.
2218 West Chicago Avenue
Chicago, Illinois 60622
(312) 489-4230

Farm and Rural Women

Illinois Farm Bureau Women's
Committee
c/o Mary Anne Chevalier
1701 Towanda Avenue
P.O. Box 2901
Bloomington, Illinois 61701
(309) 828-0021

Fashion and Design

The Fashion Group of Chicago
c/o Dorie Bell
125 North Wabash Avenue
Chicago, Illinois 60602
(312) 782-7368

Women in Design
c/o Barbara Standish/Perceptions, Inc.
307 North Michigan Avenue
Chicago, Illinois 60601
(312) 782-5020

Film

Chicago Women's Video Group
c/o Denise Zaccardi
832 West Lakeside Avenue
Chicago, Illinois 60640
(312) 334-2976

Videopolis
2004 North Halsted Street
Chicago, Illinois 60614

Health

DES Action Group/Illinois
407 East Adams Street
Springfield, Illinois 62701

Suburban Women's Health Center
837 South Westmore Street
Lombard, Illinois 60148
(312) 495-9330

Homemakers and Domestic Workers

Wages for Housework
333 North Humphrey Street
Chicago, Illinois 60302
(312) 848-2879

Labor Movement

Coalition of Labor Union Women/
    Chicago Chapter
c/o Muriel Tuteur
323 South Ashland Street
Chicago, Illinois 60607
(312) 243-3147

Women Employed
5 South Wabash Avenue, Suite 415
Chicago, Illinois 60603
(312) 782-3902

Law

National Association of Women
    Lawyers
c/o American Bar Association
1155 East 60th Street
Chicago, Illinois 60637
(312) 947-4000

Women's Law Caucus
DePaul University
25 East Jackson Boulevard
Chicago, Illinois 60604
(312) 321-7700

Medicine

Women's Medical Organization,
    Women's Resource Center
Rockford School of Medicine
1601 Parkview Avenue
Rockford, Illinois 61101
(815) 987-7279

Women in Medicine Committee
American Medical Student Association
1171 Tower Road
Schaumburg, Illinois 60196

Motherhood

Feminist Family Forum
c/o Marilyn Salomon
2116 North Bissell Street
Chicago, Illinois 60614
(312) 929-0115

Parent Support Network
c/o Kitty Hall
1616 East 50th Place, Apt. 3E
Chicago, Illinois 60615
(312) 288-8729

Music

Women in Music
c/o Thelma L. Norris
1810 West Pratt Street
Chicago, Illinois 60626
(312) 761-8765

Politics and Government

Women's Caucus for Political Science,
    Midwest Region
c/o Irene Fraser Rothenberg
1942 Orrington Avenue
Evanston, Illinois 60201
(312) 475-3260

COWL (Conference of Women
    Legislators)
160 North LaSalle Street, Suite 1801
Chicago, Illinois 60601

Professional Women

Northwestern University's Professional
    Women's Association
2001 Sheridan Road
Evanston, Illinois 60201
(312) 274-7214

Rape

Rape Crisis Force of Lake County
1002 Valley Drive
Wildwood, Illinois 60030
(312) 367-1080

Champaign County Women Against
Rape
112 West Hill Street
Champaign, Illinois 61820
(217) 356-0731

Chicago Council on Crimes Against
Women
c/o Midwest Women's Center
53 West Jackson Boulevard, Room 623
Chicago, Illinois 60604
(312) 663-4163

Coalition of Concerned Women in the
War on Crime
c/o Curie Pennick
2412 South Michigan Avenue
Chicago, Illinois 60616
(312) 225-3700

Illinois Coalition of Women Against
Rape
c/o Mary Rogel
5655 South University Avenue
Chicago, Illinois 60637

Real Estate

WIRE (Women in Real Estate)
c/o Florence Hanson
6608 West Cermak Road
Berwyn, Illinois 60402
(312) 795-7100

Women's Council of Realtors
430 North Michigan Avenue
Chicago, Illinois 60611
(312) 440-8082

Religious Groups

Chicago Catholic Women
22 East Van Buren Street
Chicago, Illinois 60605
(312) 427-4351

Ecumenical Women's Center
1653 West School Street
Chicago, Illinois 60657
(312) 348-4970

Korean United Methodist Women
c/o Shinae Chun
Korean United Methodist Church
3246 West George Street
Chicago, Illinois 60618
(312) 463-2742

Leadership Conference of Women
Religious
3902 North Ridgeway Street
Chicago, Illinois 60618
(312) 478-6024

Ministry with Women Project
c/o The Wesley Foundation
1203 West Green Street
Urbana, Illinois 61801
(217) 344-1120

Network
22 East Van Buren
Chicago, Illinois 60605
(312) 427-4351

Women and the Ministry Support
Group
Bethany Theological Seminary
c/o Nancy Faus
Butterfield and Meyers Roads
Oak Brook, Illinois 60521
(312) 620-2241

Science

Women in Research
c/o Shirley Levis
1006 Dobson Street
Evanston, Illinois 60202
(312) 864-8641

Sports and Leisure

HER (Health Education Recreation
Enterprises)
541 Indian Hill Court
Naperville, Illinois 60540

International Net Set
c/o Jane Whitchurch, President
3263 Sprucewood Lane
Wilmette, Illinois 60091
(312) 251-1428

Midwest Women's Expedition
Exchange
c/o Loop Center YWCA
37 South Wabash Avenue
Chicago, Illinois 60603
(312) 372-6600

Midwest Women's Rugby Football
Union
c/o Elissa Augello
1117 Leonard Place
Evanston, Illinois 60201
(312) 864-3992

OLE! (Outdoor Learning Experiences)
c/o Hester Newcomb
1052 Conrad Court
Elk Grove, Illinois 60007
(312) 894-2494

Support Groups

AWARE
c/o Nancy Coates
612 Park Street
Batavia, Illinois 60510
(312) 584-0255

Lavender Prairie Collective
P.O. Box 2096, Station A
Champaign, Illinois 61801
(217) 352-2701 or 384-1905

Post-Masectomy Support Group
Loop Center YWCA
37 South Wabash
Chicago, Illinois 60603
(312) 372-6600

People's Resource Center
107 West Indiana Street
Wheaton, Illinois 60187
(312) 682-3844

Women Support Women Group
Ecumenical Women's Center
1653 West School Street
Chicago, Illinois 60657
(312) 348-4970

Theater and Performing Arts

Chicago Women's Theatre Group
c/o Marilyn Kollath, Executive
Director
7100 North Greenview Street
Chicago, Illinois 60626
(312) 973-7080

Women's Rights and Political Issues

Alton Equal Rights Amendment
Information Center
217 West 3rd Street
Alton, Illinois 62002
(618) 465-0280

The Center for a Woman's Own
Name
261 Kimberly Street
Barrington, Illinois 60010
(312) 381-2113

Evanston Women's Liberation Center
2214 Ridge Street
Evanston, Illinois 60201
(312) 475-4480

Fox Valley Women's Coalition
c/o Kane County Info
1035 East State Street
Geneva, Illinois 60134
(312) 232-9100
Genny Montes

Illinois Democratic Women's Caucus
c/o Marge Markin
1429 North Astor Street
Chicago, Illinois 60611
(312) 642-5551

Illinois Women's Agenda
c/o Midwest Women's Center
53 West Jackson Boulevard, Room 623
Chicago, Illinois 60604
(312) 663-4163
Ellen Benjamin

Illinois Women's Lobby
c/o Avis Rudner
950 West Washington
Oak Park, Illinois 60302
(312) 524-0869

Rockford Coalition
c/o WOMANSPACE Center
5350 East Springbrook Road
Rockford, Illinois 61111
(815) 877-0118

University of Chicago Feminist
Organization
c/o University of Chicago
1212 East 59th Street
Chicago, Illinois 60637
(312) 684-3189

Women in Affirmative Action
c/o Agnes Barclay
People's Gas, Light and Coke
Company
122 South Michigan Avenue, #708
Chicago, Illinois 60603
(312) 431-4658

WOMANSPACE Center
5350 Springbrook Road
Rockford, Illinois 61111
(815) 877-0118

Women's Studies and Education

Chicago Area Women's History
Conference
c/o Virginia Stewart
P.O. Box 4348
Chicago, Illinois 60680
(312) 996-2742

Chicago Area Women's Studies
Association
c/o Paula Wolff
Business and Management Department
Northeastern Illinois University
5500 North St. Louis Avenue
Chicago, Illinois 60625
(312) 583-4050, ext. 760

Council on Women's Programs
c/o Pat Handzel
Oakton Community College
7900 North Nagle Street
Morton Grove, Illinois 60053
(312) 967-5120, ext. 350

Illinois Education Association Women's
Caucus
100 East Edwards Street
Springfield, Illinois 62701
(217) 544-0706

INDIANA

Business and Management

Northwest Indiana Women's Bureau
34 Conkey Street
Hammond, Indiana 46320
(219) 937-2440

Community Centers

Everywoman's Center
6354 West 37th Street
Indianapolis, Indiana 46224
(317) 632-4637

Education

Ball State University Association for
Women Deans, Administrators
and Counselors
c/o Jean Helfron
Administration Building, Room 6
Ball State University
Muncie, Indiana 47306
(317) 285-6673

Health

Woman Alive
229 Ogden Street
Hammond, Indiana 46325
(219) 838-7707

Rape

Calumet Women United Against Rape
P.O. Box 2617
Gary, Indiana 46403
(219) 938-7000

IOWA

Baby and Child Care

Cesarean Support Group
c/o Center for Women
Briarcliff College
3303 Rebecca Street
Sioux City, Iowa 51104
(712) 279-5406
  Pat Kizzier

Business and Management

Executive Women's Breakfast Club
c/o Beverley Blessing and Diane
    Hockett
P.O. Box 5262
Des Moines, Iowa 50304

The Women's Resource and Action
    Center
130 North Madison Street
Iowa City, Iowa 52242
(319) 353-6265
  Mary Maxwell

Nexsus (Women's Breakfast Club)
c/o Betsy Bowles
Penguin Studio
2712 Kingman Boulevard
Des Moines, Iowa 50311

c/o Center for Women
Briarcliff College
3303 Rebecca Street
Sioux City, Iowa 51104
(712) 279-5406
  Pat Kizzier

Health

Emma Goldman Clinic for Women
215 North Dodge Street
Iowa City, Iowa 52240
(319) 331-2111

Encore
Sioux City YWCA
619 6th Street
Sioux City, Iowa 51101
(712) 258-0127

HERA
436 South Johnson Street
Iowa City, Iowa 50304

Low-Income Women

Women Aware
c/o Center for Women
Briarcliff College
3303 Rebecca Street
Sioux City, Iowa 51104
(712) 279-5406
  Pat Kizzier

Motherhood

After Care Support Group
c/o Catholic Charities
18th and Jackson Streets
Sioux City, Iowa 51104
(712) 252-4545

Earlybird Support Group
c/o Center for Women
Briarcliff College
3303 Rebecca Street
Sioux City, Iowa 51104
(712) 279-5406
  Pat Kizzier

мом (Moving On to Motherhood)
c/o Center for Women
Briarcliff College
3303 Rebecca Street
Sioux City, Iowa 51104
(712) 279-5406
  Pat Kizzier

Religious Groups

The Church of the Mother
P.O. Box 1544
Iowa City, Iowa 52240

Single Women's Group
c/o Catholic Charities
18th and Jackson Streets
Sioux City, Iowa 51104
(712) 252-4545
  Margaret Mangold

Widowed Women

Solitaires
c/o Center for Women
Briarcliff College
3303 Rebecca Street
Sioux City, Iowa 51104
(712) 279-5406
  Pat Kizzier

KANSAS

Community Centers

Women's Center of Topeka
1268 Western Street
Topeka, Kansas 66604
(913) 357-7650

Insurance

Insurance Women of Wichita
c/o Barbara Dole
714 Union Center
Wichita, Kansas 67202
(316) 267-9221

Peace and Home Association of
  Wichita

c/o Roxanne Meyer
135 South Minnesota Street
Wichita, Kansas 67211

Women's Rights and Political Issues

Alliance for Equality in Sports
c/o Jan Garton
1010 Karla Lane
Manhattan, Kansas 66502
(913) 537-8715

Kansas City Women's Liberation
  Union
3950 Rainbow Street
Kansas City, Kansas 66103
(913) 363-2864

KENTUCKY

Arts and Crafts

David Appalachian Crafts
St. Vincent's Mission
General Delivery
David, Kentucky 41616
(606) 886-2377
  Mary Pineau, Director of Crafts
  Program

Match, Inc.
P.O. Box 68
Berea, Kentucky 40403
(606) 986-8422
  Nina Poage

Battered Women

DASH, Inc. (Domestic Abuse Support
and Housing)
c/o Carol Ganom
Mountain Comprehensive Care
Prestonburg, Kentucky 41653

Underground Network for Battered
Women
c/o Jo Broomsa
Rural Route 5, Box 97-A
Inez, Kentucky 41224

Business and Management

Business and Professional Women's
Group
c/o Elaine Musselman, Managing
Director
Harris and Company
9th Floor, Starks Building
Louisville, Kentucky 40202
(502) 584-2193

Community Centers

Brescia Women's Center
120 West 7th Street
Owensboro, Kentucky 42310
(502) 685-3132

Women's Center
Alternatives for Women

1628 South Limestone, Suite 301
Lexington, Kentucky 40508

Farm and Rural Women

The Fellowship Center
528 Main Street
Williamsburg, Kentucky 40769
(606) 549-1617
    Marion Colette

Health

Mud Creek Health Project
Box 170
Craynor, Kentucky 41614
(606) 587-2209
    Eula Hall, Administrator

New Womankind
P.O. Box 18102
Beuchel, Kentucky 40218

Women's Rights and Political Issues

Kentucky Women's Agenda Coalition
934 Breckenridge Lane
Louisville, Kentucky 40207
    Pam Elam or Allie C. Hixson

Kentucky Women's Rights
    Organization
P.O. Box 128
Prestonburg, Kentucky 41653

LOUISIANA

Battered Women and Crime

Women Against Crime
2001 Canal Street
New Orleans, Louisiana 70112
(504) 529-3232

Community Centers

Loyola University Women's Center
6363 St. Charles Avenue
New Orleans, Louisiana 70118
(504) 865-3625
    Carol Mawson, Director

Health

New Orleans Women's Health
    Collective
1117 Decatur Street
New Orleans, Louisiana 70116

Law

Association for Women Attorneys
P.O. Box 51262
New Orleans, Louisiana 70152
(504) 524-4302
    Dorothy Waldrut, President

Medicine

New Orleans Chapter/American
   Medical Women's Association
c/o Dr. Marilyn Skinner, President
1527 Antoine Street
New Orleans, Louisiana 70115
(504) 891-3001

Support

Southern Mutual Help Association
212 North Hebert Street
Jeanerette, Louisiana 70544

MAINE

Baby and Child Care

Maine Access to Alternatives in
   Childbirth
R.F.D. 1, Box 74
Dixmont, Maine 04932
(207) 257-3943
   Ariel Wilcox

Battered Women

Spruce Run Association
44 Central Street
Bangor, Maine 04401
(207) 947-0496

Communications and the Media

Women's Media Network
c/o Karen Saum
Box 111
Hope, Maine 04847

Divorced and Widowed Women

Transit
22 Monument Square
Portland, Maine 04111
(207) 773-7123

Health

Maine Feminist Health Project
183 Water Street
Augusta, Maine 04330

Maine Feminist Health Project
105 Dresden Avenue
Gardiner, Maine 04345

Maine Health Collective
c/o Donna Roux
Box 472
York Beach, Maine 03910

Portland Women's Health Council
Box 8335
Portland, Maine 04102

Lesbian Women

Maine Lesbian Feminists
Box 125
Belfast, Maine 04915

Sports and Leisure

Women's Rugby Groups
c/o Pat Cribby
59 Parrott Street
South Portland, Maine 04106

Women's Rights and Political Issues

Women's Lobby
P.O. Box 15
Hallowell, Maine 04347

MARYLAND

Art

Baltimore Women's Art Community
1110 St. Paul Street
Baltimore, Maryland 21201
    S. B. Sowbel and Susan Waters-Eller

Baby and Child Care

Birth
1304 Ludlow Drive
Temple Hills, Maryland 20031

Battered Women

House of Ruth
P.O. Box 7276
Baltimore, Maryland 21218
(301) 889-RUTH
    Mary Louise Mussoline, Director

Business and Management

Executive Women's Council, Greater
    Baltimore
c/o Eastford Professional Services
304 West Chesapeake Avenue
Towson, Maryland 21204
(301) 825-7841

Executive Women's Network
New Directions for Women
2517 North Charles Street
Baltimore, Maryland 21216
(301) 366-8570
    Marian Goetze, Coordinator

Community Centers

New Responses
6509 Westland Road
Bethesda, Maryland 20034
(301) 530-1584

Women's Growth Center
339 East 25th Street
Baltimore, Maryland 21218
(301) 366-4769

A Woman's Place
150 Maryland Avenue
Rockville, Maryland 20850
(301) 424-0727

Women Together
5609 Cross Country Boulevard
Baltimore, Maryland 21209
(301) 367-7262

Divorced and Widowed Women

Maryland Center for Displaced
    Homemakers
737A Park Avenue
Baltimore, Maryland 21217

Ethnic and Minority Women

Black Feminist Speakers
c/o Beverly Smith
149 Windsor Street, Apt. 3
Cambridge, Maryland 02139

Health

Rural Health Research/BCHS/PHS
5600 Fisher's Lane
Rockville, Maryland 20852

Labor Movement

Women Employed in Baltimore
12 East 25th Street
Baltimore, Maryland 21218
(301) 889-6677
    Diane Tiechart

Politics and Government

Maryland Association of Elected
    Women
c/o Bert Booth
Delegate, General Assembly
309 Lowe House Office Building
Annapolis, Maryland 21401
(301) 269-2545

Prostitutes

HUM (Hookers Union of Maryland)
70 West Franklin Street
Hagerstown, Maryland 21740
(301) 733-4577

Women's Rights and Political Issues

Self Help for Equal Rights
P.O. Box 105

Garrett Park, Maryland 20766
(202) 496-5056

Women's Coalition of Howard County
c/o Human Rights Commission
8950 Route 108, Gorman Plaza, Room 214
Columbus, Maryland 21044
(202) 997-7600

MASSACHUSETTS

Abortion

Abortion Action Coalition
P.O. Box 2727
Boston, Massachusetts 02208

Art

Boston Area Women's Artists
c/o Colleen T. McGee
10 Peabody Street
Newton, Massachusetts 02158

Boston Women's Graphic Collective
69 Harvey Street
North Cambridge, Massachusetts 02138
(617) 661-1559
    Nancy Sableski
    (617) 876-2446

National Center for Women in the Performing and Media Arts
Emerson College
Boston, Massachusetts 02116
(617) 267-6038

WEB (Women Exhibiting in Boston)
88 Calumet Street
Roxbury Crossing, Massachusetts 02120
    Sandra Nossiter and Connie Trowbridge Albrecht

Baby and Child Care

Birth Day
128 Lowell Avenue
Newtonville, Massachusetts 02160

COPE (Coping with the Overall Pregnancy Experience)
37 Clarendon Street
Boston, Massachusetts 02116
(617) 357-5588

Homebirth
89 Franklin Street, Suite 200
Boston, Massachusetts 02110

Business and Management

Boston Luncheon Club
c/o Deane Laycock, Trust Officer
Fiduciary Trust Company
P.O. Box 1647
Boston, Massachusetts 02105
(617) 482-5270

Women's Lunch Group
c/o Nancy Korman
35 Wykeham Road
West Newton, Massachusetts 02165
(617) 969-3678

Women's Network Luncheon
Middlesex Community College
Divison of Community Services
P.O. Box T
Bedford, Massachusetts 01730
(617) 275-1590
    Barbara Sherman, Coordinator

Business Owners and Entrepreneurs

Boston Association of Women Business
  Owners
c/o Florence M. Berke, President
16 Coolidge Road
Marblehead, Massachusetts 01945
(617) 227-2525

Women's Entrepreneurs Club
c/o Holly Alderman
Armitage Press
18 Brattle Street, Room 253
Cambridge, Massachusetts 02138
(617) 613-4824

Community Centers

Women's Center
15 Chestnut Street
New Bedford, Massachusetts 02747
(617) 996-3341

Valley Women's Center
200 Main Street
Northampton, Massachusetts 01060

Education

New England Minority Women
  Administrators
c/o Carol Carter
University of Massachusetts at Amherst
New Africa House, Room 218
Amherst, Massachusetts 01003
(413) 545-0131

Film

Feminist Film Project
c/o Thalia Films
20 Boylston Street
Cambridge, Massachusetts 02138
  Lynne Conroy

Film Women of Boston
355 Boylston Street
Boston, Massachusetts 02117
(617) 267-9617

Health

Athol Women's Health Center Group
235 Main Street
Athol, Massachusetts 01331

Boston Women's Health Book
  Collective
Box 192
West Somerville, Massachusetts 02144
(617) 924-0271
  Judy Norsigian

DES Action/Massachusetts
P.O. Box 117
Brookline, Massachusetts 02146

Framingham Women's Health Project
73 Union Avenue
Framingham, Massachusetts 01701

Resolve
c/o Barbara Eck Menning
P.O. Box 474
Belmont, Massachusetts 02178
(617) 484-2424

Salem Women's Health Collective
140 Washington Street
Salem, Massachusetts 01970

Somerville Women's Health Project
326 Somerville Avenue
Somerville, Massachusetts 02143

Women's Community Health Center
639 Massachusetts Avenue, Room 210
Cambridge, Massachusetts 02139

*Homemakers and Domestic
  Workers*

Wages for Housework
P.O. Box 94
Brighton, Massachusetts 02135
(617) 782-7685

Labor Movement

Worcester Women Working
306 Main Street
Worcester, Massachusetts 01608
  Maureen Sweeney

Law

Massachusetts Women Lawyers
    Association
c/o Kathy Clements
8 Beacon Street
Boston, Massachusetts 02108
(617) 723-4688

Lesbian Women

Gay Professors Women's Association
P.O. Box 308, Boston University
    Station
Boston, Massachusetts 02115

Pomegranate Productions
Box 7222
Watertown, Massachusetts 02172
(617) 924-0336

Motherhood

Mother's Morning Out, North
c/o Maria Anastasi
1332 Hanover Street
Boston, Massachusetts 02113
(617) 742-9570

Music

Arlington Street Women's Caucus
Box 297
Arlington, Massachusetts 02174
(617) 887-8229
    Ruth Evans

Office and Clerical Workers

9 to 5
140 Clarendon Street
Boston, Massachusetts 02116
(617) 536-6003
    Ellen Cassidy

12 to 1
111-A Draper Hall
University of Massachusetts
Amherst, Massachusetts 01003

Politics and Government

WEMO (Women Elected Municipal
    Officials)
Massachusetts League of Cities and
    Towns
6 Beacon Street
Boston, Massachusetts 02108
(617) 742-2334

Prostitutes

PUMA, Inc.
102 Charles Street, Room 780
Boston, Massachusetts 02114

Religious Groups

Unitarian Universalist Women's
    Federation
25 Beacon Street
Boston, Massachusetts 02108

Sports and Leisure

Artemis Institute
22 Ashcroft Road
Medford, Massachusetts 02155
(617) 395-6877
    Dana Densmore

Earthwatch
10 Juniper Road, Box 127 WW
Belmont, Massachusetts 02178
(617) 489-3030

The Infinite Odyssey
571 Grant Street
Waltham, Massachusetts 02154
(617) 899-6050

National Women's Bowling Association
c/o Debbie Ayars
370 J Montague Road
Sunderland, Massachusetts 01375

Women's Athletic Club
Boston YWCA
140 Clarendon Street
Boston, Massachusetts 02116
(617) 536-7940

Women Martial Arts Teachers
c/o Dana Densmore
22 Ashcroft Road
Medford, Massachusetts 02155
(617) 395-6877

Theater and Performing Arts

Women's Theatre Division of Reality
   Theatre
c/o Linda Putnam
539 Tremont Street
Boston, Massachusetts 02116
(617) 524-0028

Women's Theatre Group
c/o Everywoman Center
506 Goodell Hall
University of Massachusetts at Amherst
Amherst, Massachusetts 01002
(413) 545-0883
   Annette Townley

Women's Rights and Political Issues

Origins
169 Boston Street
Salem, Massachusetts 01970
(617) 745-5873

Women's Advocacy Service
Box 45
West Tisbury, Massachusetts 02575

Women's Studies and Education

Cambridge–Goddard Feminist Studies
5 Upland Road
Cambridge, Massachusetts 02139

CONCERNS (The Committee for the
   Concerns of New England
   Colleges and Universities)
c/o HERS
Wellesley College
Wellesley, Massachusetts 02181
(617) 235-7173

HERS New England (Higher Education
   Resource Service)
Cheever House
Wellesley College
Wellesley, Massachusetts 02181
(617) 235-7173 or 235-0320, ext. 789
   Dr. Lilli Hornig

Women's Educational Center
46 Pleasant Street
Cambridge, Massachusetts 02139
(617) 354-8807

Women's Inner-City Educational
   Resource Service
134 Warren Street
Roxbury, Massachusetts 02119
(617) 442-9150

MICHIGAN

Art

Women's Caucus for Art
c/o Elaine Godfrey
87 Carriage Way
Ypsilanti, Michigan 48197

Baby and Child Care

The Birth Center
c/o Kellog & Sinclair
141 West Margaret Street
Detroit, Michigan 48203

International Childbirth Education
   Network
c/o Jane Wirth
5701 Perrine Road
Midland, Michigan 48640
(515) 631-5198

Battered Women

Everywoman's Place
23 Strong Street
Muskegon, Michigan 49441
(616) 726-4493

Business and Management

New Girls Network
c/o Eleanor Luedtke
4001 West McNichols Road
Detroit, Michigan 48221
(313) 222-5391

Communications and the Media

Women's Media Center
Michigan Union, Room 337
Ann Arbor, Michigan 48104

Community Centers

Women's Resource Center
226 Bostwick Street
Grand Rapids, Michigan 49503
(616) 456-8571

Health

ALMA (American Lesbian Medical
   Association)
c/o Ambitious Amazons
P.O. Box 811
East Lansing, Michigan 48823

Community Women's Clinic
c/o Women's Crisis Center
306 North Division Street
Ann Arbor, Michigan 48104

Detroit Women's Health Project
18700 Woodward Street
Detroit, Michigan 48203

DES Action/Michigan
P.O. Box 66
East Lansing, Michigan 48823

Feminist Women's Health Center
15251 West Eight Mile Road
Detroit, Michigan 48235
(313) 341-5666

Feminist Self-Help Center
5325 South Cedar Street
Lansing, Michigan 48910

HER-SELF
225 East Library Street
Ann Arbor, Michigan 48108
   Kay Weiss

Lesbian Women

Lesbian Connection
P.O. Box 811
East Lansing, Michigan 48823
(517) 371-5257

Prostitutes

Alleycat
Prostitution Education Project
P.O. Box 1824
Ann Arbor, Michigan 48106
(313) 428-7233

CUPIDS (Citizens to Upgrade
   Prostitution in Detroit and
   Suburbs)
c/o Alleycat
P.O. Box 1824
Ann Arbor, Michigan 48106
(313) 428-7233 or 663-3809

Women's Rights and Political Issues

Women's Mobilization Collective
317 Braun Court
Ann Arbor, Michigan 46107

Women United for Action
103 Alexandrine Street
Detroit, Michigan 48201

MINNESOTA

Art

WARM: A Women's Collective Art
Space
414 First Avenue, North
Minneapolis, Minnesota 55403
(612) 332-5672
Diane E. Gorney, Coordinator

Twin Cities Women's Graphics
Collective
2953 Bloomington Avenue, South
Minneapolis, Minnesota 55411

Baby and Child Care

Genesis
5101 Queen Avenue South
Minneapolis, Minnesota 55410

Business and Management

AGOG (All the Good Old Girls)
c/o Pat Bengsten
603 Second Street, South
Mankato, Minnesota 56001
(507) 345-4629

AGOG (All the Good Old Girls)
P.O. Box 20121
Minneapolis, Minnesota 55420
(612) 888-6234
Ann Peterson, Executive Director

Minneapolis/St. Paul Association of
Women Business Owners
c/o Marlene Johnson, President
Split Infinitives
400 Sibley Street
St. Paul, Minnesota 55101
(612) 291-7400

Community Centers

St. Cloud Area Women's Center
1900 Minnesota Boulevard
St. Cloud, Minnesota 56301
(612) 252-8831

Twin Cities Women
430 Oak Grove Street, B-10
Minneapolis, Minnesota 55403
(612) 871-2555

Health

Elizabeth Blackwell Clinic
2000 South 5th Street
Minneapolis, Minnesota 55405

Sports and Leisure

Women's Advocates
584 Grand Avenue
St. Paul, Minnesota 55105

Woodswomen
3716 4th Avenue, South
Minneapolis, Minnesota 55409
(612) 825-1131 or 882-1868

Theater and Performing Arts

At the Foot of the Mountain Collective
c/o Aurora Bingham
3144 Tenth Avenue, South
Minneapolis, Minnesota 55407
(612) 871-2102

Circle of the Witch Collective
2953 Bloomington Avenue, South
Minneapolis, Minnesota 55407
(612) 729-6200

Minnesota Dance Support Network
616 8th Street, Southeast
Minneapolis, Minnesota 55414

Women in Performing Arts
4208 Nawadaha Boulevard
Minneapolis, Minnesota 55406

Women's Studies and Education

Emma Willard Task Force on
Education
University Station
P.O. Box 14229
Minneapolis, Minnesota 55414

MISSISSIPPI

Civic and Cultural Groups

Mississippi Society of Colonial Dames
of the XVII Century
c/o Mrs. Bruce H. Nicholson
5614 Brentwood Street
Jackson, Mississippi 39211
(601) 956-2508

Community Centers

Jackson Women's Center
P.O. Box 3234
Jackson, Mississippi 39207

Lowell Women's Center
Route 1, Box 975
Ruleville, Mississippi 38971

Ethnic and Minority Women

National Council of Negro Women,
Mississippi Section
c/o Mrs. Nellie M. Adams
303 Jefferson Avenue
Okolona, Mississippi 38860

Lesbian Women

Lesbian Front
P.O. Box 8342
Jackson, Mississippi 39204

Women's Rights and Political Issues

Women for Progress
c/o Dorothy Stewart
110 Malvern Place
Jackson, Mississippi 39206
(601) 981-2774

MISSOURI

Art

Community of Women Artists
c/o M. Durham
6609 Clemens Street
St. Louis, Missouri 63130

Women's Caucus for Art
c/o Rosalind Kimball Moulton
402 North Ann Street
Columbia, Missouri 65201

Women's Caucus for Art
c/o Natalie Cain
5320 Holmes Street
Kansas City, Missouri 64110
(816) 523-5260

Baby and Child Care

Golden Light Birthing
c/o Mau Blossom
Route 6
Doniphan, Missouri 63935
(314) 996-3339

Business and Management

American Business Women's
Association
9100 Word Parkway
Kansas City, Missouri 64114
(816) 361-6621
Ruth Bufton, Executive Director

St. Louis Women's Commerce
Association
c/o Linda Barton
The Works
4746 McPherson
St. Louis, Missouri 63108
(314) 361-1800

Business Owners and Entrepreneurs

St. Louis Association of Women
Business Owners
c/o Carolyn O'Brien
Shamrock Investment
P.O. Box 28412
St. Louis, Missouri 63141
(314) 586-4549

Health

St. Louis Women's Health Collective
Women's Resource Center
Box 1182
St. Louis, Missouri 63130

Music

Women's Jazz Festival, Inc.
c/o Dianne Gregg, President
P.O. Box 22321
Kansas City, Missouri 64113
(816) 361-1901

Politics and Government

Women into Public Leadership
c/o Marjorie Allen
Allendale
14601 Holmes Street
Kansas City, Missouri 64165

Prostitutes

OCELOT
3932 Warwick #6
Kansas City, Missouri 64111
(816) 753-7638

MONTANA

Baby and Child Care

BABIES (Better Alternative Birth
    Education, Information, and
    Services)
355 Montana Street, #7E
Missoula, Montana 59801
(406) 728-9589

Community Centers

Women's Place
1130 West Broadway
Missoula, Montana 59801
(406) 243-7606

Farm and Rural Women

Focus on Women
Montana State University
Bozeman, Montana 59717
(406) 994-2012
    Scotty Giebink, Director

Women's Studies and Education

Bitterroot Educational Resources for
    Women
315 South 4th Street
Missoula, Montana 59801

NEBRASKA

Business and Management

The Twig Daniels Group
c/o Judy Wesley
1630 Q Street
Lincoln, Nebraska 68508
(402) 475-8048

Communications and the Media

Women's Communication Center
1432 North Street
Lincoln, Nebraska 68508

Divorced and Widowed Women

Nebraska Legislative Task Force on
    Displaced Homemakers
c/o Nebraska Commission on the
    Status of Women
301 Centennial Mall
Lincoln, Nebraska 68509
(402) 471-2039
    Ina Mae Rouse, President

Support Groups

Women's Support Group Program
c/o YWCA
1432 N Street
Lincoln, Nebraska 68508
(402) 432-2802

Women's Rights and Political Issues

The Telephone Tree of the Nebraska
    Coalition for Women
c/o Ada Munson, State Chair
7340 Englewood Drive
Lincoln, Nebraska 68510
(402) 489-7207

Women's Legislative Network
League of Women Voters
1614 N Street
Lincoln, Nebraska 68508
(402) 475-1411
    Ann Wilson

Women's Studies and Education

Women's Study Group
Doane College
Crete, Nebraska 68333
(402) 826-2161

NEVADA

Battered Women

Committee to Aid Abused Women
1235 Pyramid Way
Sparks, Nevada 89431
(702) 358-4150
    Joni Kaiser, Director

Health

Community Action Self-Help
960 West Owens Street
Las Vegas, Nevada 89106

NEW HAMPSHIRE

Community Centers

Concord Women's Center
8 North Main Street
Concord, New Hampshire 03301
(603) 224-4104

Every Women's Center
c/o YMCA
72 Concord Street
Manchester, New Hampshire 03101

Women's Resource Center of the
    YWCA
40 Merrimac Street
Portsmouth, New Hampshire 03801
(603) 436-0162

Divorced and Widowed Women

Institute for the Study of Women in
    Transition
5 Market Street
Portsmouth, New Hampshire 03801
(603) 436-8071
    Betty Daniel-Green

Health

New Hampshire Feminist Health
    Center
38 South Main Street
Concord, New Hampshire 03301

New Market Health Center
84 Main Street
New Market, New Hampshire 03857
(603) 659-3106

Labor Movement

New Hampshire Association of
    Working Women
8 North Street
Concord, New Hampshire 03301

Politics

Another Place
Route 123
Greenville, New Hampshire 03048
(603) 878-1510

NEW JERSEY

Art

Women's Caucus for Art
c/o Judith Brodsky
59 Castle Howard Court
Princeton, New Jersey 08540
(609) 921-3348

Baby and Child Care

Maternal and Infant Care Consumer
    Coalition
c/o Allison Wachstein
45 Rock Spring Avenue
West Orange, New Jersey 07052
(201) 731-6212

Business and Management

New Jersey Association of Women
    Business Owners
c/o Elizabeth T. Lyons, President
1050 George Street, No. 3L
New Brunswick, New Jersey 08901

Community Centers

Alternatives for Women NOW
517 Penn Street
Camden, New Jersey 08102
(609) 964-8033

The Women's Advisory Exchange
11 Green Hill Road
Madison, New Jersey 07940
(201) 377-9031

The Women's Center of Morris
c/o Morristown Unitarian Fellowship
812 Normandy Heights Road
Morristown, New Jersey 07960
(201) 267-0484

Women's Center of Unitarian House
    for People
Whittredge Road
Summit, New Jersey 07901
(201) 273-2383

Education

Women Educators
P.O. Box 218
Red Bank, New Jersey 07701
(201) 671-1344
    Dr. Patricia B. Campbell

Politics and Government

New Jersey Women Elected Officials
c/o Bernice Davis
Councilwoman of East Orange and
    Essex County Freeholder
Hall of Records
Newark, New Jersey 07102
(201) 961-7057

Prostitutes

HUSH (Help Undo Sexual Hypocrisy)
Box 1924
Atlantic City, New Jersey 08401

Women's Rights and Political Issues

Center for the American Woman and
    Politics
Eagleton Institute of Politics
Rutgers University
New Brunswick, New Jersey 08901
(201) 828-2210
    Kathy Stanwick, Project Director

NEW MEXICO

Art

New Mexico Women in the Arts
c/o Janice Raithel
Department of Art
University of New Mexico
Albuquerque, New Mexico 87131
(505) 277-5861

Baby and Child Care

ABBE (Association for Better Birth
    Experiences)
Box 374
Alamogordo, New Mexico 88310
(505) 437-4658
  Beth Farell

Southwest Maternity Center
504 Luna Southwest
Albuquerque, New Mexico 87102
(505) 243-5584
  Mary Helen Carroll, Director

Battered Women

Battered Women's Project
P.O. Box 1501
Sante Fe, New Mexico 87501
  Cynthia Dames

Film

New Mexico Feminist Filmmakers
    Collective
302 First Northern Plaza East
Sante Fe, New Mexico 87501

Health

Women's Health Services
700 Franklin Street
Sante Fe, New Mexico 87501

NEW YORK

CARASA (Coalition for Abortion Rights
    and Against Sterilization Abuse)
P.O. Box 124, Cathedral Station
New York, New York 10025

Women's Abortion Action Alliance
150 Fifth Avenue, Room 315
New York, New York 10011

Architecture

Alliance of Women in Architecture
Box 5136, FDR Station
New York, New York 10022

Archive of Women in Architecture
The Architecture League of New York
41 East 65th Street
New York, New York 10021
  Marita O'Hare

Art

AROW (Art Resources Open to
    Women)
348 State Street, 2nd Floor
Schenectady, New York 12305
(518) 346-5101
  Pallas C. Lombardi and Janice
  Willard

Central Hall Artists
52 Main Street
Port Washington, New York 11050
(516) 883-9700
  Helen Meyrowitz

Creative Women's Collective
236 West 27th Street, 12th Floor
New York, New York 10001
(212) 924-0665
  Jacqueline Skiles

The Exhibitionists
92-20 Union Hall Street
Jamaica, New York 11432
(212) 658-7439

The Feminist Art Studio
136 East State Street
Ithaca, New York 14850
  Anne Rhodes

The Feminist School
601 Allen Street
Syracuse, New York 13210
  Joan Lukas Rothenberg

Floating Gallery
579 Broadway
New York, New York 10012
(212) 966-5215
  Donna Marxer

The Independent Artists Group
40 Lovell Road
New Rochelle, New York 10804
(914) 633-8475
  Roslyn Kirsch

The New York Feminist Art Institute
P.O. Box 798, Canal Street Station
New York, New York 10013

New York Society of Women Artists
45 East 89th Street
New York, New York 10028
  Nancy Dryfoos

The Nine Plus or Minus
48 Grand Street
New York, New York 10013

Soho 20
99 Spring Street
New York, New York 10012
(212) 226-4167
  Marjorie Abramson

Where We At Black Women Artists
103 Broadway
Brooklyn, New York 11211
(212) 388-7230
  Kay Brown, Coordinator

The Woman's Salon
c/o Sallie Finch Reynolds
24 Bay Avenue
Sea Cliff, New York 11579

Women Artists in Brooklyn
899 East 21st Street
Brooklyn, New York 11210
(212) 859-4447
  June Blum

Women in the Arts Foundation
435 Broome Street
New York, New York 10013
(212) 966-5894

Women's Caucus for Art
c/o Kathy Schnapper
340 West 28th Street, 20B
New York, New York 10001

The Women's Forum: Women at the
    Metropolitan Museum of Art
Fifth Avenue and 82nd Street
New York, New York 10028

The Women's Interart Center
549 West 52nd Street
New York, New York 10019

The Women's Studio Workshop
Box V
Rosendale, New York 12472

Baby and Child Care

Association of Mothers for Educated
    Childbirth
1161 Beach and 9th Street
Far Rockaway, New York 11691

Lay Non-Medical Midwives for
    Natural Homebirth
1364 East 7th Street
Brooklyn, New York 11230

Battered Women

New York Coalition for Battered
    Women
15 Rutherford Place
New York, New York 10003

Business and Management

Albany Women's Forum
c/o Pat McCord
Albany City Mental Health Association
75 New Scotland Avenue, Room 155
Albany, New York 12208
(518) 462-5439

The Director's Research Committee of
the Financial Women's
Association of New York
P.O. Box 5303, Grand Central Station
New York, New York 10017

The Fashion Group of New York
9 Rockefeller Plaza
New York, New York 10020
(212) 247-3940
Lee Ennis, Executive Director

Federation of Women Shareholders of
American Business
P.O. Box 190, Grand Central Station
New York, New York 10017
Wilma Soss, Director

Financial Women's Association
c/o Susan Fisher
Wells, Rich, Greene
767 Fifth Avenue
New York, New York 10022
(212) 758-4300 or 759-6554

Fortune 500 Business and Professional
Women's Club
P.O. Box 3057, Grand Central Station
New York, New York 10017
(212) 734-8160

In-House Network of the Equitable
Life Assurance Society
c/o Alina Novak
1285 Avenue of the Americas
New York, New York 10019
(212) 921-3005

Wise Women Institute
P.O. Box 297, West Station,
New York, New York 10014

Women's Economic Roundtable
c/o Susan Fisher
Wells, Rich, Greene
767 Fifth Avenue
New York, New York 10022
(212) 758-4300 or 759-6554

Women's Forum, Inc.
221 East 71st Street
New York, New York 10021
(212) 535-9840

Business Owners and Entrepreneurs

New York Association of Women
Business Owners
c/o Karen Olson
Home Life Insurance
110 East 95th Street
New York, New York 10022
(212) 688-0615

Westchester County Association of
Women Business Owners
Malorie Edelson
25 Bellwood Road
White Plains, New York 10603
(914) 592-3188

Communications and the Media

New York Feminist Writers' Guild
c/o Ellen Frankfort
682 Broadway
New York, New York 10012

Women in New Directions
50 Bellport Lane
Bellport, New York 11713

Women's Media Group
P.O. Box 2119, Grand Central Station
New York, New York 10017

Women's Writers' Center, Inc.
Williams Hall
Cazenovia College
Cazenovia, New York 13035
(315) 655-3466, ext. 138

Community Centers

All the Queen's Women
36-23 164th Street
Flushing, New York 10027
(212) 359-9204

Brookhaven Woman's Center
320 Main Street
Port Jefferson, New York 11777
(516) 473-8663

Brooklyn in Touch
c/o Natalie Abatemarco
261 Fourth Avenue
Brooklyn, New York 11215
(212) 857-7171

The Feminist Center for Human
    Growth and Development
303 Lexington Avenue
New York, New York 10016
(212) 686-0869

Islip Women's Center
855 Montauk Highway
Oakdale, New York 11796
(516) 589-7188

Nassau Center for Neighborhood
    Women
c/o Ellen Meade
1 Hillvale Road
Albertson, New York 11507
(516) 621-4587

Westchester County Women's Center
West 2nd Street and South 6th Avenue
Mount Vernon, New York 11101
(914) 664-7988

The Women's Center
Barnard College
606 West 120th Street
New York, New York 10027

The Women's Center of the Riverside
    Church
490 Riverside Drive
New York, New York 10027
(212) 749-7000

The Women's Center of Yonkers
38 Palisade Avenue
Yonkers, New York 10701
(914) 969-5800

Consumer Action

CAN (Consumer Action Now)
355 Lexington Avenue, 16th Floor
New York City, New York 10017
(212) 682-8915
    Lola Redford, President

Employment

Everywoman Opportunity Center, Inc.
190 Franklin Street
Buffalo, New York 14201
    Betsey Hopkins, Executive Director

Ethnic, Minority, and Neighborhood Women

Carroll Gardens Neighborhood
    Women
c/o Connie Noschic
386 Sackett Street
Brooklyn, New York 11231
(212) 624-3475

National Council of Negro Women's
    Center
198 Broadway
New York, New York 10038
(212) 964-8934

Williamsburg–Greenpoint
    Neighborhood Women
c/o Elizabeth Speranza
60 Conselyea Street
Brooklyn, New York 11211
(212) 782-1889

Film

Association of Independent Video and
    Filmmakers
99 Prince Street
New York, New York 10012
(212) 966-0900

The Collective for Living Cinema
52 White Street
New York, New York 10013
(212) 925-2111
  Renee Shafransky

Women Artist Filmmakers
69 Mercer Street
New York, New York 10012
(212) 966-5944
  Alida Walsh

Health

Buffalo Women's Self-Help Clinic
c/o Buffalo Women's Center
498 Franklin Street
Buffalo, New York 14212

Chelsea Women's Health Team
188 Eighth Avenue
New York, New York 10011

DES Action/New York
Long Island Jewish Hillside Medical
  Center
New Hyde Park, New York 11040

DES-Watch
P.O. Box 141
Jericho, New York 11753

DES-Watch
P.O. Box 12
Wantagh, New York 11793

Eastern Women's Center
14 East 60th Street
New York, New York 10022

Feminist Health Research Committee
9 Susan Court
White Plains, New York 10605

Feminist Health Works
487 A Hudson Street
New York, New York 10014
(212) 929-7886

Health Organization Collective of New
  York/Women's Health and
  Abortion Project

36 West 22nd Street
New York, New York 10010

Healthright, Inc.
41 Union Square, Room 206-9
New York, New York 10003
(212) 675-2651

Ithaca Women's Health Care
  Collective
101 North Geneva Street
Ithaca, New York 14850

National Women's Health Coalition
222 West 35th Street
New York, New York 10016

Radicalesbians Health Collective
  Women's Center
36 West 22nd Street
New York, New York 10010

Rochester Women's Health Collective
713 Monroe Avenue
Rochester, New York 14607

Women for Improved Group Health
  Services
c/o Elinor Polansky
390 First Avenue
New York, New York 10010

WHAM (Women's Health Action
  Movement)
175 Fifth Avenue, Room 1319
New York, New York 10010

Women's Health Alliance of Long
  Island
P.O. Box 645
Westbury, New York 11590

Women's Health Forum and Women's
  Health Center
175 Fifth Avenue
New York, New York 10010

Women's Occupational Health
  Resource Center
c/o American Health Foundation
New York, New York 10017
(212) 953-1900
  Dr. Jeanne Stillman

Woodstock Women's Health Collective
P.O. Box 579
Woodstock, New York 12498

Homemakers and Domestic Workers

Black Women for Wages for
  Housework
100 Boerum Place
Brooklyn, New York 11201
(212) 834-0992

Bronx Household Technicians
c/o Corri Miller
2323 Aqueduct Avenue, Apt. 1B
Bronx, New York 10468
(212) 367-2435

Medicine

American Medical Women's
  Association
1740 Broadway
New York, New York 10019

Motherhood

The Sisterhood of Black Single
  Mothers
1360 Fulton Street
Brooklyn, New York 11216
(212) 638-0413

Maternity Center Association
48 East 92nd Street
New York, New York 10028

Office and Clerical Workers

Women Office Workers
680 Lexington Avenue
New York, New York 10022
(212) 688-4160
  Joy Hornung

Photography

Professional Women Photographers
525 West 23rd Street
New York, New York 10011

(212) 989-9704
  Nickola Sargent and Dianora
  Niccolini

Politics and Government

Center for Women in Government
SUNYA Draper Hall, Room 302
1400 Washington Street
Albany, New York 12222
(518) 455-6211
  Nancy Perlman

Prostitutes

Scapegoat
c/o Marie Maggu
1540 Broadway, #300H
New York, New York 10036
(212) 757-6300

Religious Groups

Women's Rabbinical Alliance
c/o Hebrew Union College
40 West 68th Street
New York, New York 10023

Sports and Leisure

Greater New York Athletic Association
c/o Bob Glover (coach)
522 Fifth Avenue, Suite 431
New York, New York 10036
(212) 580-2310

Theater and Performing Arts

Action for Women in the Theatre
c/o SSD&C
675 West End Avenue
New York, New York 10024
(212) 675-5174
  Nancy Rhodes, Coordinator

The Alviva Players
262 Central Park West
New York, New York 10024
(212) 362-2277
  Mira J. Spektor

Women's Caucus of the Dramatists
    Guild, Inc.
234 West 44th Street
New York, New York 10036
(212) 398-9366

Women's Rights and Political Issues

Coalition Against Sterilization Abuse
c/o TWWA
244-48 West 27th Street
New York, New York 10011

Coalition of Grass Roots Women
1133 Broadway
New York, New York 10010

Committee to End Sterilization Abuse
Box 839, Cooper Station
New York, New York 10003

Women Against Pornography
579 Ninth Avenue
New York, New York 10036
(212) 594-2801
    Lynn Campbell

Women's Studies and Education

Project Second Chance
State University of New York
New Paltz, New York 12561
(914) 257-2172

NORTH CAROLINA

Baby and Child Care

Birth Alternatives
802 Washington Street
Winston-Salem, North Carolina 27101

Business and Management

Brevard Women's Club
P.O. Box 1142
Brevard, North Carolina 28712

New Girl Network
Life Span Center
Salem College
Winston-Salem, North Carolina 27108
(919) 721-2807

North Carolina Triangle Association of
    Women Business Owners
c/o Mary Diener, President
Diener and Associates
P.O. Box 12052
Research Park, North Carolina 27709
(919) 549-8945

Women's Forum of North Carolina
c/o Martha C. McKay, Chair
P.O. Box 2514
Chapel Hill, North Carolina 27514
(919) 929-7139

Communications and the Media

The Durham Women's Radio
    Collective
c/o WDBS
Box 4742
Durham, North Carolina 27706

Community Centers

A Woman's Place
110 Henderson Street
Chapel Hill, North Carolina 27514
(919) 967-8006

Farm and Rural Women

Council on Appalachian Women
P.O. Box 1458
Mars Hill, North Carolina 28724
(800) 438-4921
    Jeanne Hoffman, Director

Health

Durham Women's Health Co-op
Central YWCA, Room 29
515 West Chapel Hill Street
Durham, North Carolina 27701

NORTH DAKOTA

Banking

Women's Banking Center
First Bank of North Dakota
Fargo, North Dakota 58102
  Donna Chalimonczyk
  (701) 235-1793

Business and Management

The Old Girls Network
c/o Donna Chalimonczyk

1625 South 14½ Street
Fargo, North Dakota 58103
(701) 235-1793

Women's Centers

Women's Information Collective
P.O. Box 234
Twainley Hall
Grand Forks, North Dakota 58201

OHIO

Art

The Oven Productions
P.O. Box 18175
Cleveland, Ohio 44118
(216) 321-0692

Women's Art League of Akron
c/o Pauline Smead
258 Northland Drive
Akron, Ohio 44278
(216) 633-0901

Women's Caucus for Art
c/o Charlotte Hanten
566 Mineola Avenue
Akron, Ohio 44320
(216) 864-9701

Battered Women

Phoenix House
Columbus, Ohio
(614) 294-3381
  Carol Jorgenson, Director

Business and Management

Akron Women's Network
c/o Amy Coen Dienesch, Membership
  Coordinator
39 East Market Street
Akron, Ohio 44308

Career Women in Industry
574 Building
Dow Chemical Company
Midland, Ohio 48650

Woman's City Club
1349 East McMillan Street
Cincinnati, Ohio 45206
(513) 218-5866

Community Centers

Athens Women's Collective/Caucus
Baker Center
Ohio University
Athens, Ohio 45701

Dayton Women's Center
1309 North Main Street
Dayton, Ohio 45405
(513) 223-3296

Oberlin Women's Service Center
92 Spring Street
Oberlin, Ohio 44074
(513) 774-4377

Women Space
1258 Euclid Avenue, No. 200
Cleveland, Ohio 44115
(216) 696-3100
  Jane Campbell, Director

Women Together
P.O. Box 6331
Cleveland, Ohio 44101
(216) 281-0600

Employment

Career Advancement Network
3805 North High Street, Suite 310
Columbus, Ohio 43214
(614) 267-0958
  Dorothy Geiger, President

Cincinnati Women Working
9th and Walnut Streets
Cincinnati, Ohio 45202
(513) 381-2455
  Katie Whelan

Dayton Women Working
YWCA Room 318
141 West Third Street
Dayton, Ohio 45402
(513) 228-8587

Jobs Club
3805 North High Street, Suite 310
Columbus, Ohio 43214
  Dorothy Geiger

Women's Ohio Volunteer Employment
  Network
199 West Tenth Avenue
Columbus, Ohio 43201
(614) 422-1681 or 488-7260
  Mary E. Miller, Director

Ethnic and Minority Women

Ohio Black Women's Leadership
  Caucus
422 West Princeton Avenue
Youngstown, Ohio 44511

Health

Free Afternoon Women's Clinic
123rd Street and Euclid Avenue
Cleveland, Ohio 44106

Self-Help Group
c/o Linda Goubeaux

37½ East Frambes Street
Columbus, Ohio 43201

Homemakers and Domestic Workers

Wages for Housework
1356 West 59th Street
Cleveland, Ohio 44102

Black Women for Wages for
  Housework
456 Wildwood Street
Akron, Ohio 44320

Labor Movement

Cleveland Women Working
1258 Euclid Avenue
Cleveland, Ohio 44115
(216) 566-8511

Music

Women's Music Union
P.O. Box 02076
Columbus, Ohio 43212
(614) 263-7298

Rape

Women Against Rape
P.O. Box 02084
Columbus, Ohio 43202
(614) 291-9751

Religious Groups

Women's Ecumenical Network
c/o Greater Cleveland Interchurch
  Council
2230 Euclid Avenue
Cleveland, Ohio 44115
(216) 621-5925

Sports and Leisure

Goodyear Wingfoot Runners
c/o Goodyear
Department 960
114 East Market Street
Akron, Ohio 44316

Support Groups

Women Helping Women
9th and Walnut Streets
Cleveland, Ohio 45202
    Lucy Crane, Board President

Women's Rights and Political Issues

Women's Action Collective
127 East Woodruff Street
Columbus, Ohio 43201
(614) 291-7756

Women's Law Fund, Inc.
Keith Building
Cleveland, Ohio 44115
(216) 621-3443
    Jane Picker

Women's Studies and Education

Brown Bag Noon Hour Workshops
Spare Room
Lazarus Department Store/Downtown
South High and Towne Streets
Columbus, Ohio 43230
(614) 463-3688

Young and Teenage Women

Friends in Action
380 South 5th Street
Columbus, Ohio 43215
(614) 224-4389

OKLAHOMA

Community Centers

Women's Center of Tulsa
1240 East Fifth Place, Room 200
Tulsa, Oklahoma 74135
(918) 584-4444

Women's Resource Center
207½ East Gray Street
Norman, Oklahoma 73069
(405) 364-9424

Health

Oklahoma Women's Health Coalition
12225 Candytuft Lane
Oklahoma City, Oklahoma 73132

Sports and Leisure

DOLLS (Dedicated Outdoor Lunker
    Lovers Society)
P.O. Box 45-604
Tulsa, Oklahoma 74145
    Rose M. Ricklefs, President

OREGON

Baby and Child Care

Birth Center Lucinia
207 West 10th Street
Eugene, Oregon 97401

Business and Management

Institute for Managerial and
    Professional Women
P.O. Box 93

Portland, Oregon 97207
(503) 244-1006
    Alice Armstrong, Executive Director

Women Entrepreneurs/Portland
c/o Carol Angstman Maul
14225 Southwest Daphne Street
Beaverton, Oregon 97005
(503) 646-4577

Women in Sales and Marketing
Network
c/o Sunny Calvert
Tab Products
1525 Southeast 10th Avenue
Portland, Oregon 97214
(503) 233-4878

Community Centers

Women's Resource Center of Lincoln
County
9087 Southwest Hubert Street
Newport, Oregon 97365
(503) 265-7751

Education

OWEA (Oregon Women in Educational
Administration)
c/o Pat Schmuck
CEPM
University of Oregon
1472 Kincaid Street
Eugene, Oregon 97401
(503) 686-5074

Engineering

Society for Women Engineers
c/o Sue Frey
CH2M Hill
Western Boulevard
Corvallis, Oregon 97330
(503) 752-4271

Health

Ashland Women's Health Center
295 East Main Street
Ashland, Oregon 97520

DES Action/Oregon
3268 Northeast Almeda Street
Portland, Oregon 97212

Northwestern School of Practical
Midwifery
P.O. Box 14
West Linn, Oregon 97068
(503) 659-8295

Southeast Women's Health Center
3537 Southeast Hawthorne Street
Portland, Oregon 92714

Women's Health Clinic
4160 Southeast Division Street
Portland, Oregon 94702
(503) 234-9774

Law

The Queen's Bench
c/o Holly Hart
430 Southwest Morrison Street
Portland, Oregon 97204
(503) 226-3651

Older Women

The Older Women's Network
3502 Coyote Creek Road
Wolf Creek, Oregon 97497

Politics and Government

Women in Public Management
c/o Jane Hartline
Informational Services
Department of Public Administration
P.O. Box 751
Portland, Oregon 97207
(503) 229-3711

Science

Association for Women in Science
Corvallis Group of the Oregon
Chapter
c/o Ann Brodie
Biochemistry Department
Oregon State University
Corvallis, Oregon 97331
(503) 754-3169

Sports and Leisure

Keep Listening
P.O. Box 446
Sandy, Oregon 97055
(503) 287-0380 or 622-3895

Oregon Women's Land
Box 1713
Eugene, Oregon 97401

Women's Basketball Team (lawyers
  only)
c/o Lois Beran
Bank of California Towers
407 Southwest Broadway
Portland, Oregon 97205
(503) 222-3531

Women's Soccer Team (lawyers only)
c/o Jennifer Johnson
900 Southwest 5th Street
Portland, Oregon 97204
(503) 224-3380

Women's Rights and Political Issues

Women's Rights Project of the
  American Civil Liberties Union
c/o Lois Beran
Bank of California Towers
407 Southwest Broadway
Portland, Oregon 97205
(503) 222-3531

Women's Studies and Education

Career Women in Science Honors
  Program
Oregon State University
Corvallis, Oregon 97331
(503) 754-1459
  Margaret Meehan, Director

The Oregon Network
c/o Pat Schmuck
CEPM
University of Oregon
1472 Kincaid Street
Eugene, Oregon 97401
(503) 686-5074

OSU Women Studies Symposium
Center for Women's Studies
Oregon State University
Corvallis, Oregon 97331
(503) 754-3186 or 754-1135
  Jean Dost, Director

PENNSYLVANIA

Art

A Rose by Any Other Name
c/o Giovanni's Room
1426 Spruce Street
Philadelphia, Pennsylvania 19102
(215) 732-9612

Women's Caucus for Art
c/o Maurie Kerrigan
422-B South 21st Street
Philadelphia, Pennsylvania 19146

Women in the Arts
P.O. Box 5015
Harrisburg, Pennsylvania 17110
(717) 233-3967
  Susan Kogan

Baby and Child Care

Association of Women Directors of
  Infant Child Care Centers
c/o Evelyn Moats Munger
117 Hillside Road
Wayne, Pennsylvania 19087
(215) 688-6394

International Childbirth Education
  Network
c/o Patricia Corsi
173 Victoria Drive
Monongahela, Pennsylvania 15063
(412) 258-4718

Battered Women

Marital Abuse Project
P.O. Box 294
Wallingford, Pennsylvania 19086
(215) 565-6272

Women Against Abuse
P.O. Box 12233
Philadelphia, Pennsylvania 19144
(215) 386-7777 or 843-2438

Women's Center and Shelter of
    Greater Pittsburgh
616 North Highland Avenue
Pittsburgh, Pennsylvania 15206
(412) 661-6066

Business and Management

Executive Women's Council of Greater
    Pittsburgh
c/o Executive Steno Services
4120 Jenkins Arcade
Pittsburgh, Pennsylvania 15222
(412) 741-5591
    Ann Lang

Philadelphia Forum for Executive
    Women
c/o Betsy Gemmill
Girard Bank
Girard Plaza
Philadelphia, Pennsylvania 19101
(215) 585-2000

Philadelphia Women's Network
c/o Diane Freaney
Director of Business Analysis
INA Corporation
1600 Arch Street
Philadelphia, Pennsylvania 19101
(215) 241-4000

The Woman's Network
325 West Avenue
Wayne, Pennsylvania 19087
(215) 687-9485
    Dorothy Jurney, Executive Director

Business Owners and Entrepreneurs

Greater Pittsburgh Association of
    Women Business Owners
c/o Ruth Ryals
Pittsburgh Pension Planners
55 Wyoming Avenue
Pittsburgh, Pennsylvania 15211
(412) 931-3900

Community Centers

Fishtown Women's Community
    Center
1340 Frankford Avenue
Philadelphia, Pennsylvania 19125

Kensington Women's Resource Center
174 Allegheny Avenue
Philadelphia, Pennsylvania 19133
(215) 739-1430

Women's Resource Network
4025 Chestnut Street
Philadelphia, Pennsylvania 19104
(215) 387-5556

Employment

Job Options for Women on Probation
Blackstone Building, Room 704
112 Market Street
Harrisburg, Pennsylvania 17101

Options for Women
8419 Germantown Avenue
Philadelphia, Pennsylvania 19118

Women in Transition
4025 Chestnut Street
Philadelphia, Pennsylvania 19104
(215) 387-5556

Health

DES Action Group
University of Pennsylvania Women's
    Center
112 Logan Hall
Philadelphia, Pennsylvania 19174

DES Action/Pennsylvania
c/o Kathe Balter
1812 Pine Street
Philadelphia, Pennsylvania 19104

Elizabeth Blackwell Health Center for
Women
112 South 16th Street
Philadelphia, Pennsylvania 19103

Philadelphia Women's Health
Collective
5030 Newhall Street
Philadelphia, Pennsylvania 19144

Women for Sobriety, Inc.
Box 618
Quakertown, Pennsylvania 18951

Women's Health Caucus
2127 Green Street
Philadelphia, Pennsylvania 19130

Women's Health Concerns Committee
112 South 16th Street
Philadelphia, Pennsylvania 19102
(215) 563-0839

Homemakers and Domestic Workers

Philadelphia Wages for Housework
Action Group
602 South 48th Street
Philadelphia, Pennsylvania 19143
(215) 748-7303

Wages for Housework
602 South 48th Street
Philadelphia, Pennsylvania 19143
(215) 726-7926 or 748-7303

Law

Women's Law Project
112 South 16th Street, Suite 1012
Philadelphia, Pennsylvania 19102
(215) 564-6280

Medicine

Center for Women in Medicine
The Medical College of Pennsylvania

3300 Henry Avenue
Philadelphia, Pennsylvania 19129

Gay Nurses Alliance
P.O. Box 5687
Philadelphia, Pennsylvania 19129

Rape

WOAR (Women Organized Against
Rape)
1220 Sansom Street
Philadelphia, Pennsylvania 19107
(215) 922-3434

Religious Groups

Interfaith Projects of Working Women
c/o Tabernacle Church
3700 Chestnut Street
Philadelphia, Pennsylvania 19104

Sports and Leisure

Center for Women and Sports
Sports Research Institute
Pennsylvania State University
White Building
University Park, Pennsylvania 16802

Encounter Four
c/o Kayla Melville
Butler County Community College
Butler, Pennsylvania 16001

Erie Runhers
c/o Wendy Fiorenzo
813 Oakmont Street
Erie, Pennsylvania 16505

Women's Studies and Education

HERS Mid-Atlantic (Higher Education
Resource Services)
3601 Locust Walk
University of Pennsylvania
Philadelphia, Pennsylvania 19104
(215) 243-5426
    Dr. Cynthia Secor

RHODE ISLAND

Baby and Child Care

New Beginnings, Inc.
A Birth Center
P.O. Box 541
Warwick, Rhode Island 02886
(401) 737-1599

Rhode Islanders for Safe Alternatives
in Childbirth
99 Overhill Road
Providence, Rhode Island 02906

Community Centers

Women's Center
37 Congress Avenue
Providence, Rhode Island 02907
(401) 781-4080

Health

Rhode Island Women's Health
Collective

P.O. Box 1313
Providence, Rhode Island 02903
(401) 274-9264
Hillary Salk

Rhode Island Women's Health
Collective
c/o YWCA
423 Broad Street
Central Falls, Rhode Island 02863

Women's Health Conference
120 Fourth Street
Providence, Rhode Island 02906

Labor Movement

Rhode Island Working Women
100 Washington Street
Providence, Rhode Island 02903
(401) 331-6077
Sue Goldberger

SOUTH CAROLINA

Community Centers

Columbia Women's Center
1900 Haywood Street
Columbia, South Carolina 29205

Divorced and Widowed Women

Transition Resources
P.O. Box 512
Orangeburg, South Carolina
(803) 536-5972
Jeanne Lipscomb, Director

Health

Abortion Interest Movement
25 Country Club Drive
Greenville, South Carolina 29605

Self-Help Clinic
c/o Babette Walsh
15 Riverside Drive
Charleston, South Carolina 29403

SOUTH DAKOTA

Art

Custer Art Colony
Box 43
Custer, South Dakota 57730
  Evelyn Brauner, President

Community Centers

Brookings Women's Center
802 11th Avenue
Brookings, South Dakota 57006
(605) 688-4518

Divorced and Widowed Women

WIT (Women in Transition/formerly
  Pillsbury Bake-Off Girls)
c/o Libby Shreves
2501 South Kiwanis, Apt. 212
Sioux Falls, South Dakota 57105
(605) 338-1132

Ethnic and Minority Women

CANTE OHITIKA WIN (Brave-Hearted
  Women)

P.O. Box 474
Pine Ridge, South Dakota 57770

North American Indian Women's
  Association
c/o Hildreth Venegas
720 East Spruce Street
Sisseton, South Dakota 57262
(605) 698-3387

Women of All Red Nations
c/o Lorelei Means
General Delivery
Porcupine, South Dakota 57779
(605) 455-2563

Health

Women and Chemical Dependency
c/o Jennifer Rhodes
26 East Dartmouth Street
Vermillion, South Dakota 57069
(605) 624-9495

Wounded Knee Women's Health
  Collective
807 Fairview Street
Rapid City, South Dakota 57701

TENNESSEE

Business and Management

Mountain Women's Exchange
c/o Marie Cirillo
Clairfield, Tennessee 37715
(615) 424-6832

Community Centers

Knoxville Women's Center
406 Church Street
Knoxville, Tennessee 37902
  (615) 546-1873

Nashville Women's Center Health
  Group
1112 19th Avenue, South
Nashville, Tennessee 37212

Women's Resources Center
499 South Patterson
Memphis, Tennessee 38111
(901) 458-1407

Employment

Coal Employment Project
Box 3195
Oak Ridge, Tennessee 37830
(615) 482-3428
  Betty Jean Hall

Health

Health Group-YWCA
200 Monroe Avenue
Memphis, Tennessee 38103

TEXAS

Art

MAS (Mujeres Artistas del Soroeste)
P.O. Box 18275
Austin, Texas 78760
 Santa Barraza

TACO (Texas Art & Cultural
 Organization)
c/o Mary Ross Taylor
4601 University Oaks
Houston, Texas 77004
(713) 527-8522

Women's Caucus for Art
c/o Martha Terrill
4142 University Boulevard
Houston, Texas 77030

Baby and Child Care

The Maternity Center
1119 East San Antonio Center
El Paso, Texas 79901
(915) 533-8142
 Shari Daniels

Greater Houston Association of
 Women Business Owners
c/o Mary Locke, President
Word Processing Enterprises
3131 Briarpark Drive, Suite 700
Houston, Texas 77042
(713) 780-0713

Business and Management

River Oaks Business Women's
 Exchange Club
c/o Zola Cater
6800 Main Street, Suite 107A
Houston, Texas 77030

Clergymen's Wives

Talk 'n' Thought, Inc.
c/o Clara Bing Binford
1801 Heights Boulevard
Houston, Texas 77008
(713) 864-5130

Community Centers

Austin Women's Center
711 San Antonio Street
Austin, Texas 78701
(512) 472-3775

Everywoman Center
Richland Community College
c/o Community Services
12800 Abrams Street
Dallas, Texas 75243
(214) 746-4447

Women's Center of Dallas
2001 McKinley Street, No. 300
Dallas, Texas 75201
(214) 651-9795

Health

Houston Women's Health Center
c/o Cloud
1920 Richmond Street, No. 2
Houston, Texas 77006

Politics and Government

Texas Association of Elected Women
c/o Jan Shannon
Texas Municipal League
1020 Southwest Tower
Austin, Texas 78701
(512) 478-6601

UTAH

Art

Women's Caucus for Art
c/o Darlene Gunnerson
5907 Shangri Lane
Salt Lake City, Utah 84121

Community Centers

Women's Centers Directors in Utah
c/o Dr. Shauna Adix, Director
Women's Resource Center
University of Utah
293 A Ray Olpin Union
Salt Lake City, Utah 84112
(801) 581-8030

Education

The Consortium for Women in Higher
    Education
c/o Carol Reed, President
Utah Technical College—Provo
1395 North 150 East
Provo, Utah 84057
(801) 373-7890, ext. 46

HERS-West (Higher Education
    Resource Services)
c/o Dr. Shauna Adix, Director
Women's Resource Center
University of Utah

293 A Ray Olpin Union
Salt Lake City, Utah 84112
(801) 581-8030

Women's Resource Center
293 A Ray Olpin Union
University of Utah
Salt Lake City, Utah 84112
(801) 581-8030
    Dr. Shauna Adix, Director

Employment

The Phoenix Institute
383 South 600 East
Salt Lake City, Utah 84102
(801) 532-6095
    Jinnah Kelson, Director

The Utah Commission on Careers and
    Unemployment for Women
965 South 22nd East
Salt Lake City, Utah 84108
(801) 532-6095 or 582-7429
    Jinnah Kelson

Health

Feminist Women's Health Center
363 East Sixth Street
Salt Lake City, Utah 84104

VERMONT

Art

Images: A Women's Drawing
    Cooperative
c/o Nancy Storrow
Putney, Vermont 05346

Health

Green Mountain Health Center
36 High Street
Brattleboro, Vermont 05301

Southern Vermont Women's Health
    Center
187 North Main Street
Rutland, Vermont 05701

Vermont Women's Health Center
336 North Avenue
Burlington, Vermont 05402

Theater and Performing Arts

Vermont Women's Theatre
c/o Roz Payne
P.O. Box 164
Richmond, Vermont 05477

Women's Studies and Education

Women's Research Project
P.O. Box 81
Bennington, Vermont 05201
(802) 442-3180

VIRGINIA

Art

Women's Caucus for Art
c/o Heather Holden
1329 West Main Street
Richmond, Virginia 23220
(804) 358-2727

Baby and Child Care

International Childbirth Education
 Network
c/o Pam Housler
1310 Jerome Street
Chesapeake, Virginia 23324
(804) 543-7385

Community Centers

Williamsburg Area Women's Center
P.O. Box 126
Williamsburg, Virginia 23185
(804) 229-9944

Health

Women's Health Collective
P.O. Box 3760, University Station
Charlottesville, Virginia 22903

Social Sciences

Professionals in Social Sciences Support
 Group
c/o Emily Brown
1300 Wilson Boulevard, Suite B2-6
Arlington, Virginia 22209

Women's Rights and Political Issues

ACLU Southern Women's Rights
 Project
1001 East Main Street, Suite 512
Richmond, Virginia 23219
(804) 643-6419

Ad Hoc Religious Committee for ERA
c/o Emily Benson
2300 Gherkin Avenue
Vienna, Virginia 22180
(703) 281-9319

Mormons for ERA
c/o Sonia Johnson
Route 2, Box 233
Sterling, Virginia 22170
(703) 430-2650

WASHINGTON

Architecture

SHE (Sisters for a Human
 Environment)
11034 14th Avenue, Northeast
Seattle, Washington 98125

Art

Feminist Art Co-op
c/o Sara Hartman
4740 21st Street, Northeast
Seattle, Washington 98105
(206) 523-6919

Women Artists
1525 10th Street
Seattle, Washington 98122
(206) 324-5580

Women Artists Group of the
    Northwest
Box 9462
Seattle, Washington 98109
(206) 632-4747

Baby and Child Care

Birth Awareness Center
P.O. Box 855
Ellensburg, Washington 98926
(509) 674-2907

International Childbirth Education
    Network
c/o Ruth Ann Hill
12051 4th Avenue, Northwest
Seattle, Washington 98177

Business and Management

Greater Seattle Women in Business
c/o Gail Forte
256 Securities Boulevard
Seattle, Washington 98107
(206) 623-4838

Women in Touch
c/o Kay D. Anderson
Snohomish County Clerk
Snohomish County Courthouse
Everett, Washington 98201
(206) 259-9543

The Women's Network
1107 East Olive Street
Seattle, Washington 98122
(206) 323-6490
    Jean Donohue, Executive Director

Civic and Cultural Groups

Daughters of the Pioneers of
    Washington
c/o Mrs. Russell Clark
110 West Olympic Place

Seattle, Washington 98119
(206) 283-8052

Communications and the Media

League of American Pen Women
c/o 418 Northeast 82nd Street
Seattle, Washington 98115
(206) 525-8826

Education

The Washington Council of
    Administrative Women in
    Education
c/o Monica Schmidt, Assistant
    Superintendent
Superintendent of Public Instruction
Old Capitol Building
Olympia, Washington 98504
(206) 753-6701

Engineering

Society of Women Engineers
1928 Forest Avenue
Richland, Washington 99352

Fashion and Design

Friends of the Rag
Box 4107
Seattle, Washington 98104
(206) 624-0432
    Indian Owen

Women in Design
c/o Pat Hansen
1006 Turner Way East
Seattle, Washington 98112
(206) 632-3580

Health

Alice Hamilton Women's Clinic
P.O. Box 525
Tacoma, Washington 98401

Country Doctor Women's Clinic
402 15th Avenue, East
Seattle, Washington 98102

Elizabeth Blackwell Women's Clinic
1409 East Maplewood Street
Bellingham, Washington 98225

Lesbian Health Collective
6817 Greenwood Avenue, North
Seattle, Washington 98103

Open Door Women's Clinic
5012 Roosevelt Way, Northeast
Seattle, Washington 98105
(206) 524-7404

Women's Association of Self-Help
11100 2nd Street, Northeast
Bellevue, Washington 98009
(206) 454-9274

Women's Health Resource Center
203 West Holly Street
Bellingham, Washington 98225

Labor Movement

Seattle Working Women
1118 5th Avenue
Seattle, Washington 98101
(206) 624-2985
  Dorothy Hayden

Prostitutes

Seattle COYOTE
Box 4255
Seattle, Washington 98105

Sports and Leisure

Feminist Karate Union
701 North 76th Street
Seattle, Washington 98103

National Women's Rowing Association
c/o Carol Brown
2015 24th Street, East
Seattle, Washington 98112
(206) 325-7558

Support Groups

Ph.D. Candidates Support Group
University of Washington
Seattle, Washington 98105

Women Out Now Prison Project
P.O. Box 22199
Seattle, Washington 98122

Theater and Performing Arts

Women's Coffee Coven
Seattle Feminist Entertainment Center
P.O. Box 5104
Seattle, Washington 98105

WEST VIRGINIA

Community Centers

Shenandoah Women's Center
P.O. Box 1083
Martinsburg, West Virginia 25401
(304) 263-8522
  Donna Perrone, Director

Women's Information Center
221 Willey Street
Morgantown, West Virginia 26505

Health

Kanawha Valley Women's Health
  Group
1114 Quarrier Street
Charleston, West Virginia 25301

WISCONSIN

Art

Wisconsin Women in the Arts
610 Langdon Street, Room 728
Madison, Wisconsin 53706
(608) 263-2954

Baby and Child Care

International Childbirth Education
    Association
P.O. Box 20852
Milwaukee, Wisconsin 53220

Business and Management

Tempo
c/o Colleen Henderson
Manager of Investor Relations
Rexnord, Inc.
3500 First Wisconsin Center
Milwaukee, Wisconsin 53202
(414) 643-2510

Community and Neighborhood Centers

Women Pro Se, Inc.
c/o Janet Tierney
3719 West Fond du Lac Street
Milwaukee, Wisconsin 53216
(414) 445-2066

Women's Center
124 Blackhawk Commons
Oshkosh, Wisconsin 54901
(414) 424-1491

The Women's Center
419 North Grand Avenue
Waukesha, Wisconsin 53201
(414) 547-4600

Women's Resource Center
2101 A Main Street
Stevens Point, Wisconsin 54481
(715) 346-4851

Employment

Skilled Jobs for Women
111 South Hamilton Street, No. 16
Madison, Wisconsin 53703
    Dede Graff

Farm and Rural Women

Wisconsin Women for Agriculture
c/o Audrey Sickinger
Route 1
Cato, Wisconsin 54206
(414) 775-4257

Health

Amazon Women's Coalition
2211 East Kenwood Boulevard
Milwaukee, Wisconsin 53211

Health Writers
306 North Brook Street
Madison, Wisconsin 53715

Women's Rights and Political Issues

Task Force on Women
c/o Joanne Vogel
8901 Hilltop Road, Route 1
Cato, Wisconsin 64206
(414) 682-6615

Women's Coalition
2211 East Kenwood Street
Milwaukee, Wisconsin 53211
(414) 964-6117

Women United for Action
1012 North 3rd Street, Room 414
Milwaukee, Wisconsin 53202

Wisconsin Women's Network
625 West Washington Street
Madison, Wisconsin 53703
(608) 255-9809
    Gene Boyer, Chair

WYOMING

Health

AWARE
P.O. Box 505
Jackson, Wyoming 83001

Women's Resource Center
P.O. Box 3135, University Station
Laramie, Wyoming 82070

Sports

The Happy Hoofers
c/o Tina Bullock
1002 East Jefferson Road, Apt. 203
Cheyenne, Wyoming 82001